The Life, Personality and Writings of Al-Junayd

The Life, Personality and Writings of Al-Junayd

A Study of a Third/Ninth Century Mystic

with

an Edition and Translation of his writings

by

ALI HASSAN ABDEL-KADER

Gibb Memorial Trust

Published by

The E. J. W. Gibb Memorial Trust

First published 1976
Reprinted 2014

ISBN 978-0-718902-23-0

A CIP record for this book is available from the British Library

Further details of the E. J. Gibb Memorial Trust and its publications
are available at the Trust's website

www.gibbtrust.org

Printed and bound by CPI Group (UK) Ltd, Croydon, CR0 4YY

THIS VOLUME

IS ONE OF A SERIES

PUBLISHED BY THE TRUSTEES OF

THE "E. J. W. GIBB MEMORIAL"

The funds of this Memorial are derived from the Interest accruing from a Sum of money given by the late MRS. GIBB *of Glasgow, to perpetuate the Memory of her beloved Son*

ELIAS JOHN WILKINSON GIBB

and to promote those researches into the History, Literature, Philosophy and Religion of the Turks, Persians and Arabs, to which, from his Youth upwards, until his premature and deeply lamented Death in his forty-fifth year, on December 5, 1901, his life was devoted.

تِلْكَ آثَارُنَا تَدُلُّ عَلَيْنَا ٭ فَانْظُرُوا بَعْدَنَا إِلَى ٱلآثَارِ

" *These are our works, these works our souls display;*
Behold our works when we have passed away."

CONTENTS

CONTENTS

INTRODUCTION

BAGHDĀD IN THE THIRD CENTURY

Baghdād, in the third century of the Hijra (ninth century A.D.), little more than a century old, had already passed through various stages of evolution—social, economic, political and also spiritual. Many contacts of varying degrees of intimacy with Byzantine, Persian and Indian civilizations had been made in the preceding period in this metropolis, and in this century the influence of these manifold contacts was to develop in every sphere of culture. This was especially noticeable in the academic world, in the fields of theology, jurisprudence, philology, literature and philosophy.

Certain extremist tendencies were translated into political movements in the panorama of this century. We may refer—in the sociological sphere—against the background of a cultured and prosperous society whose wealth was drawn from a far-flung trade—to the social unrest of the lowest class, the Zinj, the slaves of Baṣra, who rebelled in 264 A.H., and also to the religious and equalitarian revolt of the Carmathians in 278 A.H.

In the religious sphere a new movement came into the foreground: the Mystical School of Baghdād. This 'Irāqī school had, from its very inception, certain features which distinguish it from all other ṣūfī schools. Thus they speak of *shaṭḥ* or overflowing (Überschwang); *'ibāda* or adoration of God; and *lisān* or tongue, eloquence, in an original and exclusive way.[1] Contemporary literature records the fact that the School of Baghdād held different views from those held by other ṣūfī schools, and notes especially their difference with the School of Khurasān, with which Baghdād maintained continuous contact and debate.[2]

This Ṣūfī School of Baghdād was recognized as highly significant at the time, and exercised a profound influence not only on contemporary Muslim thought, but also on all ṣūfīs up

---

[1] Abū'l Maḥāsin, An-Nujūm Azzāhira, v. 3, p. 169.
Qushayrī, Risāla, p. 103.

[2] Qushayrī, p. 89.

to the present day. It began afresh its questioning on God and man, putting great stress on personal experience, thus shaking every established traditional concept—shaking and, at the same time, giving new life and colour to Islamic tradition and lifting it to new ethical and visionary planes. This Ṣūfī School of Baghdād, which raised the ethical ideals and the innermost feelings of the Muslim religious spirit to their loftiest heights, has not yet been adequately explored. With the discovery of new material, new research work on some aspects of the school became possible, and scholars like Massignon, Nicholson, R. Hartmann, Arberry and Margaret Smith have made notable contributions.

An original and contemporary document of this school, a work by Abū'l Qāsim al-Junayd, has recently come to light, but has not yet been studied. Al-Junayd, as we shall see, became the master and inspired teacher of the Baghdād School in the latter half of the third century, and the more we study his personality, the more light is shed on the Ṣūfī School of Baghdād in particular, and on the significant early development in Ṣūfism in general.

In these pages we shall endeavour to give a picture both of the personality and of the doctrine of al-Junayd, as drawn from the original sources.

SURVEY OF SOURCES

It would have been very helpful for the study of al-Junayd's life and doctrine if the two original books written by his two intimate disciples—*Tabaqāt an Nussāk* by Abū Sa'īd Ibn al-A'rābī and *Ḥikāyāt al-Awliyā'* by Muḥammad Ja'far al-Khuldī—were still accessible.

IBN AL-A'RĀBĪ: Abū Sa'īd Aḥmad ibn Muḥammad ibn Ziyād ibn Bishr ibn al-A'rābī was born in Baṣra, but eventually settled down in Mecca, where he died at the age of 94 in 341 A.H. He was a traditionalist and jurist, but at the same time a ṣūfī. During his sojourn in Baghdād, before ultimately settling in Mecca, he frequented the circle of the Baghdād ṣūfīs and was a disciple of al-Junayd, al-Qalānisī and 'Amr al-Makkī[1] Later on, when he lived in Mecca, he was the Shaykh al-Ḥarām, the leading scholar in the Sacred Land. From Mecca—the centre of the Pilgrimage—where he taught for more than thirty years, he spread not only the *Ḥadīth*, in which he was profoundly versed, but also the esoteric teachings and way of the Mystics which he learnt by experience in the School of Baghdād. Many contemporary scholars who came to Mecca as pilgrims, in particular those from Africa and Spain, studied under him and subsequently quoted his teachings as disciples. Thus, for example, it is known that the first book on the Ḥadīth which reached Cordova in Spain and which was recognized as authoritative, was the *Kitāb as-Sunan* of Abū Dāwūd al-Baṣrī (died 275 A.H.). The scholars of Cordova received this important book through the agency of Abū Sa'īd al-A'rābī, who had himself been a disciple of Abū Dāwūd.[2] Scholars from Spain and Africa also took Abū Sa'īd's own books back to their home countries. In all probability other ṣūfī books reached the western Islamic world through Abū Sa'īd of Mecca. It is fair, then, to assume that the new mystical thought of the realm of the East first became known to the distant West by way of Mecca, through this great *Shaykh*. Thus the torch of philosophy appears to have been carried from Baghdād to Mecca, and thence by the pilgrims to Spain. Here, as a result, very lively discussions amongst scholars on all the issues of thought and doctrine took place.[3]

It appears that Abū Sa'īd ibn al-A'rābī was an authority on al-Junayd, whose spiritual leadership he gratefully acknowledged. He said in his *Ṭabaqāt an Nussāk*—quoted by Makkī—after giving the names of various mystics, " the last of these mystics was al-Junayd, and no one after him is worth mentioning."[4] Of this important book—*Ṭabaqāt an Nussāk*—many

---

[1] Abū Nu'aym, *Ḥilyat al-Awliyā'*, v. 10, p. 375. Ibn al-'Imād, Shadharāt, v. 2, p. 354.

[2] Al-Ishbīlī, *Fihrist*, p. 286, ff.

[3] Cf. Asin Palacios, Obras Escogidas I, p. 46.

[4] Qūt al-Qulūb, v. 2, p. 41.

fragments have been preserved in quotations in the books of the following generation, as we shall see.[1]

AL-KHULDĪ: Abū Moḥammad Ja'far ibn Nuṣayr ibn al-Qasīm al-Khawwāṣ al-Baghdādi al-Khuldī, who was born in 252 A.H. and who died in 348 A.H., also started his career as a traditionalist, and later on turned to ṣufīsm. He had learned to sift and select Tradition and used this discrimination in collecting the sayings and anecdotes of the famous ṣūfīs of his time. He said: " Had I not turned to the ṣūfīs, I would have set before you the Tradition of the Prophet from the whole world."[2]

He was a novice of Baghdād and was one of the favoured and intimate pupils of al-Junayd. He repaid his teacher's favour by recording every detail of al-Junayd's life known to him and handed down to posterity his master's sayings. This task is done so well that Khuldī's work is a major source not only for al-Junayd but for his teacher Saqaṭī, and also for Saqaṭī's teacher al-Karkhī.

His work, *Ḥikāyāt al-Awliyā'*, was well known in Baghdād and judged by all to be a remarkable book. It was said: " The people of Baghdād say: ' The wonders of the world are three, the Allegoric utterances of Shiblī (ishārāt), the Mystical subtleties (Aphorisms—nukat) of al-Murta'ish, and the Anecdotes (ḥikāyāt) of Ja'far.' "[3]

These two outstanding books, Abū Sa'id al-A'rābī's *Ṭabaqāt*

---

[1] Cf. Abū Sa'id's other works.
Al-Ishbilī in his *Fibrist* composed in 712 A.H. records the following:
(1) *Kitāb al-Ikhtiṣāṣ fi dhikr al-Faqr wa'l ghinā'*.
(2) *Kitāb al-Ikhlāṣ wa Ma'ānī 'Ilm al-Bāṭin.*
(3) *Kitāb Ikhtiṣār aṭ-Ṭarīq.*
(4) *Kitāb al-Maḥabba.*
(5) *Kitāb al-Ṣabr wat-Tasabbur.*
(6) *Kitāb al-'Umr wa'sh-Shayb.*
(7) *Kitāb Ma'ānī azzuhd wa'l Māqalāt fīhi.*
(8) *Kitāb Ṭabaqāt an-Nussāk.* (*Fibrist*, p. 284.)
Ibn al-Imād (1032–1089 A.H.) records the following:
(9) *Kitāb Ta'rīkh al-Baṣra.* (Shadharāt, p. 354.)
Sarrāj in his *Luma'* gives us an extract of a book of Abū-Sa'īd's, entitled:
(10) *Kitāb al-Wajd.*
(11) *Risāla fi'l-Mawā'iẓ wa'l Fawā'id wa ghayri dhalika.*
(12) *Kitāb al-Qubal wa'l-mu'ānaqa wa'l-muṣāfaḥa.*
Of these numbers 7, 11 and 12 are in Brockelmann, G. A. L.

[2] Supplement I, p. 358.

[3] Sulamī, *Ṭabaqāt* Aṣ-ṣufiyya, fol. 80a.

an Nussāk and Ja'far al-Khuldī's *Ḥikāyāt al-Awilyā'*, were very highly esteemed and widely read for many generations. These works are unfortunately no longer extant, but, when we read contemporary and other Arabic literature, we constantly meet quotations from them. They are the ultimate sources from which all later writers have directly or indirectly drawn their material—and to them we owe most of what we know about the period of the great ṣūfīs and their separate and individual contributions to the development of ṣūfī teaching at the critical and initial stages.

It was largely because both al-'A'rābī and al-Khuldī were recognized as authoritative traditionalists that this recognition of their authority extended to their works on the history of ṣufīsm. We too have no choice but to accept their authority. It becomes abundantly clear from their books that both these great Shaykhs came to al-Junayd, already disciplined in the exacting school of Ḥadīth. They came to him for spiritual guidance and, in listening to al-Junayd's teaching, became completely moulded by the integrity of their teacher's mental discipline and fully permeated by his spiritual approach. Such quotations of their works as are still available for us have been accepted in this study as authentic.

AS-SARRĀJ: Abū Naṣr 'Abdullah ibn 'Alī as-Sarrāj aṭ-Ṭusī, the author of the *Kitāb al Luma' fī at-Taṣawwuf*, who died in 378 A.H., was a pupil of Ja'far al-Khuldī. In the Kitāb al-Luma' we find that he, the author, quotes many facts about al-Junayd, both from stories related to him by al-Khuldī and also from Khuldī's books which he used. Thus on one occasion he writes of his relationship with al-Khuldī in these words: "Ja'far al-Khuldī told me, while he was studying under him that he had heard al-Junayd say . . . ."[1] This important book has fortunately survived and we owe its publication to Nicholson (1914), and to Arberry (1947), who completed it with an important newly discovered section. Sarrāj, in his *Kitāb al-Luma'*, gives us an authentic and full account of al-Junayd's teachings, quotes many of his aphorisms and describes the man in his relationship with contemporary ṣūfīs. This work is our unique available source for the bulk of information we have about

[1] Sarrāj, *Luma'*, p. 251.

al-Junayd. Some of the more esoteric quotations from Junayd's letters are preserved only in this work. The reason may well be that later writers were reluctant to adduce them, since, though they were couched in veiled terms, these passages might have been interpreted as impugning the purity of their faith. This book is then of prime importance in our study.

AL-MAKKĪ: Abū Ṭālib Muḥammad ibn 'Alī 'Aṭīya al-Makkī, who died in 386 A.H., the author of the *Kitāb Qūt al-Qulūb fī Mu'āmalāt al-Maḥbūb*, was a pupil of Abū Sa'id al-A'rābī. He came from Jibal in Persia and was brought up in Mecca, whence he came to Baghdād and studied under Sarrāj. Later he went to Baṣra, where he was too late to meet Abū'l Hasan ibn Sālim al-Baṣrī alive, but where he accepted his teaching from his works and disciples. In his book, *Qūt al-Qulūb*, Makkī drew much material about al-Junayd from his teacher Abū Sa'īd al-A'rābi.

A century later, Khaṭīb, the *sunni* historian, says of Makkī, that he used to give utterance to such confused statements about God that his teaching was regarded as heretical and his discourse shunned by the masses. But to-day when we read *Qūt al-Qulūb* we are inescapably drawn to Makkī by the sincere profession of inspired sūfī experience. We have before us one of the finest works of mystical expression. It is at one and the same time simple and sincere, learned and felt, inspired and inspiring. As a " document humaine " it must always be one of the treasures of Arabic literature. But great works of spiritual import make great demands on those who study them. The influence of the *Qūt al-Qulūb* on later generations of Muslim thinkers is directly proportional to their genius. Thus, al-Ghazzālī, universally recognized as a leading exponent of muslim thought, so fully accepted the teachings of Makkī that the famous *Iḥyā 'Ulūm Al-Dīn* can, with justification, be described as an enlargement and popularization of the *Qūt al-Qulūb*. The significance of the *Qūt al-Qulūb* in this study is not so much in the detail, which is sparse, as in the fact that the spiritual atmosphere which it so effectively creates is that atmosphere in which al-Junayd and his school flourished.

AL KALĀBĀDHĪ: a contemporary of al-Makkī, abū Bakr Muḥammad ibn Isḥāq al-Kalābādhī is another important authority on early ṣūfīsm. We know of him little beyond the fact that he was a Ḥanafī lawyer and died in Bokhara in 388 A.H. His book, *Kitāb al-Ta'arruf li-Madhhab at-Taṣawwuf*, recently edited and translated by Arberry, describes the principles and practices of the ṣūfīs as known to him. It is important because it is the earliest extant endeavour to reconcile such points of difference as were thought to exist between the ṣūfī attitude and the accepted tenets of Islam. *Al-Kalābādhī's* book is thus a source for ṣūfī doctrine of the period, an original defence of the validity of the ṣūfī attitude and a work of unimpeachable impartiality since *al-Kalābādhī* was an orthodox sunni.

Kalābādhī's *Kitāb at-Ta'arruf li madhhab at-Taṣawwuf* won immediate popularity throughout the whole muslim world, where it was accepted as authoritative. We are particularly fortunate in having at our disposal a printed edition of an almost contemporary translation and commentary in Persian by Abū Ibrāhīm ibn Isma'īl ibn Muḥammad ibn 'Abdullah al-Mustamlī al-Bukhārī. Mustamlī, who died in 434 A.H. and who was a professional theologian, a native of the same town as Kalābādhī, may well have been his pupil. It is not an unlikely inference that he gives his interpretation on Kalābādhī's discourse at first or, at most, second hand. However, Mustamlī, in his commentary, departs from the caution and prudence of Kalābādhī and is full of information about the rather more advanced views of such diverse types as al-Hallāj and al-Junayd. Unfortunately, it has been possible to use Mustamlī only as an occasional reference, and it is to be hoped that some future scholar will make a study of what appears to be a first-rate source for the history and development of the early ṣūfī esoteric school.

AS-SULAMĪ: Abū 'Abd ur-Rahman Muhammad ibn al-Ḥusayn ibn Mūsa as-Sulamī an-Nīsābūrī (born about 330 A.H., died 412 A.H.) wrote extensively on ṣūfī subjects. His *Ṭabaqāt aṣ-Sūfiyy'a*, extant in manuscript,[1] was a popular work which appears to have served as a source for most later writers on the early ṣūfīs. 'Abdullah al-Anṣārī al-Harawī (died 481 A.H.) used to lecture on the lives of the ṣūfīs, taking as his text the *Ṭabaqāt aṣ-Sūfiyya* and adding observations of his own. One of his

[1] British Museum, Add. 18520.

disciples took these lectures down in the " local language of Herāt." It was on this version that Jāmī based his well-known " Lives of the Saints "—*Nafaḥāt ul Uns*. Adh-Dhahabī has also used this book in the *Ta'rīkh al-Islām*. For us, however, as-Sulamī is the repository of much of the anecdotal material about al-Junayd and the ṣūfīs of his period. But, though the Ṭabaqāt also serves as a source for the aphorisms of al-Junayd, as-Sulamī has us still more deeply in his debt for his quotations of al-Junayd's doctrinal teachings in the *Ḥaqā'iq At-Tafsīr* which is a prime source for early ṣufīsm, to-day extant only in manuscript in the Dār-al-Kutub in Cairo. Here we may do more than sit at the feet of al-Junayd; we see al-Junayd's learning, inspiration and teaching set side by side and point by point next to that of his contemporaries. In this framework al-Junayd's originality and importance stand out beyond question.

ABŪ NU'AYM: Reference has been made to the *Ḥilyat al-Awliyā' wa Ṭabaqāt al-Aṣfiyā'* of al-Hafiz abū Nu'aym Ahmad ibn 'Abdullah al-Iṣfahānī, who died in 430 A.H. In this remarkable book most of the genuine ṣūfī traditions have been collected and handed down to us. Al-Iṣfahānī drew his material from al-A'rābī, al-Khuldī and a dozen or so authors quoted by name, who are new to us because their works are lost. This work, recently printed in Cairo, which contains material of great value on early ṣūfīsm in general, has been used in this study in particular as the unique source for many of al-Junayd's Rasā'il (letters).

AL KHAṬĪB: The voluminous *Ta'rīkh Baghdād* of al-Ḥāfiẓ abū Bakr Aḥmad ibn 'Alī al-Khaṭīb al-Baghdādī, who died in 463 A.H., has been used extensively as a source for historical detail. Khaṭīb has closed many a gap left open by the other sources, and lit up many a dark corner in the labyrinth of our studies.

QUSHAYRĪ; HUJWĪRĪ: From the same century, the fifth, we have used the two well-known works: the *Risāla* of Abu'l Qāsim 'Abd al-Karīm ibn Hawāzin al-*Qushayrī* an-Nīsābūrī (died 465 A.H.), and the *Kashf al-Maḥjūb* of Abū l'Ḥasan Abī ibn 'Omar ibn Abi 'Ali al-Jullābī al-*Hujwīrī* (died 470 A.H.), translated by Nicholson. These two works, which provide the fullest statement on ṣūfī tenets, have been used constantly, as much for factual information as for the interpretation of technical terms and arguments used by al-Junayd.

The sources which have been listed are, then, the total of the primary sources used in this study of al-Junayd. Secondary sources are listed in the bibliography.

RASA'IL AL-JUNAYD: In recent years a manuscript of the letters of al-Junayd has come to light. The object of our book is to make the contents of al-Junayd's letters, as preserved in this Istanbul manuscript, *Shahit Ali* MS. 1374, accessible to the English reader. We have undertaken to edit and to translate them. In preparing the translation reference has been made to the sources listed above and, in comparing the matter in the *Rasā'il* with what is available elsewhere, three points come to the fore: first, that the picture of al-Junayd's doctrine is filled in significantly; second, that al-Junayd's position as the outstandingly original and authoritative formulator of ṣūfī thought has hitherto not been recognized; and finally, that these *Rasā'il* embody the secret teaching of al-Junayd, which was reserved exclusively for the elect.[1]

These are the personal documents of a great mystic of the third century A.H., which, written in a half-colloquial, half-elevated and always intimate style, reach the loftiest heights of mysticism and are, in fact, unequalled in Arab literature. For us they are of unique value in finding our bearings in the wide sea of early Islamic mysticism.

These *Rasā'il* reveal the system of al-Junayd's thought. Al-Junayd sets down in writing the fundamental principles of Islamic mysticism and, in making his synthesis of ṣūfī thought, prepares that path which was later to be followed by many generations of ṣufīs.[2]

It would be true to say that what Ash-Shāfi'ī did for jurisprudence in his *risāla*, al-Junayd did for ṣūfīsm in his *Rasā'il*. Ash-Shfiā'ī, by his synoptic comprehension and vast

---

[1] Arberry remarks about this manuscript: "Only one copy of the work has survived, and that by the hand of the well-known pupil of Ibn 'Arabī, Isma'il ibn Sawdakin (d. 646–1248), so that it is permissible to conjecture that the book was a guarded secret of the Ṣūfīs, who communicated it to one another privately, without divulging its contents to the general public." See Al-Kharrāz Introduction, p. vii of *Kitāb al-Ṣidq*. See also MS., fol. 31.

[2] About other preserved fragments of al-Junayd's writings see p. 81. The Istanbul MS. is of first-rate importance.

learning, was able to initiate principles of Muslim jurisprudence which were so fundamental that later generations of jurists were happy to elaborate them, but unable either to add to them or change them. It is in this sense that al-Junayd is the father of ṣūfīsm.

PART I

THE LIFE, PERSONALITY AND WRITINGS OF AL-JUNAYD

Chapter I

AL-JUNAYD'S EARLY LIFE AND EDUCATION

Al-Junayd's Family

Though Abu-l-Qāsim al-Junayd ibn Muḥammad ibn al-Junayd al-Khazzāz al Qawārīrī was born and brought up in Baghdād, the fact that his ancestors came from the Persian town of Nihāwand in the province of Jibāl was known to his contemporaries in Baghdād.[1] Nihāwand was considered to be the most ancient town in the province of Jibāl and to have existed even before the flood. It was conquered by the Arabs between 17 and 21 A.H. (638/641 A.D.) at the time of 'Umar. In this campaign the Arabs found themselves faced by a strongly fortified town reputed to contain great treasure. Its conquest was achieved only at the price of heavy sacrifices and cost the conquerors the life of their general, Nu'aym ibn Mukarram al-Muzanī. But the victory stood the Arab cause in good stead, since Nihāwand opened the road into the interior and beyond. Its name is coupled with deeds of heroism and rich booty in the pages of Arab history. The Persian writers held that Nihāwand was both one of the most beautiful and also one of the coldest places in Persia.[2] The town owed its wealth to the fruitful soil of the surrounding districts, which was put to good use in the production of vegetables and fruit. Its inhabitants were shrewd merchants who were able to build up a considerable export trade with Mesopotamia. According to

Khaṭīb, *Tārikh Baghdād*, 7, 242.

[1] Ibn al-Faqīh *Kitāb-al-Buldān* (Bibliotheca Geographorum Arabicorum, ed. de Goeje), p. 258, 16. Yāqūt, *Mu'jam al-Buldān*, v. 8, p. 329.

Iṣṭakhrī: "Nihāwand is situated on a hill and the houses are of clay. There are fine gardens and many fruits which, on account of their quality and profusion, are exported to Mesopotamia."[1] Ibn Ḥawqal, too, calls Nihāwand an important town with much trade and fine agricultural land.[2]

In view of the foregoing, it is not unlikely that al-Junayd's ancestors, as citizens of Nihāwand, came originally from hardy mountain stock and had, as is customary in the East, probably been engaged in the export trade to Mesopotamia for several generations. It is possible that trade relations with Baghdād may have induced the family to emigrate there, but we do not know exactly when they settled in the metropolis. However, the occupations of the immediate members of al-Junayd's family are known to us from their names. Al-Junayd's father is referred to as a Qawārīrī, i.e. a glass merchant; al-Junayd himself is known as a Khazzāz, i.e. a merchant of raw silk; while his uncle, as-Sarī, is called as-Saqaṭī, i.e. a merchant dealing in spices and seasonings. Al-Junayd, as we see, was brought up in the milieu of merchants from merchant stock. Little is known about his childhood, beyond the fact that his father died while he was still a boy. His maternal uncle, as-Saqaṭī, took the orphan into his home and brought him up.

The Date of Al-Junayd's Birth

Though the date of al-Junayd's birth is not recorded, the date of his death is given as 296, 297 or 298 A.H. (908, 909, 910 A.D.). It is the last date which is best attested.[3] As we shall see later, over and above his preoccupations as a merchant, he studied law and ḥadith in his youth with Abū Thawr, who died in 240 A.H. We are told that he was twenty when he studied under him and, since this discipline takes from three to five years, the most likely date of birth is 215 A.H. After completing these studies, he turned to ṣūfīsm, when he sat under al-Ḥārith al-Muḥāsibī. Judging from the profound comprehension which al-Junayd acquired of al-Muḥāsibi's teaching, the respect in

[1] Iṣṭakhrī, *Masālik al-Mamālik* (B.G.A.), v. 7, p. 199, 15.

[2] Ibn Ḥawqal, *Al-Masālik wa al-Mamālik* (B.G.A.), v. 2, p. 258, 18.

[3] See Khaṭīb, *Tārīkh Baghdād*, v. 7, p. 248. Ibn al-Jawzī, *Muntaẓam*, v. 6, p. 105. Ibn Khallikān, v. 1, p. 147.
Sam'ānī, *Ansāb*, p. 464 B. (The night of NAWRŪZ, 298 A.H.)

which al-Junayd always held his teacher and the extreme difficulty of the subject, it is not too much to assume that al-Junayd came to al-Muḥāsibī as a man of thirty and studied for some ten years. On the basis of the foregoing, I am inclined to the opinion that al-Junayd was born round about 210 A.H. This would make him about ninety when he died, and we may note in passing that there was a strain of longevity in the family on his mother's side, since his uncle, as-Saqaṭī, was in the nineties when he died.

EARLY EDUCATION OF AL-JUNAYD

Fiqh and Ḥadīth

As has been mentioned, he began his studies with law and *ḥadīth* (Tradition of and about the Prophet) on the advice of his uncle. Al-Junayd relates that one day as he was leaving his uncle, Sarī as-Saqaṭī, asked him to whose *majlis* (assembly) he was going. He replied: "To that of Ḥārith al-Muḥāsibī." Sarī then said: "Yes, go and accept his learning and his discipline, but beware of his speculative reasoning and his refutation of the Mu'tazilites." "And, as I was going out," adds al-Junayd, "I heard Sarī say, 'May God make you a traditionalist who is a ṣūfī, and not a ṣūfī who is a traditionalist!'"[1] Makkī goes on to explain that knowledge of the tradition and the Sunna should come first, and that afterwards, by practising ascetiscism and devotion, al-Junayd might advance in knowledge of ṣūfīsm and become an expert ṣūfī, but that the reverse process of trying to attain to the higher degree of ṣūfīsm without being well grounded in orthodox theology was dangerous. On this point we have al-Junayd's further testimony: "I studied law according to the school of such authorities on ḥadīth as Abū 'Ubayd and Abū Thawr, and later I associated with al-Ḥārith al-Muḥāsibī and Sarī ibn Mughallas. That has been the reason of my success, because our knowledge must be controlled by going back to the Qur'ān and the Sunna. Whoever has not learned the Qur'ān by heart and has not formally studied ḥadīth, and has not learned law before embarking on ṣūfīsm, is a man who has no right to lead."[2]

---

[1] Makkī, *Qūt l-Qulūb*, vol. 2, p. 35. Cf. Sulamī, *Ṭabaqāt*, fol. 11a.

[2] Subkī, *Ṭabaqāt*, v. 2, p. 36.

So we see that al-Junayd devoted himself at the beginning to orthodox studies, the Ḥadīth and Sunna, which stood him in good stead both in creating his style and in the evolution and crystallization of his thought when he became a *ṣūfī* and taught mysticism. Thus, the roots of his *ṣūfism* were laid deep in the orthodox tradition and, as a result, his teaching was acceptable to *sūnnī* and *ṣūfī* alike in his day and a prized heritage for posterity.[1]

We see that he studied jurisprudence under the recognized authorities on it at this time in Baghdād. Ibn Khallikān writes: " Al-Junayd studied law under Abū Thawr. Some say that he took the doctrine of Sulaymān al-Thawrī and the jurist Ibn Surayj was his associate and friend."[2] Abū Thawr Ibrāhīm b. Khālid al-Kalbī al-Baghdādī, who died in 240 A.H., was the outstanding jurist of his day in Baghdād. Abu Thawr began to practise as a member of the 'Irāqī school of thought. This school differed from the traditionalist school of Hijāz in so far as its members were more open to juristic analysis, more aware of foreign legal traditions, and giving expression to its appreciation of precedent by collecting and recording new cases. It was only when Shāfi'ī came to Baghdād that Abū Thawr, under his influence, left the school of 'Irāq for the school of Tradition (*Ḥadīth*). He may perhaps not have been equally accomplished as a teacher of the *ḥadīth* as he was a jurist. Abū Ḥātim ar-Rāzī, in his book " al-Jarḥ wa'l-Ta'dīl " (" Refutation and Justification," a work assessing the relative merits of the traditionalists), said of him: " He was a man whose conclusions were based on theory rather than *ḥadīth*; sometimes he was right; sometimes he was wrong. His place is not amongst the widely versed traditionalists."[3]

There is reason to believe that, had al-Junayd not turned to mysticism, he would have been a distinguished jurist. Subkī says in his praise that, when only twenty years old, he sat at the feet of Abū Thawr, and that in this circle his juristic decisions were recognized.[4] It should be noted in passing that

---

[1] Ibn Taymiya, Minhāj al-Sunna, v. 3, p. 86. Ibn Qayyim, *Madārij al Sālikin*, v. 1, p. 137.
[2] Ibn Khallikān, *Wafayāt*, v. 1, p. 146.
[3] Sam'anī, p. 485.
[4] Subkī, *Ṭabaqāt*, v. 2, p. 28.

the middle thirties would to-day be regarded as a very early age to achieve this level of juristic maturity.

The biographers classify al-Junayd as a "Thawrī." Some hold that this designation points to his teacher, Abū Thawr; others hold that it refers to the legal school of Abū Sufyān al-Thawrī (161 A.H., 111 A.D.), which was well known and widely followed in Baghdād for a number of generations.[1] According to Abu'l Maḥāsin al-Taghribardī, the former opinion is the right one.[2] From the fact that only few *ḥadīths* of his are preserved, we may see that in this respect al-Junayd resembled his teacher Abū Thawr.[3]

His other associate, Ibn Surayj, the jurist, was a Shafi'ite. It is said that he was the first to "open the door of thinking," and taught people dialectic in law.[4] It is also said that during the third century three men stood out in different spheres: Ibn Surayj in law, Ash'arī in theology and Nasā'ī in *ḥadīth*.[5]

Ibn Surayj appears to have been a close friend of al-Junayd. It is said that once, when Ibn Surayj had delivered a fine discourse, one of the circle expressed his admiration and asked: "Where did you get the idea?" He replied: "It was one of the benefits I had from my sessions with al-Junayd."[6] It is also related that Ibn Surayj said: "Before to-day, when you told me, I did not know the answers to these questions." Al-Junayd replied: "God inspired me and put the words into my mouth. They come neither from books nor from study. They are grace from God." Ibn Surayj asked: "How did you attain this insight?" and al-Junayd replied: "It comes from my communion with God for forty years."[7] The intimacy which these stories presuppose gives good reason for the assumption that al-Junayd's authority and standing were recognized by the leading men of his day. Ibn Surayj, who died in 306 A.H., wrote several books which are no longer extant.

---

[1] Ibn Kathīr, *Bidāya*, v. 11, p. 114.
[2] *Nujūm*, v. 3, p. 169.
[3] *Tārīkh Baghdād*, v. 7, p. 242.
Subkī, *Ṭabaqāt*, v. 2, p. 33.
[4] Subkī, *Ṭabaqāt*, v. 2, p. 87.
[5] Ibid., p. 89.
[6] Qushayrī, p. 19.
[7] Ibn Kathīr, *Bidāya*, v. 11, p. 114.

'Ilm al-Kalām

That al-Junayd was not a scholastic theologian is implied by the story of the advice given him by his uncle, Saqaṭī, already quoted. Ibn Khaldūn relates of al-Junayd that one day he passed by a group of *mutakallimīn* (scholastic theologians), who were expounding their opinions with a great flow of words. He asked: "Who are these people?" He was answered: "These are people who use proofs to show that God has none of the attributes in order of that which is created and no signs of imperfection." Al-Junayd then said: "To deny a fault which could not possibly exist, is a fault (of judgment)."[1]

We have stories of *mutakallimīn* of the time who met and admired al-Junayd. We are told that Abū al-Qāsim al-Kalbī, a leading Mu'tazilite, said: "I saw in Baghdād a *shaykh* called al-Junayd. My eyes have never seen anyone like him. The writers come to him for style; the philosophers seek him for his profound thoughts; the poets come to him for imagery; the theologians for the content of his discourse; and the level of his talk was always higher than theirs in perception, eloquence and learning."[2]

We read, moreover, an apocryphal story that, when Ibn Kullāb[3] had written his book refuting the other sects, he asked: "Is there any other sect I have not yet refuted?" They answered him: "Yes, the ṣūfīs." He asked: "Who is their leader?" and they answered: "Al-Junayd." So Ibn Kullāb went to al-Junayd and asked him about his doctrine. Al-Junayd said to him: "Our doctrine is the separation of the eternal from that which was originated in time; abnegation of fellow-men brethren and native places, and no thought of the past or the future." When Ibn Kullāb heard this answer he was amazed, and said: "This is a thing which we cannot discuss or treat dialectically." After that, he attended al-Junayd's circle and asked him about *tawḥīd* (unification). Al-Junayd answered him with an expression showing knowledge of the mysteries and wisdom. Ibn Kullāb asked him to repeat it, but al-Junayd merely spoke another sentence and, when Kullāb asked al-Junayd

---

[1] Ibn Khaldūn, *Muqaddima* (ed. Quatremere), v. 3, p. 43.

[2] Khāṭib, *Tā'rīkh Baghdād*, v. 7, p. 243.

[3] Abū Muḥammad b. Kullāb, 'Abdullāh b. Sa'īd al Qaṭṭān.

to explain it to him, he was told: "If it came from my own tongue I could dictate it to you." And then Ibn Kullāb recognized al-Junayd and acknowledged the sublimity of his inspiration.[1] That it is unlikely that Ibn Kullāb actually had dealings with al-Junayd we know from al-Subkī. He says: "I saw the note of al-Dhahabī on this story which said . . . 'this is wrong, because Ibn Kullāb lived in the time of Ibn Ḥanbal; how could he, therefore, have met al-Junayd?' What al-Dhahabī said is quite true, since it appears that Ibn Kullāb died shortly after 240 A.H."[2] However, the anecdote is significant in so far as it reflects a view widely held by later generations both of al-Junayd's authority as a teacher and his attitude to the *mutakallimīn*.

---

[1] Yāfi'ī, *Mir'āt al-Janān*, v. II, p. 233.
[2] Subkī, *Ṭabaqāt*, v. 2, p. 51.

Chapter II

JUNAYD'S MYSTICAL SOURCES

AL-JUNAYD'S TEACHERS IN *ṢŪFĪSM*

As al-Junayd indicates, his first acquaintance with the mystic way was in his uncle as-Saqaṭī's house when he was a little boy. He says: "When I was seven years old and playing in front of Saqaṭī, when a party of men were with my uncle who were talking about 'gratitude to God' (Shukr), my uncle said to me: 'Oh boy, what is gratitude to God?' and I replied to him that 'gratitude was that one should not disobey God who bestows gifts.' Whereupon my uncle said: 'It may well be, my boy, that your gift from God will be your tongue.'" Al-Junayd continues: "My eyes still fill with tears when I think of what as-Saqaṭī said."[1]

Sarī as-Saqaṭī

As already stated, Sarī as-Saqaṭī was a merchant who dealt in spices and seasonings. One day, when a fire occurred in the bazaar, he was told that his shop had been burned. He replied: "Then I am freed from the care of it." Afterwards, it was discovered that his shop had not been burned, although all the shops surrounding it had been destroyed. On discovering this, Sarī gave all he possessed to the poor and devoted himself exclusively to *ṣūfīsm*.[2]

As-Saqaṭī attained the age of ninety-eight years, as we learn from al-Junayd: "I have seen no one more bent on worship than as-Saqaṭī—in the whole ninety-eight years of his life it was unknown for him to lie down, except in his last illness."[3] He died about 253 A.H.[4] His birth thus should have been about 153 A.H. This means that he lived in the first period of the

[1] Qushayrī, p. 81.
[2] Hujwīrī, p. 110.
[3] Khaṭīb, *Ta'rīkh Baghdād*, v. 9, p. 192.
[4] Ibid., according to Qushayrī in 257. See p. 10. According to Ibn 'Asākir in 251. (See *Tahdhīb*, v. 6, p. 79.)

'Abbāsid dynasty. He lived through the reigns of seven or eight Khalifs and was a witness of all those great events in thought and philosophy which took place in the golden age of 'Irāq. As-Saqaṭī was famous for his devotion and his abstinence.—*Wara'*. On this subject many stories are related. When his name was mentioned to the *Imām* ibn Ḥanbal, he remarked: "Oh you mean the Shaykh who is well-known for his scrupulousness about food?"[1] As-Sulamī said of him: "Sarī was the first in Baghdād to teach Unification (*tawḥīd*) through the way of mysticism, and the first to teach the knowledge of reality; he was also the leader of the Baghdādis in the symbolic utterances (ishārāt).[2] Qushayrī said: "He was unique in his time in devoutness and abstinence, in his high state of mind and in the knowledge of unification."[3]

It appears that as-Saqaṭī's reputation was high both with the leaders, governors, generals and scholars of his time, and also with the people at large. Later he withdrew from the public eye and spent his time with a selected few.[4] Among his pupils, apart from al-Junayd, were an-Nūrī, Ibn Masrūq aṭ-Ṭūsī, Muḥammad ibn al-Faḍl al-Saqaṭī, Ibrahīm al-Makhramī, al-'Abbās al Shaklī.[5]

With regard to the teaching which as-Saqaṭī imparted to al-Junayd, it seems that he carried on discussions with him and put questions to him as Socrates did with his pupils. Al-Junayd says: "When as-Saqaṭī wants me to profit by his teaching he puts questions to me."[6] We have an illustration of this method in the following incident as described by al-Junayd: "Sarī' questioned me one day about love and I answered: 'Some say that love is identity of feeling, others say it is to prefer another to oneself, while others say something else.'" Sarī pinched the skin of his arm, which was so taut and dry that he was not able to pull it out, and he said: "By God, if I said that this skin dried on these bones through loving Him, I should be

---

[1] Abū Nu'aym, *Ḥilya*, v. 10, p. 126.
[2] Sulamī, fol. 10a.
[3] Qushayrī, p. 10.
[4] Ibn 'Asākir, *Tahdhīb*, v. 6, p. 77.
[5] Khaṭīb, v. 9, p. 190.
[6] Qushayrī, p. 82.

telling the truth."[1] On another occasion al-Junayd relates: "I came to as-Sarī one day and found him different from usual, and I asked him: 'What is the matter?' He replied: 'A young man came to me and asked about repentance. I answered: "Repentance is not to forget your sin." The young man objected and said: "On the contrary, repentance is to forget your sin." 'Al-Junayd said to as-Sarī: "What the young man said is my own view."' 'As-Sarī asked me: "Why?" and I replied: "If you have been on bad terms with God and are afterwards raised to being on good terms, to think of your former state is bad."' As-Sarī was silent.[2] That as-Sarī recognized the stature of al-Junayd is evident from the following anecdote. One day as-Sarī was asked whether the status of a disciple could be higher than that of his spiritual mentor, and he replied: "Yes, there is manifest proof of this; the status of al-Junayd is above mine."[3] We have another instance in the fact that, when as-Sarī was dying, al-Junayd said to him: "Oh, as-Sarī, the people will not see anyone like you when you are gone." As-Sarī answered: "But they will not see anyone as kind and gentle as you are."[4]

Al-Junayd tells us that, at the beginning, he was reluctant to become a teacher as long as as-Sarī was alive, until one night he dreamt that the Apostle of God said to him: "Oh, al-Junayd, speak to the people, for God hath made thy words the means of saving a multitude of mankind." When he awoke, the thought occurred to him that his status was superior to that of as-Sarī's, since the Apostle had commanded him to preach. At daybreak as-Sarī sent a disciple to al-Junayd with the following message: "You would not discourse to your disciples when they urged you to do so, and you rejected the intercession of the Shaykhs of Baghdād and my personal entreaty. Now that the Apostle has commanded you, obey his orders." Al-Junayd said: "My former fancy went out of my head. I perceived that as-Sarī was acquainted with my outward and inward thoughts in all circumstances, and that his status was above mine, since he was acquainted with my secret thoughts, whereas

---

[1] Ibid., p. 10.
[2] Ibid., p. 47.
[3] Hujwīrī, p. 128.
[4] Ibn 'Asākir, v. 6, p. 79.

I was ignorant of his status. I went to him and begged his pardon and asked him how he knew that I had dreamed of the Apostle. He answered: 'I dreamed of God, who told me that He had sent the Apostle to bid you preach.' "[1]

As-Sarī, like Socrates, has left nothing in writing. Most of what we have of his sayings have come down to us from al-Junayd. It may be that sometimes he put his own thoughts into the mouth of as-Sarī. Seeing that as-Sarī had such a tremendous influence on al-Junayd, we realize that, without al-Junayd, we would know nothing of the importance of as-Sarī. If we wish to picture the relationship between as-Saqaṭī and al-Junayd, we may compare them with Socrates and Plato. Al-Junayd worked out the systematic structure of ṣūfīsm and put it in writing. As-Saqaṭī spoke on the problems of ṣūfīsm in an almost platonic dialogue. He used to hold discussions, put up questions and lead his circle to an appreciation of the issues involved. He was without question a practising ṣūfī.

We may regard as-Saqaṭī as the founder of the Ṣūfī School of Baghdād. This school differed from contemporary ṣūfī schools in Syria and in Khorasan. The Baghdād school's main topic was Unification, *Tawḥīd*, and it developed the "knowledge" of Unification. The school is distinguished by its symbolic expressions and by its discussions on the mystic state and station of the ṣūfī. The members of the school are, therefore, called "The Masters of Unification," *Arbāb al-Tawḥīd*, like al-Junayd, an-Nūrī and ash-Shiblī.[2] This school has another feature, in that the 'Irāqīs were famous by virtue of their eloquence. Al-Junayd remarked on this, stating: "Syria is the home of chivalry, 'Irāq of eloquence and Khorāsān of sincerity."[3] We are told that as-Sarī heard the great traditionalists of his time, such as al-Fuḍayl, Hushaym, Ibn 'Ayyāsh, Yazīd b. Hārūn, Sufyān b. 'Uyayna and others. The implication is, then, that as-Sarī had had the benefit of the academic training available in his time and that his status in the contemporary academic world was not without recognition. His ṣūfīsm was, therefore, based on academic knowledge and developed in keeping with

[1] Hujwīrī, p. 129.
[2] Sarrāj, page of *Luma'* (Arberry ed.), p. 12.
[3] Qushayrī, p. 103.

the principles of academic interpretation of holy writ. It was the esoteric nature of the subject which tended to be new in Islām rather than the method employed in reaching his conclusions.

Ma'rūf al-Karkhī

As-Sarī was a pupil of the great ṣūfī Abū Maḥfūz Ma'rūf ibn Fīrūz al-Karkhī (died 200 or 201 A.H.). As-Sarī' used to say: " What I have learned is from the blessing of my association with Ma'rūf."[1] Ma'rūf was of Persian descent. It is said that he was a client (*Mawlā*) of the Imām 'Alī ibn Mūsa al-Riḍā and, having been a non-Moslem, accepted Islām at the hands of al-Riḍā. Ma'rūf lived in Baghdād in the time of Hārūn al-Rashīd in the Karkh quarter of the city, and thus was generally called Ma'rūf of Karkh. Abū 'l-Maḥāsin Taghribardī says that his parents were Sabeans coming from the region of Wāsiṭ; but al-Daqqāq said that they were Christians.[2] These Sabeans or Mandaeans or Elkhasāites (the Sabeans of the Qur'ān) had their centre in the marsh land between Baṣra and Wāsiṭ, where some of them still survive. They were called by the Moslems the *Mughtasilah* (Washers), on account of their frequent ceremonial ablutions. Their founder is said to have been Elkhasāi and, as their name Mandaeans (gnostics) implies, they are the remnants of a very ancient gnostic sect.[3]

According to Ibn-an-Nadīm in the Fihrist, Mani, the founder of the Manicheans, was in his youth one of the Mughtasila.[4] Accordingly, Professor Kessler formulated his theory that the doctrines of the Mughtasila were the principal source of Mani's system.[5] Al-Bīrūnī says that the Sabeans in Samarkand were the survivors of the Manicheans in the lands of Islām.[6]

R. Hartmann points out many Mandaean influences in ṣūfī doctrine and terminology.[7] To support this, we may refer to

---

[1] Abū Nu'aym, *Ḥilyā*, v. 10, p. 123.
[2] Nujūm, v. 2, p. 167.
[3] Nicholson, JRAS, 1906, p. 319. The Sabeans according to Nöldeke (*Mandaische Gramtik*, p. 1) were not Mandaeans but more likely Elkhasaites.
[4] *Fibrist*, p. 457.
[5] See Legge, *Forerunner and Rival of Christianity*, v. 2, p. 305.
[6] Bīrūnī, *Al 'Āthār al-Bāqiya*, p. 209.
[7] Der Islam, v. 6, p. 46.

the ideas of Ḥaqq and Ṣidq, which appear again and again in Manichean literature. We find that they also occur very often in a particular sense in the works of al-Junayd, as in his " Book of Ṣidq " and his book of " Ulūhiyya." It may well be that al-Junayd took these notions and terms through Saqaṭī from Ma'rūf. At any rate, we can see in the sayings of Ma'rūf that he used the terms *Ḥaqq* and *Ṣidq*. It is well known Ma'rūf, as-Saqaṭī and al-Junayd were the first to speak in Baghdād of Ḥaqā'iq.

There is also the question whether there has been a Neo-platonic influence through these Mandaeans or Sabeans which reached the ṣūfīs. Hartmann maintains that the Neo-platonists were very scholarly, whereas ṣūfīsm rose from the people.[1] But, if it be true that these Mandaeans from the lower Euphrates marsh-lands were rather primitive sectarians, this is not the case with our ṣūfīs. There were, on the contrary, amongst them the most scholarly and widely cultured personalities of their time. It would be certainly worth while to raise the question whether there have been Neo-platonic influences on the early ṣūfīs. The Christian Syriac theological writers, who flourished widely in the centuries preceding the rise of Islām, were deeply steeped in the Neo-platonic current of thought. One may think of Dionysius the Arcopagite, and of Stephan bar Sudaili, a Syrian Christian mystic and pantheist (considered a heretic by contemporary churchmen), who taught and wrote before and about 500 A.D. in Edessa and Palestine. His work of mystical essays, called the " Book of the Holy Hierotheos," addressed to a disciple, stresses the secret character of these teachings. It interprets the Old and New Testament in a Neo-platonic sense, and is a witness for us of Christian Neo-platonism in Syria—rendered accessible by the translation of F. S. Marsh.[2] The Christian Neo-platonic influence on later ṣūfī thought has been further investigated by A. G. Wensinck in his edition, translation and commentary of " The Book of the Dove," written by Bar Hebraeus in 1278 A.D. One is tempted to hazard the conjecture that the long development of Neo-platonic thought in the Christian circles of Asia Minor was contempor-

[1] Ibid., p. 62.

[2] The Book of the Holy Hiorotheos, translated by F. S. Marsh, 1927.

aneous, but not intimately connected with developing ṣūfī doctrine. One looks rather to Plotinus as a probable inspiration to both schools, and to Syriac Christian writings as parallels of interest rather than direct sources of doctrine.

In fact, when we study the *Rasā'il* (letters) of al-Junayd, we find what seems to be Neo-platonic elements. To give a few examples only: The theory of the pre-existence and post-existence of the soul before and after life in this earthly body, as the reason for the longing of the soul in man to return to its origin. The nature of the " first separation from God " and of the " second separation " after mystical union. The deep search into the problem of essence and attributes, and of reality. God is the only reality, we are but phenomenal. Human attributes are only impressions (rasm) and ephemeral, mirroring faintly God's attributes, which are eternal. Neo-platonic ideas were widespread at a later period in Baghdād and made their contribution to the development of Islāmic philosophy. How far did they influence al-Junayd, his contemporaries and his teachers?

We may think of such an important work of Greek philosophy as the book known as *Aristotalis Uthulujiya—Theologia Aristotelis,*[1] which is preserved to us only in its Arabic translation. The title of this book states it contains a commentary of Porphyry on the Theology of Aristotle, translated by the Syrian 'Abd al-Masīḥ ibn 'Abd Ullah al-Ḥimṣī al Nā'imī (a Syrian Christian), and checked by al-Kindī (the early Muslim philosopher and physicist) for the Khalīf al-Mu'taṣim (218 A.H.–251 A.H.). The contents of this book, which was translated into Latin in the sixteenth century, and some fifty years ago into German by F. Dieterici, shows that we have before us not a work of Aristotle, but a treatise of Porphyry, the disciple of Plotinus and commentator of Aristotle. Within the framework of the philosophical and cosmological system of Aristotle, the author gives a summary of the whole authentic philosophical system of Plotinus.

His remarkable work on the God-head, the created Universe

---

[1] Die sogennante Theologie des Aristoteles, ed. and trans. Fr. Dieterici, Leipzig 1882–83; cf. Brockelmann, Geschichte der Arabischen Literatur, Sup. I, p. 364.

and the soul very skilfully blends the teachings of Aristotle and of Plotinus. The formal system of the teaching reminds us more of Aristotle than the poetical, spontaneous style of Plotinus.

This work, as the dates of al-Kindī and Khalif al-Mu'taṣim indicate, must have reached the intellectuals of Baghdād in the generation before al-Junayd. Either the book itself or the ideas it contained may well have become known to the ṣūfīs at that time. There are, however, no indications in al-Junayd's letters that he himself had read the book. He was not interested in systematic philosophy or in cosmology. The contents of the book which were of significance to the mystics must have reached him by word of mouth. It is sufficient here to note that the dates allow the surmise of influence through oral discussion. A more detailed analysis of comparative doctrine will be given later.

To return to Ma'rūf al-Karkhī, the following anecdote at once shows the significance of his teachings and the atmosphere in which al-Junayd developed.

"It was reported that whenever food was presented to Ma'rūf as a gift he always accepted and ate it. Someone said to him: 'Your brother Bishr b. al-Ḥārith always refuses such food,' and Ma'rūf replied: 'Abstaining causes my brother's hands to be tied, whilst Gnosis causes my hands to be stretched forth. I am only a guest in the house of my Lord . . . when He feeds me, I eat; when He does not, I have to be patient. I have neither objection nor choice.'"[1] Here we meet for the first time in ṣūfī literature a peculiar and original conception of tolerence. The ramifications of this conception are both deep and significant. Similar ideas can also be found in Saqaṭī and al-Junayd. Here are further examples:

A friend of Ma'rūf's asked him: "What has impelled you to the worship of God and caused you to withdraw?" He was silent. The friend continued: "Is it the thought of death?" "No," was the reply, "for what is death?" "The thought of the grave perhaps?" asked the friend; again, "No, for what is the grave?" The friend continued: "Perhaps the fear of

[1] *Qūt al-Qulūb*, v. 4, p. 61.

Hell and the desire for Paradise?" Ma'rūf answered: "Whatever all this may be, it is all contained in the hand of God. When you love Him, He will make you forget all these; when you become acquainted with Him, He will protect you from all these things."[1]

'Ali b. al-Muwaffaq related the following: "I dreamt I had entered Paradise. I saw there a man at a table, two angels were beside him, one on his left and one on his right; they gave him many kinds of food, which he ate. I saw another man who stood at the gates of Paradise; he looked at the faces of the people; some he allowed to enter, others he turned away. I left Paradise and continued to the Holy Court. There I saw the Pavilion of the Throne and a man was gazing steadfastly towards God—his eyelid did not flicker once. I asked Riḍwān: 'Who is this?' and he replied: 'This is Ma'rūf al-Karkhī who worships God, not through fear of Hell, nor desire for Paradise, but only for love of Him, and so God allows him to look at Him until the day of Resurrection.' I then asked: 'Who are the other two men?' and he replied: 'One is your brother Bishr b. al-Ḥārith and the other is Aḥmad b. Ḥanbal.'"[2]

Anṣarī related: "I dreamt that I saw Ma'rūf al-Karkhī before the throne of God and heard God say to his angels: 'Who is this?' They answered: 'Thou knowest best, O Lord! This is Ma'rūf al-Karkhī; he is intoxicated by Thee and will not recover his senses, except by meeting Thee face to face.'"[3]

One day Ma'rūf said to his nephew, Ya'qūb: "When you desire anything from God, invoke my name in your appeal to Him."[4]

When we consider the teachings and sayings of the various ṣūfī Shaykhs of this period, we see how close was the relationship between these three personalities, Ma'rūf, Saqaṭī and al-Junayd; their attitude, character, purpose and mystic way are essentially one and the same. It consists mainly of Theosophy, the apprehension of divine reality and Unification, whereas most other ṣūfīs had, in their mystical teachings, a more limited

---

[1] Ibid., v. 3, p. 82.
[2] *Qūt al Qulūb*, v. 3, p. 83.
[3] *Ḥilyāt al-Awliyā*, v. 8, p. 366. In Qushayri, p. 11, this dream related from Sarī as-Saqaṭī.
[4] *Ḥilyāt al-Awliyā*, v. 8, p. 364. In Qushayri also this saying related from Saqaṭī, p. 11.

and a less idealistic objective. They seem to have stressed the importance of religious practice rather than mystical theory.

We learn from different sources that Ma'rūf was an associate of Dāwūd al-Ṭā'i (died 165 A.H.) and that Dāwūd al-Ṭā'i derived from Ḥabīb al-'Ajamī (died 120 A.H.), who derived from al-Ḥasan al-Baṣrī (died 110 A.H.), who derived from 'Alī Ibn Abī Ṭālib (died 40 A.H.).[1] Yet this chain of mystic tradition is very doubtful, as it has not been proved by the historians that Ma'rūf was ever the associate of Dāwūd al-Ṭā'ī, nor that Dāwūd had met Ḥabīb al-'Ajamī. It is not correct either that al-Ḥasan met 'Ali. He met only his associates, as he was a child when 'Ali died. Thus this chain of teacher and pupil is not valid.[2]

Other historians give us a different chain of tradition for Ma'rūf. In the *Fihrist*, Ibn an-Nadīm says, quoting Abū Isḥāq, that he learned from the writings of Ja'far al-Khuldī, and also heard direct from him, that he took mysticism from al-Junayd, who derived it from as-Saqaṭī, who derived it from Ma'rūf, who derived it from Farqad al-Sabakhī (died 131 A.H.), who derived it from Ḥasan al-Baṣrī, who derived it from Anas Ibn Mālik (died 90 A.H.).[3]

Abu Ya'qūb Farqad al-Sabakhī al-Baṣrī,[4] the teacher of Ma'rūf in this *chain*, was a famous ascetic in his time; he was also a traditionalist and related some traditions from Anas b. Mālik, Sa'id b. Jubayr and from other " *Tābi'ūn* " who conversed with the companions of the Prophet; but the leading traditionalists did not approve of Farqad's tradition and refused to receive it from him.[5] What should be noted about him is that he was originally a Christian from Armenia who later became a convert to Islām.[6] As he died in 131 A.H. and Ma'rūf died in 200 A.H., it is very doubtful if Ma'rūf could have associated

---

[1] See *Kitāb asrār al-Tawḥīd*, p. 18, 38. *Qushayri*, p. 134.
[2] Ibn Taymīya, *Minhāj al-Sunna*, v. 4, p. 135, f.
[3] *Fihrist*, p. 260.

[4] السنجى بالنون والجيم NOT السبخى بالباء و الخاء

as it is corrected in *Mushtabah* of *Dhahabī*, p. 253, and in *Tuḥfat Dhawī al-Irab*, p. 161. The mistake may have occurred from the copying. (See *Mizan*, v. 2, p. 327. Nicholson, JRAS.)
[5] Shadharāt al-Dhahab, v. 1, p. 181.
[6] *Mizān*, v. 2, p. 327.

with Farqad and learned from a man who died seventy years before his own death.

On the surface this chain appears more likely than the other. But neither has an historical appeal. There is no circumstantial evidence of these associations between pupil and teacher, nor are any literary similarities adduced as a proof. Such chains of tradition for ṣufīs were often compiled at a much later date in order to prove their authority. They are, at any rate, of small account to the historian.[1]

Al-Muḥāsibī

The house of as-Saqaṭī was a meeting place for mystics, where they could discuss their problems at their leisure. As-Saqaṭī's personality appears to have attracted the leading mystical personalities of his day to his home. This provided young al-Junayd with the opportunity to meet these distinguished men, to hear them discuss and at times to be himself drawn into their discussion. It appears that it was in this way that al-Junayd got to know many of these mystics, whose teachings and aphorisms made a great impression on him.

Amongst these men was the famous mystic Abu 'Abdullah al-Ḥārith ibn Asad al-Muḥāsibī,[2] a friend of al-Saqaṭī, who visited him often. Al-Junayd relates: "Ḥārith came to our house and said: 'Come out with me, let us go for a walk.'" And al-Junayd continues: "I said to him: 'Will you drag me forth from my life of retirement, in which I feel secure, out on to the highroads with their risks, and distractions for the senses?' He said: 'Come out with us, never fear!' So I went forth with him and the road was completely deserted; we saw nothing objectionable. And when we arrived at the place where he was accustomed to sit with his friends and discuss with them,

---

[1] Ibn Khaldūn says:

"حتى لقد جعلوا مستند طريقتهم في لباس الخرقة أن عليًّا ألبسها
للحسن البصري وأخذ عليه العهد بالتزام الطريقة واتصل ذلك
عندهم بالجنيد من شيوخهم ولا يعلم هذا أحد على وجه صحيح

Muqaddima (ed. Quatrimere), v. 2, p. 164.

[2] Al-Muḥāsibī was born towards A.H. 165 (A.D. 781) at Baṣra; he was an Arab. Later he came to Baghdād and settled there.

he bade me question him, but I said: 'I have no questions to ask you.' Then he said: 'Ask me about anything that comes into your mind.' Now questions crowded in on me, and I asked him about them and he gave me answers to them straight away. Then he departed to his house and set them down in writing."[1]

From this story we see the type of relationship which obtained between Ḥārith and al-Junayd. In his youth al-Junayd liked to be alone so that he could meditate in retirement. It is to this period that the following story probably belongs. Al-Junayd said: "As-Saqaṭī remarked to me: 'I heard that you had a gathering around you in the mosque.' I said to him: 'Yes, they were my friends. We talked together in a scholarly way and benefited from one another's knowledge.' And as-Saqaṭī replied: 'Oh, Abu'l Qāsim, I see that you are beginning to spend your time with the common people.' "[2] Muḥāsibī, however, appears not to have seen any harm in his mixing with people. Al-Junayd relates that at that time he often used to say to Ḥārith al-Muhāsibī: "My delight is in solitude, but you expose me to the rough and tumble of society." And then he would say to me: "How often will you say to me: 'My delight is in solitude?' Though half of mankind were to draw near to me, I should not find any delight in their company, and though the other half were to keep away from me, I should not feel lonely because of their distance from me!"[3] His predilection for retirement is attested again by the quotation in Qushayrī: "He who would be secure in faith, and confident in body and heart, should keep away from people because the times in which we live are out of joint."[4]

Another aspect of this story is that both the Shaykh and his young pupil profited from the mutual exchange of views. Al-Junayd put his questions to Ḥārith and thus opened both for Ḥārith and for himself the road to new fields of thought. There is little room for doubt that al-Ḥārith found these discussions stimulating and inspiring and that it was his custom, after a new point had been argued, to take to his pen and record,

---

[1] Abū Nu'aym, *Ḥilyat*, v. 10, p. 255.
[2] Sarrāj, *Luma'*, p. 181.
[3] Abū Nu'aym, *Ḥilyat*, v. 10, p. 256.
[4] Qushayrī, p. 51.

with that clarity, facility and simple style for which he is justly famous, the conclusions which had been reached. He writes, however, as if the theory were his own. From this it would appear that the association between al-Junayd as an exceptional pupil, and al-Ḥārith as a teacher, took place when the mind of al-Junayd had already reached a degree of maturity.

That al-Junayd was less influenced by al-Ḥārith than he was by his uncle as-Saqaṭī appears as much from the difference in doctrine between them as it does from the difference of attitude towards the significance of ethical conduct. To-day many of the works of al-Ḥārith are extant and in perusing them we understand why al-Ghazzālī describes al-Ḥārith as " outstanding for his contributions in the field of human conduct, as recognizing both the inherent weakness of the soul and the evil of human action."[1] Al-Ghazzālī, for whom the essential works of al-Junayd were not available, studied the works of al-Ḥārith, which were then highly prized. It was in this way that Muḥāsibī's ṣūfīsm, which al-Ghazzālī fully accepted and used as the foundation of his doctrine, was later to prevail in the Muslim world, especially in the lands of the eastern caliphate, where the popularity and authority of al-Ghazzālī were amply witnessed by the fact that his works were easily available and widely spread. Al-Junayd, his uncle as-Saqaṭī and Ma'rūf, while appreciating the importance of the laws of human conduct as laid down in the *sunna*, were rather more concerned with what might be described as a dynamic, continued and overriding consciousness of the Godhead. But to put the Godhead before *sunna* was fraught with danger and not right for the laity.

Muḥāsibī took an active part in the disputes with the mu'tazilites and was known for his scholastic approach to theology, though, in this field, his pronouncements are justly famed for the exactness of his terminology and the clarity of his arguments, his chief claim to fame will always be his originality as a moralist and psychologist. The care of the soul, in order to lead it on, stage by stage, to a higher state of moral purification, was his main concern. He was not interested in the mystical knowledge of Unification and Annihilation, and

---

[1] Cf. 'Arūsī in *Nata'ij-al-afkār*, v. 1, p. 94.

the vague symbolic utterances of his ṣufī contemporaries. He warned his pupils against expressions which sounded extravagant and might well have proved dangerous. The following story illustrates his attitude: "One day Abū Ḥamza of Baghdād came to the house of Muḥāsibī. Muḥāsibī had a fine house, tastefully decorated, in which he had a king bird which would suddenly burst into song. When Abu Ḥamza heard this song, he cried out: 'It is God.' Muḥāsibī became very angry and snatched up a knife, crying: 'If you don't take back what you said I'll kill you.' Abu Ḥamza replied: 'If you cannot bear what I said just now, why do you live in such a luxurious place and wear such fine clothes?—why don't you start eating black bread and coarse fare?'" By saying this he meant to convey that Muḥāsibī's anger with him showed that he had gone but a short distance on the mystical path. Only those ṣūfīs who had achieved a high degree of spiritual elevation could allow themselves the comfort of luxury without fear of distraction. Abū Ḥamza had interpreted the luxurious state of Muḥāsibī's home as proof that Muḥāsibī had reached the stage of complete indifference to the physical circumstances in which he lived.[1] Hujwīrī adds to this story:

"Muḥāsibī's disciples exclaimed: 'Oh, Shaykh, we all know him to be one of the elect Saints and Unitarians; why does the Shaykh regard him with suspicion?' Ḥārith replied: 'I do not suspect him, his opinions are excellent, and I know that he is a profound Unitarian, but why should he do something which resembles the actions of those who believe in incarnation (*hulūlīyūn*) and had the appearance of being derived from their doctrine? If a senseless bird pipes in the manner of birds, why should he behave as though its notes were the voice of God? God is indivisible, and the Eternal does not become incarnate, or united with phenomena, or commingled with them.' When Abū Ḥamza perceived the Shaykh's insight, he said: 'Oh, Shaykh, although I am right in theory, nevertheless, since my action resembled the actions of heretics, I repent and withdraw.'"[2]

This story tells us much about the attitude of Muḥāsibī. He

---

[1] Sarrāj, "Pages from *Luma'*," p. 6.
[2] Hujwīrī, *Kashf al-Maḥjūb*, p. 182.

clearly found himself out of sympathy with the unpredictable, impulsive and solipsist attitude of those mystics whose spiritual intoxication led them to see God in the most mundane phenomena. The mind should be concentrated on God only. His own mind was so clear and sober that such behaviour did not commend itself to him. He did not embark on the esoteric, but limited his teachings to that which was clear and could be discussed in the light of reason. He kept strictly to the orthodox transcendent school of religion which, for the most part, was, and is, generally accepted in Islām. For Muḥāsibī the secret of ṣufīsm lay in a profound knowledge of the Qur'ān. Muḥammad had shown the road to God, the sunna made these instructions more explicit, and the main task of a Muslim was to submit to revelation. For al-Junayd, however, the secret of ṣūfīsm was God—not as an abstract theological conception, tied by the shackles of scholastic theology, but as a personal and impersonal Godhead. Thus it was that al-Muḥāsibī gives us of his best and leads through the maze of revelation step by step and logically to an academically sound mystical conception of the deity; whereas al-Junayd was preoccupied in the first place with a different type of problem. He is in the line of Saqaṭī, Bislāmī and Dhu'l-Nūn al-Miṣrī. He seeks God with real tears and shattering spiritual tribulations and is not satisfied to let the intellect prescribe for the soul. Is it too much to see in this a reflection of Muḥāsibī's Arab descent and academic training, while al-Junayd's quest into the absolute reflects Persian speculation and Persian descent?

E. G. Browne says: "It is with ṣūfīs like Abu Yazīd of Bistām, a Persian, and al-Junayd of Baghdād (also, according to Jāmī, a Persian) that, in the latter part of the ninth and the beginning of the tenth centuries of our era, the pantheistic element first makes its definite appearance . . . in short, with these men, whom the ṣūfīs reckoned amongst their greatest teachers, a very thoroughgoing pantheism is superadded to the quietism of the older mystics. The transition is in reality a natural one; from regarding God as the only proper object of love and subject of meditation, man as a mere instrument under His controlling power 'like the pen in the hands of the scribe,' and the Spiritual Life alone as important, to regarding God as the one Reality and the Phenomenal World as a mere Mirage or Shadow of Being, is but a short step.

" It was certainly the Persian ṣūfīs who went to the greatest lengths in developing the pantheistic aspect of ṣūfīsm, yet we must bear in mind that, as appears from a study of other forms of mysticism, the step from quietism to pantheism is neither long nor difficult."[1]

One cannot help feeling that the step from quietism to pantheism was beyond the range of perception and interest for most Muslims of Arab origin at this time. For the Arabs of the desert and their descendants in the towns it was as natural as it was inevitable to submit to canonical Islām which fully satisfied their religious impulse. Their acceptance of Islām was fraught with neither doubt nor question nor speculation. Thus it was that the speculative religious philosophies of the Persians, Greeks and Indians were alien to them and had almost no significance. The only valid example which they knew of men of other religions submitting to God and devoting their lives to seeking Him was that of the eastern Christian monks. It is, therefore, not surprising that the ṣūfīs of Arab descent may well have been in debt to these monks of the desert for some of their religious ideas as well as their rough woollen garments. The Muslims of Persian descent, however, were attracted by religious speculation and the warp of their Islām was to be woven with the weft of philosophy and of the divine.

Al-Muḥāsibī, as an Arab, seems to have been considerably influenced by his contacts with Christians. Margaret Smith says: " Further, his education most evidently did not exclude contact with Christian and Jewish teaching, from which he draws illustrations and examples for his own purpose, and to which also it may be that he owed his keen sense of the essential need for moral, rather than external, purification."[2]

Margoliouth[3] adduces examples of the influence of the New Testament in Muḥāsibī. But there is no trace of any such influence in al-Junayd.

---

[1] Browne, " History of Persia," I, pp. 427–8.
[2] Smith, " Early Mystics of Baghdād," p. 6.
See Margoliouth in " Transactions of the Third International Congress for the History of Religion," I, 292 f.

Muḥāsibī was attacked by the school of the *Muḥaddithūn* (Traditionalists). It is reported that Ibn Ḥanbal attacked him because he had paid the mutazilites the compliment of refuting their tenets in scholastic arguments, a worthy enough cause, but vitiated by the means, since in Ibn Ḥanbal's view such argument went a long way to accepting the validity of Kalām.[1] Ibn Zur'a, a great traditionalist, when he was asked about Muḥāsibī and his books, said: " Beware of these books because they are full of innovations (bid'a) and are misleading."[2] The *Muḥaddithūn*, according to Massignon, objected : to his making a distinction between the conception of '*Ilm* and '*Aql*, and between *Īmān* and *Ma'rifa*; because he admitted the created character of the *Lafẓ* (holy writ); and further because he taught that the chosen in Paradise were called to have direct intercourse with the Divinity; also because he selected, as they said, his proofs, not according to the formal correctness of their " *Isnād*," but on the basis of their essential significance and their moral influence on the reader.[3]

The reaction of his contemporaries as above indicated is, of course, significant and calls for a slightly fuller elucidation. Aḥmad ibn Ḥanbal was so convinced that in the sunna lay the essence of Islām, that he not only disallowed the validity of speculation on religious matters, but he felt it to be a positive duty to forbid absolutely any debate or argument on a doctrine of religion. In his eyes Muḥāsibī was a renegade, though he behaved as an orthodox muslim, because he entered into discussions on matters which at that time were not accepted as fit matters for debate. Ibn Zur'a's opposition is again that of the ardent traditionalist for whom a work not on traditional lines is without significance, unreliable and a source of error. Massignon's summary of the opposition with which Muhāsibī met from the *Muḥaddithūn*, whom we must regard as the leading muslims of the epoch and men of influence both in the religious and the political sphere, reveals the opposition of the puritan to the mystic.

When Muḥāsibī draws a distinction between '*Ilm* and '*Aql*,

---

[1] Subkī, *Ṭabaqāt*, v. 2, p. 39. Khaṭīb, *Tārīkh*, v. 6, p. 214.
[2] Khaṭīb, *Tārīkh*, v. 8, p. 213.
[3] Handwörterbuch des Islam, p. 541.

between acquired knowledge and intuitive discrimination, between what is handed down (*manqūl*) and what is deduced (*ma'qūl*), he is accepting the weapons which the mu'tazilites used. When Muhāsibī recognizes a difference between faith (Īmān) and gnosis (Ma'rifa), he is a ṣūfī. In admitting the created character of the words of the Qur'ān (Lafẓ) Muḥāsibī declares his position vis-a-vis the mu'tazilites and says that the words of the Qur'ān (Lafẓ) are created and temporal (makhlūq), whereas what these words convey (ma'nā) is of all time and eternal (qadīm). Direct intercourse with the Divinity in the hereafter is a ṣūfī claim. Eclecticism in tradition (ḥadīth) such as Muḥāsibī practised must appear as meretricious in the eyes of a formal traditionalist. To sum up, then, Muḥāsibī's orthodox traditionalist contemporaries regarded him as suspect primarily because he was not of them, secondarily because he entered the lists against the Mu'tazilites and, in the third place, because his ṣūfīsm so coloured all he wrote as to vitiate it from the point of view of the sunna.

Ibn Ḥanbal carried his persecution of al-Muḥāsibī to the point of banning his writings and compelling him temporarily to leave Baghdād. He was later forced, through the fanaticism of the numerous followers of Ibn Ḥanbal, to live in retirement in Baghdād. When he died in the year 243 A.H. only four persons attended his funeral.[1]

It would appear that al-Junayd was aware of Muḥāsibī's predilection and preoccupation with Kalām (scholastic theology), which had rendered his books suspect in the sight of the Ḥanbalites. For his part, al-Junayd refrained from Kalām and seems always to have followed the advice of his teacher and uncle Saqaṭī. Though by nature al-Junayd was retiring, his very real appreciation of popular feeling and reaction kept him on a safe path. His caution can be seen from his answer to a question on "retirement." He replied: "Security is achieved only by those who consciously seek it, who do not set themselves up in opposition, who renounce the temptation to seek after what knowledge of Islām forbids."[2]

---

[1] Ibn Khallikān, *Wafayāt*, v. 1, p. 158.
[2] Sarrāj, *Luma'*, p. 167.

Muḥammad al-Qaṣṣāb

We know only a few facts concerning Abū Ja'far Muḥammad ibn 'Alī al-Qaṣṣāb, the third teacher of al-Junayd. Al-Junayd himself called Qaṣṣāb his "real teacher," and said: "The people connect me mainly with Sarī, but my real teacher was Muḥammad al-Qaṣṣāb."[1] It is a fact, however, that Junayd does not give us so many quotations and incidents relating to Qaṣṣāb as he does of Sarī.

Al-Khaṭīb quotes a saying of Qaṣṣāb's adduced by Junayd. "Junayd said: Our teacher, Abū Jaf'ar al-Qaṣṣāb, was asked: 'Why does it happen that the members of your circle are detached from the general run of people?' and the reply was: 'There are three circumstances which bring this about. Firstly, God does not wish the elect to have what the laity possess. Had He wished to bestow on the elect what the laity possess, then He would have had to bestow His special privilege on the laity. Secondly, God does not wish to mark the good actions of the elect on the pages of other people. Had He so wished, He would have made them associate with other people. Thirdly, they are a group of men going only towards God; therefore, God withholds everything except Himself and keeps them exclusively for Himself.' "[2]

This small quotation suggests al-Qaṣṣab's high spirituality and what a secluded life he led. It is likely that what Junayd learned from him was not commonplace, but rather the secrets reserved for the initiated. Abū Ja'far al-Qaṣṣab died in 275 A.H.

Ibn al-Karanbī

Al-Junayd was also in continuous contact with the 'Iraqī scholars and ṣūfīs who lived in Baghdād. Of these 'Irāqīs with whom he associated, Abū Ja'far al-Karanbī al-Baghdādī[3] is said

---

[1] Khaṭīb, *Tārīkh Baghdād*, v. 3, p. 62.

[2] Ibid.

[3] Ibn al-Karanbī ابن الكَرَنْبي as in Tārīkh Baghdād; in *Luma'* ibn al-Kurrīnī ابن الكُرينى Nicholson has corrected it to ibn al-Karanbī (see *Luma'*, p. 459); in *Talbis Inblis* ibn al-Koraytī ابن الكريتي p. 350 in *Ḥilyat al-Awliyā'*, v. 10, p. 224. ibn al-Kūfī. ابن الكوفى

to have influenced most of the ascetics of Baghdād at this time. He was well known in Baghdād for his patched garments (*muraqq'a*). It is said that before he died he made a will in which he bequeathed his robe to one of his friends. This friend found that the arm of the robe weighed 13 raṭl . . . so many patches were attached to it.[1] Many other anecdotes are related concerning this robe.[2]

Ibn al-Karanbī was a pupil of Abū 'Abd Allah al-Burāthī[3] and an intimate teacher of al-Junayd,[4] who has recounted many sayings and stories of him. Once Junayd asked Ibn al-Karanbī: " What is your opinion of a man who talks knowledge, but does not practise it? " and the reply was: " If that man is you . . . continue! "[5]

One day al-Junayd offered Ibn al-Karanbī a purse of money, but it was refused. Al-Junayd said: " If you are not in need and yet will take it, you will please a Muslim's heart." So the purse was accepted.[6]

It is related, too, by al-Junayd, that, when al-Karanbī was dying, al-Junayd was sitting by his head gazing upwards at the sky. Ibn Karanbī said: " It is distant " and thereupon Junayd turned his eyes to the ground. Again he heard Ibn al-Karanbī say: " It is distant." Sarrāj explains this conversation by pointing out that God is so near to us, there is no need to look either at the sky or at the ground in order to be aware of Him.[7]

When the ṣūfīs of Baghdād were persecuted, Ibn al-Karanbī left the town. As he walked away in his old patched gown, with his long flowing beard, he made a funny face and shook his head to and fro, so that people said he was mad.[8]

It seems from these stories that Ibn al-Karanbī's personality and manner were eccentric in the extreme, but that he was simple, sincere and friendly. His life in humble seclusion must have stood out as a model before the eyes of his friends and pupils.

---

[1] *Tārīkh Baghdād*, v. 14, p. 414. *Talbīs Iblīs*, p. 191.
[2] Ibid.
[3] Abū 'Abd Alla b. Ali Ja'far al-Burathī, see v. 10, p. 224, of *Ḥilyat al-Awliyā'*.
[4] See *Luma'*, pp. 146, 210, 188. *Qūt al-Qulūb*, v. 3, p. 109. *Iḥyā'*, v. 4, p. 347.
[5] *Luma'*, p. 182. *Ḥilyat at-Awliyā'*, v. 10, p. 224.
[6] *Luma'*, p. 198. *Ḥilyat al-Awliyā*, v. 10, p. 224.
[7] *Tārīkh Baghdād*, v. 14, p. 414. *Luma'*, p. 210.
[8] Ibid.

He reached a high stage as a ṣūfī by his religious exercises, by conquering his desires, and by a true purification of his soul. Al-Junayd probably was influenced by Ibn Karanbī, not so much with regard to theory, but by his living ṣūfīsm, his manner and his way of life.

Al-Qanṭarī

Another of his associates in Baghdād was Shaykh Abū Bakr Muḥammad ibn Muslim 'Abd al-Raḥmān al-Qanṭarī. Al-Qanṭarī associated with Ma'rūf al-Karkhī and Bishr ibn al-Ḥārith al-Ḥafī[1] and was renowned in Baghdad for his piety and ascetic life.

Al-Junayd frequently visited al-Qanṭarī's house and many were the discussions which took place. On presenting himself one day at noon, he was asked by al-Qanṭarī: " Have you no work to do that you come to me at this hour? " to which Junayd replied: " If my visits to you are not work . . . then what is work? "[2]

Qanṭarī was of a retiring and reserved disposition. He was rather poor and earned a meagre livelihood by copying, for little reward, the collection of traditions compiled by Sufyān al-Thawrī. He died in 260 A.H.[3]

As already stated, Junayd met most of the 'Irāqī Shaykhs of his time, amongst whom were Abū Ya'qūb al-Zayyāt, Muḥammad al-Samīn and Ḥasan al-Bazzāz. To their opinions in discussion he listened attentively and he has himself related many of their views as authoritative.

Abū Ḥafṣ al-Ḥaddād

Al-Junayd also met in Baghdād Shaykhs who were not 'Irāqī, but who had come to the metropolis as visiting travellers. Amongst these distinguished visitors was one Abū Ḥafṣ 'Amr ibn Salama al-Ḥaddād al-Nishāpūrī, the Shaykh of Khorāsān, who was a Mu'tazilite and had written several books on scholastic theology. In referring to one of these books, *Kitāb al-Jārūf fī Takāfu' al-Adilla*, Ibn al-Nadīm stated that it was refuted by

---

1 *Ḥilyat al-Awliyā'*, v. 10, pp. 305, 309.
2 Ibid., *Tārīkh Baghdād*, v. 3, p. 256.
3 *Tārīkh Baghdād*, v. 3, p. 256.

Abū 'Alī al-Jubbā'ī, al-Khayyāṭ and al-Ḥārith al-Warrāq.[1] Al-Khayyāṭ, in his book, *Kitāb al-Intiṣār*, has referred to Abū Ḥafṣ as a " Rāfiḍī " and stated that he had adopted the theory of *Qidam al-Ithnayn*[2] (the eternity of the attribute and the essence), a belief not held by the mu'tazilites.

In addition to this lesser difference in the metaphysical sphere, we learn that Abū Ḥafs, whilst being a mu'tazilite, was also a ṣūfī. There were, in fact, numerous mu'tazilites, such as Abū Sa'īd al-Ḥoṣarī aṣ-Ṣūfī and Abū Mūsa 'Īsa ibn al-Haytham aṣ-Ṣūfī, whose full names tell us that they were ṣūfīs. Their fellow mu'tazilites are stated to have said of them that originally they were mu'tazilites but were later corrupted. It seems that Abū Ḥafṣ was one of their number.[3]

Abū Ḥafṣ's teachers were 'Abdullah ibn Mahdī al-Abīwardī and 'Alī an-Naṣrabādhī, and he also had associated with Aḥmad ibn Khuḍrūya.[4]

Al-Junayd held Abu Ḥafṣ in high esteem and said of him: " He was one of those who understood the meaning of divine reality . . . one had but to meet him to feel satisfied and enriched . . . he spoke from the depth of his heart and was a perfect scholar . . . the Shaykhs of Khorāsān are on a very high level and likewise are their followers."[5]

When Abū Ḥafṣ went to Baghdād he lived as a guest in the house of Junayd, who relates the following story of the visit: " Abū Ḥafṣ remained in my home for a year with eight of his friends. Every day I offered them fresh food, new clothes and perfumes. On his leaving I presented him and his friends with new attire and, on taking his farewell, Abū Ḥafṣ said to me: ' When you visit Nīshāpūr we shall treat you with all nobility and generosity. What you have done for us was a self-imposed task. If the poor come to you, do not worry: for when you are hungry, they will be hungry; when you are fed, they also will be fed, and their coming and going will not harass you.' "[6]

---

[1] *Fihrist* (Chester Beatty MS.), 118a.
[2] *Intiṣār*, pp. 97, 105.
[3] *Fihrist. Op. cit.*
[4] *Tārīkh Baghdād*, v. 12, p. 220.
[5] Ibid., p. 221.
[6] *Sam'ānī*, p. 158a.

It has been said that Abū Ḥafṣ did not converse well in Arabic, his mother tongue being Persian. However, when he met the Shaykhs of Baghdād, including Junayd, in the Shunīziyya Mosque, he conversed with them in elegant Arabic, so that they despaired of rivalling him in eloquence. They asked him: " What is generosity? " He said: " Let one of you begin and declare what it is." Junayd said: " In my opinion generosity consists in not regarding your generosity and in not referring to it yourself." Abū Ḥafṣ replied: " How well the Shaykh has spoken, but in my opinion generosity consists in doing justice and in not demanding justice." Junayd said to his disciples: " Rise, for Abū Ḥafṣ has surpassed Adam and all his descendants (in generosity)."[1]

It is said that Abū Ḥafṣ was rich, as his silken raiment was costly and magnificent and his house was beautifully furnished.[2] This suggests rather an aesthetic mysticism, not based on the ascetic life, but rather on a gentle and noble attitude to life. In this Abū Ḥafṣ differed from the ascetic behaviour and attitude of most members of the Baghdādī School of Ṣūfīs. This level of the Khorasan in the spiritual and material sphere impressed al-Junayd greatly.

It is not unlikely that al-Junayd had learned how to appreciate aesthetic values from the wealthy and sensitive al-Muhāsibī and that this lesson was re-learned while Abū Ḥafṣ and his companions resided with him for a year. Here were Muslims, scholars, abreast of the times in all the issues which preoccupied the learned world, who knew how to savour beauty and comfort which were ephemeral, but who, none the less, achieved a level of spirituality, a state of Tawḥīd, which inspired his respect and his admiration. Asceticism was clearly not the exclusive path to spiritual elevation and it was pointless to make an issue of abnegation. All the anecdotes about him tend to confirm the view that Abū Ḥafṣ liked luxury and accepted physical comforts without their, in any way, interfering with his mystical meditations. It may well be that al-Junayd either accepted anew or became confirmed in his view that what mattered for him primarily was the ṣūfī conception and the ṣūfī experience and

---

[1] *Hujwīrī*, p. 124.
[2] *Luma'*, p. 188.

that the high level of ṣūfīsm in Khorasān impressed him profoundly. It may well be that Abū Ḥafṣ acted as the significant motive which caused al-Junayd to cast off the ascetic side of ṣufīsm, which appeared to him to be secondary, and to embrace wholeheartedly the concentrated devotion on spiritual experience and development to which his writings so amply testify.

Abū Ḥafṣ died about 260 A.H.[1]

Yaḥya ibn Mu'ādh and Abū Yazīd al-Bisṭāmī

Another distinguished visitor to Baghdād whom al-Junayd met was Abū Ja'far Yaḥya ibn Mu'ādh ibn Ja'far ar-Rāzī (died 258 A.H.). It is related that, when Yaḥya visited Baghdād, the pious used to gather around him to converse with him and at one of these sessions, when Junayd rose to speak, Yaḥya said to him: " Keep silent, O sheep! Who are you to speak when men speak? "[2] It is probable that al-Junayd was still a comparatively young man at this date, since there remain fragments of a correspondence of great importance between Yaḥya and al-Junayd. If these fragments are genuine, as they appear to be, then they would most probably be of a later date than Yaḥya's visit to Baghdād.[3]

Yaḥya was famous for his teachings on Ma'rifa (gnosticism) and was in contact with the famous ṣūfī Ṭayfūr ibn 'Īsa ibn Sharwasān Abū Yazīd al-Bisṭāmī (died 261 A.H.). Junayd did not meet Abū Yazīd nor was there correspondence between them, but Junayd knew of him through his books and also through many friends whom they had in common, particularly Yaḥya Ibn Mu'ādh. Al-Junayd has, in fact, written a commentary on the sayings of Abū Yazīd, parts of which are still preserved.[4] The sayings of Abū Yazīd are difficult to understand, because they are couched in recondite and obscure language. Al-Junayd's commentary on Abū Yazīd's mystic ejaculations is generally not favourable; he sees them as jejune catchwords of little merit. Though in his intellectual judgment al-Junayd has to disparage what Abū Yazīd wrote, this did not

---

[1] Qushayrī, p. 17.
[2] *Tārīkh Baghdād*, v. 14, p. 209. Ibn Khallikān, v. 2, p. 296.
[3] See later " Rasā'il."
[4] *Kitāb al Luma'*, pp. 380–387.

prevent him from recognizing Abū Yazīd's spirituality and appreciating his status as a ṣūfī. He said of him: " He is amongst us like Gabriel amongst the angels."[1] None the less, the following extracts are evidence of his critical attitude. He says, for instance, in his commentary: " Abū Yazīd has described certain aspects of his knowledge of Unification, which reveal a somewhat primitive method of approach suitable only for beginners." And further: " That his descriptions are only half complete."[2]

Abū Yazīd's popularity in the ṣūfī world did not wane after his death. Such sayings of his as " There is nothing in this garment of mine except God " are quoted to this day by those that tread the ṣūfī path. But Abū Yazīd did not formulate a doctrine or work out a mystical theological system. He has been described by orientalists as a pantheist, and, if we take this to mean that he recognized his intuition in religious matters to be godly and that this intuition revealed the sentient world to him as being the unity of God, then we are compelled to point out that he and al-Junayd were far apart in their mystical approach. For Bisṭāmī in his elevated state the ephemeral world took on divinity, whereas for al-Junayd in his elevated state the ephemeral world did not exist. Al-Junayd achieved mystical union with a Godhead that was timeless, untrammelled by earthly conceptions, unshackled by intellectual considerations, Himself so beyond human description that contact with Him was ineffable.

Yūsuf b. al-Ḥusayn

Another distinguished ṣūfī who visited Baghdād at this period, and who carried on a correspondence with al-Junayd, was Abū Ya'qūb Yūsuf ibn al-Ḥusayn ibn 'Alī ar-Rāzī, who was then the Shaykh of Rayy and Jibal (died 304 A.H.). He was a skilled stylist and wrote with unusual clarity. One of his letters has most fortunately been preserved in the body of the manuscript of al-Junayd's rasā'il.[3] From the literary point of view, it is the finest specimen of contemporary ṣufī literature which has come down to us. Its intrinsic merit as a piece of

---

[1] Hujwīrī, p. 106.
[2] *Kitāb al Luma'*, Op. cit.
[3] See p. 84.

Arabic prose was recognized immediately and it was passed round and esteemed in the circle of al-Junayd's acquaintance. Even to-day, as we read it, we are reminded of the standard of prose style achieved by such men as 'Abd-ul-Ḥamīd and Ibn ul-Muqaffa'. But Yūsuf, though of Persian origin, did not indulge in flowery expression. His merit, the fineness of his style (ḥusnu Kālamihī), springs from the clarity of his perception and the integrity of his understanding. He does not allow the words to inspire the thought or befog the issue, but has clearly worked out his problem intellectually and expressed his meaning with elegance and tact. Yūsuf was clearly an outstanding intelligence and gifted with unusual perception in ṣūfī matters. He was as welcome with Aḥmad ibn Ḥanbal, the great legal mind, as he was with Dhū'n Nūn al-Miṣrī, to whom so much was revealed in mystical experience. That such a man should rate al-Junayd so high and call him the *sayyid al-ḥukamā' wal'ārifīn min ahlī'asrihi* (the leader of the learned and mystics of this our age) is not the idle flattery of the sycophant. It is the recognition by a contemporary of deep perception of the genius and spirituality of al-Junayd.[1]

Abū al-Ḥusayn appears to have been a great traveller. He visited many countries, including 'Irāq, where he met and became friends with the famous 'Irāqī ṣūfī Abū Sa'īd al-Kharrāz and probably also al-Junayd; Syria, where he met and heard the distinguished Syrian ṣūfī Aḥmad ibn Abī al-Ḥawārī; and Egypt, where he associated with Dhū'n Nūn al-Miṣrī.[2] Dhū'n Nūn (died 245 A.H.) was Abū al-Ḥusayn's principal guide in ṣūfīsm. Yūsuf used to quote Dhū'n Nūn constantly and was largely instrumental in spreading his ideas in Khorasān. Dhū'n Nūn visited Baghdād for a short time,[3] but we cannot discover whether or not he met al-Junayd. In passing, it should be noted that there are very few quotations or references to Dhū'n Nūn in al-Junayd's sayings and writings.

Junayd's Travels

Junayd rarely travelled, but remained mostly in Baghdād,

---

[1] *Ḥilyat al-Awliyā'*, v. 10, p. 240.
[2] *Tārīkh Baghdād*, v. 14, p. 314. Abī Ya'la, *Ṭabaqāt al-Ḥanābila*, p. 279.
[3] Ibn Khallikān, v. 1, p. 126.

although he did make the pilgrimage once.[1] It appears from Qushayrī that al-Junayd made the pilgrimage in his early youth.[2] Baghdād, however, was the centre of travel and trade and the centre of spiritual life, so that he had the opportunity of meeting many distinguished people in his home town.

Conclusion

This survey shows that the contacts and relations of al-Junayd with the famous ṣūfīs and religious thinkers who were his contemporaries, both in 'Irāq and in distant lands, were both wide and numerous.

His vast and many-sided learning and his clarity of thinking enabled him to absorb this variety of thought and teachings of his period, and to transform them through the medium of his personality, and, by adding his own ideas and experiences, to reach his own mystical way and his own philosophical system. He preserved all that was sound in the thoughts of the individual ṣūfīs, putting them in a certain order. We may say, as Hartmann remarks,[3] he " Islamized Mysticism and integrated the thoughts of the ṣūfīs, many of which at first may have appeared strange in the framework of Islām. He cut short the intellectual and moral extravagances without relinquishing the essence." He joined, so to speak, the many wild mountains streams of ṣūfīsm into a firm and constant river-bed. He, in fact, has joined and united Mysticism with Orthodoxy. He is thus rightly called the " Shaykh al-Ṭarīqa," the " Master of the Way."[4] Through him, we may say, ṣufīsm reached its fulfilment.

For this, Junayd has been accepted and praised by all authorities in Islām, Mystics and conservative Orthodox alike. They have called him the " scholarly ṣufī," the " chief of the community," " the peacock among the divines." Even traditionalists like Ibn Taymīya and Ibn al-Qayyim, who were very anti-ṣufī, accepted his authority and appreciated his *tarīqa*, and spoke highly of him.[5]

---

[1] Sarrāj, *Luma'*, p. 207, but ibn Khallikān reported that he made the pilgrimage 30 times, which is doubtful.

[2] Qushayrī, p. 147.

[3] Der Islam, v. 6, p. 69.

[4] Sulamī, *Ṭabaqāt*, fol. 32.

[5] Ibn Taymīya, *Minhāj*, v. 3, p. 85. Ibn Qayyim, *Madārij*, v. 7, p. 137.

Chapter III

THE MYSTICAL SCHOOL OF BAGHDĀD

The early founders of the Mystical School of Baghdād were Saqaṭī and Muḥāsibī. Saqaṭī was of Persian origin, while Muḥāsibī was an Arab; both, however, were Sunnites, that is, they followed the orthodox tradition of Islām. Saqaṭī represented, we might almost say, the advanced wing in his daring research into the Unity of God (*Tawḥīd*), while Muḥāsibī represented the conservative wing in his conscious moderation and in his concern with the practical moral issues.

The Esoteric Character of the School

The main topic for the School of Baghdād was certainly *Tawhīd*. They were called by their contemporaries *Arbāb at-Tawḥīd*, the " People of Tawḥīd."[1] They pursued the knowledge of Tawḥīd to dangerous heights. They developed their doctrine, worked out their system and taught it in secret. It was in keeping with this secrecy that they used to formulate their teachings and ideas in a special esoteric terminology (Ishārāt), invented for this purpose.

It is reported that al-Junayd restricted the number of people with whom he spoke on ṣūfīsm to no more than twenty.[2] No doubt he felt that his teaching was of a very secret nature and might be a source of danger if publicly known, because it was liable to be misunderstood. When he wrote to a friend, he would word his letter very cautiously. In one such letter he says: " What prevented me from communicating with you was the thought that my letter might fall into the hands of someone without your knowledge. Some time ago I wrote a letter to a friend in Iṣfahān; someone opened it, but found it difficult to understand, for which I was very sorry indeed. One must be kind to these people and careful of what one says and talk to

[1] Sarrāj, pages from *Kitāb al-Luma'*, Arabic Text, p. 12.
[2] Makkī, *Qūt al-Qulūb*, v. 2, p. 30. *Iḥyā'*, v. 1, p. 42.

them in a manner which they understand. May God keep you safe and in peace! . . . You must control your tongue and know your contemporaries. Talk to the people so that they can understand and omit that which they cannot understand."[1]

Sarrāj, in the *Kitāb al-Luma'* records several stories which describe the efforts of the ṣūfīs of this period to keep their teachings secret. He tells us, for instance, the following story: " 'Amr ibn 'Uthmān al-Makkī had notes which contained special and private knowledge, but these fell into the hands of one of his students, who ran away with them. When 'Amr al-Makkī heard this, he said: 'I am afraid his hands, feet and head will be cut off.' It was said that the young man who stole the letters was al-Ḥusayn al-Ḥallāj, and he was killed later on account of this, and thus the prophecy which 'Amr al-Makkī had uttered was fulfilled."[2]

Certain ṣūfīs have gone so far as to say that Ḥallāj was killed because he revealed the secret teachings of the ṣūfīs to the laity. 'Aṭṭār says: "One of the great ṣūfīs stated that, on the day on which Ḥallāj was crucified, he spent the whole night under the cross praying. When day broke, the ṣūfī heard a voice saying: 'We have revealed to him a secret of the kings.' "[3] 'Aṭṭār also relates that Shiblī said: "During this night I remained praying and at dawn I went to sleep. In my sleep I saw the day of Resurrection and heard the voice of God saying: 'This was because he has divulged our secret to others.' "[4]

From these stories we can see how the ṣūfīs of Baghdād at this period advisedly tried to conceal their teachings from the public at large. They knew that the laity were not capable of understanding them.

The ṣūfīs held that ultimate religious truths contained an element of mystery and that none should reveal this element of mystery to the uninitiated. They held that the revealing of the secret of the nature of Divinity was heresy. Some of them taught that if the secret of the nature of Divinity were revealed that prophecy would cease. Further, they taught that prophecy

---

[1] Risālat al-Junayd to Abī Bakr al-Kisā'ī, *Luma'*, p. 239.
[2] Sarrāj, pages from *Kitāb al-Luma'*, p. 9.
[3] 'Aṭṭar, *Tadhkirat al-Awliyā'*, v. 2, p. 26.
[4] Ibid., p. 12.

had a secret which, if revealed, would cause knowledge to cease and that, if the secret of knowledge were revealed, natural law would cease.[1] So we see that the ṣūfīs were fully aware of the nature of their esoteric knowledge and that it could not be communicated to the orthodox because of its superficially heretical appearance.

Characteristic of the atmosphere in which these thinkers lived is Junayd's feeling that the knowledge of the Divine was so vast and high that his circle and he himself possessed only a small fragment of it, and even of this they could share out and explain only a little. He hints that there may have been a decline in such knowledge from the previous generation even to his time. He says: "The carpet of the knowledge of which we are now talking has been wrapped up for twenty years. We are talking at present merely on its fringe." He also said: "I have discussed with people for years knowledge which I did not understand and of which I was ignorant. I have not opposed myself to this, though I have by no means always accepted and loved it without knowing." He said further: "In the olden days we used to gather together to talk with one another about many-sided knowledge. Nowadays, nobody cares for it or asks me about it."[2]

Thus we see that Junayd, in his old age, felt that ṣūfīsm had flourished more and that people were more sincere and more seriously inclined to ṣūfīsm in the far-off days of his youth, and that more knowledge had been revealed to those men with whom he had lived when he was young. He was, we gather, somewhat disappointed during the period of his old age, when he had many sad experiences and felt isolated.

Persecutions of the School

Towards the end of Junayd's life, the School of Baghdād suffered much. The ṣūfīs were accused of being atheists, infidels and believers in re-incarnation. Every member of the school, including al-Junayd, was publicly accused of heresy. Sarrāj has stated that, although al-Junayd had a profound knowledge of many things, was honoured and recognized as an outstanding

---

[1] Ghazzālī, Op. cit., p. 199. Makkī, Op. cit., p. 133.
[2] Makkī, *Qūt al-Qulūb*, v. 2, p. 41.

religious man and an equally great man in intellectual stature, and although he continued his religious worship, in spite of all this, the people bore witness against him as being an infidel.[1]

Many historians have related the story of the persecution of the Ṣūfī School of Baghdād. Ghulām al-Khalīl raised the case against the ṣūfīs before the Khalīf al-Muwaffaq. Junayd described himself as being simply a Jurist by profession and thus escaped the court.[2] The others were taken before the court. The accusation was that these men discussed the Love of God, while Ghulām al-Khalīl held that no love between God and man was possible, and that it was therefore heretical to use that expression about God. He held that love was an attribute only of the creature and not of the Creator, and that nobody was allowed to say: " I love God and God loves me."[3]

The ṣūfī school, al-Junayd, Nūrī, Abū Sa'īd and others, on the other hand, held that there was love between God and man. Qushayrī interpreted love (*Maḥabba*) towards God as follows: " *Maḥabba* is a condition which man feels in his heart, too subtle to be expressed in words. This subtle spiritual state leads the worshipper to recognize the greatness of God, instills in him the desire, above all things, to please God, makes him unable to tolerate God's absence, induces in him constant excitement at the thought of God; he finds no rest without God and feels an intimate comfort in continual thought of Him. Yet the idea of the love of man for God does not imply physical attraction and possession. How could it do so—since the true Infinite is too holy to be fully attained or reached or comprehended. It is more to the point to describe the man who knows maḥabba as being completely lost and overwhelmed in the beloved, than to refer to the relationship as one of possession. If the lover were described as submerged in the beloved, it would be more adequate than if they were described as being together."[4] But this love between God and man seemed, at the time, not to be an orthodox doctrine. The teaching that " I

---

[1] Sarrāj, page from *Luma'*, p. 9.
[2] Qushayrī, p. 112. Ibn al-Jawzī, *Talbīs Iblīs*, p. 172.
[3] Sarrāj, page from *Kitāb al-Luma'*, p. 5. See Ghazālī, *Iḥya*, v. 4, p. 330.
[4] Qushayrī, p. 144.

love God and God loves me" may have scandalized many a traditional mind.[1]

This was the main thesis of the accusation. Sarrāj quotes other accusations, for instance, that the ṣūfīs were said to be promoting superstition and pantheistic views. A case was opened against Nūrī, Abū Ḥamza, Raqqām, Shahhām and Sumnūn. Sarrāj says that: "Sumnūn, a friend of Junayd, was called 'the lover.' He was handsome and talked with charm. It is related that a woman disciple of Sumnūn's fell in love with him. When he knew that she loved him, he turned her out of his circle. This woman then went to al-Junayd and asked him: 'What do you think of a man who was my way to God, but then God vanished and the man remained?' Junayd knew what she meant and did not answer her. The woman had wished to marry Sumnūn, but, when he turned her out in a haughty way, she went to Ghulām al-Khalīl, his adversary, saying: 'These men,' mentioning some names, 'did not behave correctly towards me.' So Ghulām al-Khalīl took up this and other complaints and brought the case before the Khalīfa."[2]

The main point in the accusation seems to have been the terms "Love" and "Passion," which can be interpreted in various ways. It seems that the accusation against the Ṣūfī School of Baghdād confused theological objections to their teachings with objections to their behaviour.

It appears that the Qāḍī (High Judge) of Baghdād handed over the case to the Khalīfa in his capacity as supreme judge. The Khalīfa Muwaffaq decided to acquit the ṣūfīs, probably finding that there was not sufficient evidence against them. Most probably his decision was motivated by reason of state and governmental interest and not as much, as some ṣūfī authors declared, by a special sympathy on the part of the monarch towards the teachings of the ṣūfī school. All we know of this ruler is that he showed himself to be a matter-of-fact statesman and a soldier.

Yet, though they were acquitted and did not undergo any

---

[1] See further about "Maḥabba, Shawq, 'ishq" Ghazzālī, Iḥyā', p. 4, p. 286, ff. Ibn Qayyim, Madārij., v. 3, p. 4, ff.

[2] Sarrāj, page of *Luma'*, p. 8.

physical harm, this persecution, supported by a part of public opinion, was most unfortunate for the Ṣūfī School of Baghdād, and its members withdrew more and more from public life and became increasing silent and cautious.[1]

These events must have left their imprint on the soul of al-Junayd and cast a shadow over his later life. It was for him an experience leading to withdrawal.

It was probably at that time, under the influence of this trial and its wider social context, that al-Junayd began to base his teachings, more and more, on the Qu'rān, the Ḥadith and the Sunna. He probably felt that, for the good of the people, it was wiser to restrain the unbridled outbursts of individual ṣūfī thinkers. He led those " wild turbulent mountain streams " of religious enthusiasm into the benevolent channels clearly indicated for the good of the wise as well as the simple, by the tradition of Islām, so that they should not endanger the general orders of things.

MEMBERS OF THE SCHOOL

Friends of Junayd—an-Nūrī

The Baghdād School of Ṣūfīsm at this time had many distinguished members who were either friends or pupils of al-Junayd.

Among his friends and companions we think of Abū al-Ḥusayn Aḥmad ibn Muḥammad an-Nūrī. Nūrī's family originated from Khorāsān, but he was born and brought up in Baghdād. He was, like Junayd himself, a pupil of Saqaṭī, and in matters relating to the mystical way, he and Junayd were in agreement.[2] They were intimate friends and Junayd deeply appreciated Nūrī. The name " Nūrī " was given to him because, when he spoke in a dark room, the whole room would appear illuminated by the light of his spirituality and by the light of truth. Nūrī knew by intuition the innermost thoughts of his disciples, so that Junayd said of him: " Abū al-Ḥusayn knoweth the minds of man."[3] Nūrī also stressed the importance of self-

---

[1] See more details in Sarrāj, op. cit. *Qūt al-Qulūb*, v. 3, p. 114. Hujwīrī, p. 62. *Iḥyā'*, v. 4. p. 330. Ibn al-Jawzi, op. cit., pp. 169, 172, 371.

[2] Hujwīrī, p. 189.

[3] Ibid., p. 104.

sacrifice and self-abnegation, which was most difficult for a man of learning to practise, but which was an essential condition for the state of a ṣūfī. He was by no means as cautious as Junayd, and eventually was prosecuted by the authorities, and had to face the hostility of the people. He died soon after his acquittal in 295 A.H. It is related that Junayd said: "Since the death of Nūrī, no one has spoken about the essential Truth."[1] When Junayd was dying he requested that he should be buried at the side of Nūrī, but this wish was not carried out.[2]

Abū Sa'īd al-Kharrāz

Another friend of Junayd's was Abū Sa'īd Aḥmad ibn 'Īsa al-Kharrāz, who was considered one of the most distinguished ṣufīs of Baghdād at that period. He, too, was a pupil of Saqaṭī and was one of the earliest mystics to write books.[3] It is said he was the first to explain the doctrine of *fanā'* and *baqā'*. He practised self-mortification and Junayd is reported to have said: "If God asked us to do what Kharrāz is doing, we would soon perish, for we could not do it." Someone asked: "What is Kharrāz doing?" and Junayd replied: "He remains at his weaving loom year after year, but never does he forget to mention God between each two woofs."[4] Kharrāz died in 277 A.H.

Ibn 'Aṭā' al-'Ādamī

Abū al-'Abbās Aḥmad ibn Muḥammad ibn Sahl ibn 'Atā' al-'Ādamī was another friend of Junayd. They were most intimate and met on the same spiritual level. Eventually, however, a difference of opinion occurred between them and they separated and became opponents. The dispute arose regarding the rich and the poor.[5] Ibn 'Atā' maintained the superiority of those rich people who thanked God for His gifts. He argued that at the Resurrection they would be called to account for the use they had made of their wealth, and that giving such an account entails the hearing of the Divine Word—

---

[1] Qushayrī, p. 20.
[2] *Tārikh Baghdād*, v. 5, p. 130.
[3] *Ḥilyat al-Awliyā'*, v. 10, p. 246.
[4] *Nujūm*, v. 3, p. 76.
[5] *Tārikh Baghdād*, v. 3, p. 28.

without any medium between them—in the form of a reproach, and a reproach is always addressed by the beloved to the lover. Junayd, on the other hand, considered the poor superior, and he answered: " If He will call the rich to account, He will ask the poor for their apology . . . and to be asked for an apology is better than to be called to account."[1] This question appears to have been a bone of contention, both in private and in public, between the two friends, and was ultimately the cause of their separation.[2] Ibn 'Atā' died in 309 A.H.

Ruwaym

Another intimate friend of al-Junayd was Abū Muḥammad Ruwaym ibn Aḥmad, who was a great scholar and well versed in the reading and interpretation of the Qu'rān. He wrote several works on ṣūfīsm, which are often quoted, although they have not been preserved. It appears that in later years Junayd also separated from Ruwaym because, towards the end of his life, Ruwaym ranged himself on the side of the rich, gained the Khalīf's confidence and became *Qāḍī* at the Court of Baghdād.[4] Junayd was then heard to remark: " We are devotees accidentally occupied with the world, and Ruwaym is a man occupied with the world who is devoted to God." Ruwaym died in 303 A.H.

The following is a brief account of a few other distinguished friends of Junayd, who contributed to the fame of the School of Baghdād:

Abū Ḥamza Muḥammad ibn Ibrāhīm al-Baghdādī, who belonged to the circle of Saqaṭī and was one of the leading ṣufīs of Baghdād. He is said to have been the first of the ṣūfīs to speak in public.[3] He died in 269 A.H.

Abū' Abdullah 'Amr ibn 'Uthmān al-Makkī, who was a patrician of Baghdād and from whom Junayd also separated on the occasion of Makkī accepting the post of a Qāḍi.[4] Makkī was the first teacher of Ḥallaj before Junayd. He died in 297 A.H.

Abu'l Ḥasan Muḥammad ibn Isma'il Zohayr al-Nassāj, who

---

[1] Hujwīrī, p. 23.
[2] See *Qūt al-Qulūb*, v. 2, p. 191, and *Luma'*, p. 220.
[3] *Muntaẓam*, v. 3, p. 68. Ṣafadī, *al-Wāfī*, p. 344.
[4] Shadharāt, v. 2, p. 225.

was a great Shaykh and also a pupil of Saqaṭī. Junayd held Nassāj in high esteem and is reported to have said of him: "He is the best of us."[1] Both Shiblī and Khawwāṣ were converted to mysticism in Nassāj's circle. He sent Shiblī to Junayd, wishing to express his respect for the latter. Nassāj lived to a very ripe old age and probably survived Junayd by many years.

Abū Aḥmad Muṣ'ab al-Qalānisī, who, as a mystic, held as high a position in Baghdād as al-Junayd. One of Qalānisī's pupils was Abū Sa'īd al-'Arabī. Qalānisī died in 270 A.H.[2]

Abū'l Ḥasan Sumnūn ibn Ḥamza was an associate of Saqaṭī, Qaṣṣāb and Qalānisī. Sumnūn left some very fine poems and spoke of love with such beautifully tender words that he was called "the lover." He was an intimate friend of Junayd and died shortly before him, in the same year—298 A.H.[3]

Abū'l 'Abbās Aḥmad ibn Muḥammad ibn Masrūq, from Ṭūs, but lived in Baghdād. He belonged to the circle of Muḥāsibī and of Saqaṭī. He died in 298 A.H.[4]

Abū Ja'far al-Ḥaddād al-Kabīr, another well-known member of the school.[5]

These then were the leading members of the School of Baghdād, contemporaries of al-Junayd, who were to be found gathered around Saqaṭī, Muḥāsibī and the other great Shaykhs of this older generation.

JUNAYD'S PUPILS

The next generation were pupils both of al-Junayd and of his contemporaries whom we have mentioned previously.

Jurayrī

Of these pupils we should mention Abū Muḥammad Aḥmad ibn Muḥammad ibn al-Ḥusayn al-Jurayrī. He was a scholar in every branch of learning, especially in Law, and was also well versed in Theology. His status in ṣūfīsm was very high and he was a pupil of both Saqaṭī and Junayd. Al-Junayd had the

---

[1] Hujwīrī, p. 144. Qushayrī, p. 25.
[2] See *Muntaẓam*, v. 5, p. 79. Qushayrī, p. 133. *Luma'*, p. 217.
[3] *Ḥilyat al-Awliyā'*, v. 10, p. 309. *Tārīkh Baghdād*, v. 9, p. 234.
[4] *Ḥilyat al-Awliyā'*, v. 10, p. 213. *Tārīkh Baghdād*, v. 5, p. 100.
[5] *Tārīkh Baghdād*, v. 14, p. 412.

highest regard for al-Jurayrī, so much so that he is reported as having said to him: " Teach my pupils, discipline and train them."[1] Indeed, when Junayd was dying, he was asked by those around him: " Who will succeed you? " He replied: " Abū Muḥammad al-Jurayrī."[2] After Junayd's death, Jurayrī therefore took his place as a teacher of Junayd's circle of pupils. Al-Jurayrī died in 311 A.H. By an unfortunate mischance, when a pilgrim, he was crushed to death in the stampede on the Mecca high road during the battle of Obeir.[3]

Shiblī

Another remarkable pupil of Junayd was Abū Bakr Dulaf ibn Jahdar al-Shiblī. He was at first a chamberlain to the Khalīf, but later was converted to ṣūfīsm at a gathering at the house of Nassāj. He relinquished his official post and became a disciple of Junayd. Apparently al-Shiblī was rather hot-headed and over-enthusiastic and Junayd, although he liked him greatly, is reported as having said: " Shiblī is always drunk . . . if he became sober, he would be an *Imām* from whom people would benefit."[4] It is related that one day, when Shiblī entered the bazaar, the people said: " He is mad." To which Shiblī replied: " You think I am mad, and I think you are sane. May God increase my madness and your sense."[5] There is another anecdote which is characteristic of Shiblī. One day, filled with rapturous ecstasy, he approached Junayd. On observing that Junayd was sad, he enquired as to the cause of the trouble, and Junayd said: " He who seeks shall find." Shiblī at once replied: " No, he who finds shall seek! "[6] Shiblī was noted for his subtleness in the use of symbolic allusions (*ishārāt*), and in his many short aphorisms, of which there are frequent examples in the classical collections of *shaṭḥ*. He was also conspicuous for his deliberate eccentricities and his queer ascetic practices. In the story of al-Ḥallāj the role attributed to Shiblī is very important. He seems to have continued venerating al-Ḥallāj

---

[1] Hujwīrī, p. 148.
[2] *Tārīkh Baghdād*, v. 4, p. 432.
[3] Ibid., p. 433.
[4] *Luma'*, p. 404.
[5] Hujwīrī, p. 415.
[6] Hujwīrī, p. 414.

in secret, after having denied him in public. Dogmatically, he had the same attitude as Junayd, but in his way of speech and behaviour he differed from him in the extreme.

In the classical *Silsila* he forms a link in the chain between his teacher Junayd and his pupil Naṣrābādī. Shiblī was a Baghdādi, born and brought up in the metropolis. He died in 334 A.H. and his tomb is still visited in the A'zamīya quarter of Baghdād.[1]

Ḥallāj

One of the most famous pupils of al-Junayd was Abū'l Mughīth al-Ḥusayn ibn Manṣūr al-Ḥallāj. He was brought up in Tustar and was a pupil of Sahl al-Tustarī, but later he came to Baghdād and joined 'Amr al-Makkī. It is said that Ḥallāj, in a temper, broke his friendship with 'Amr al-Makkī and went to Junayd. Junayd asked him for what purpose he had come, to which Ḥallāj replied: " For the purpose of associating with the Shaykh." Junayd replied: " I do not associate with madmen. Association demands sanity; if that is wanting, the result is such behaviour as yours towards Sahl b. 'Abdallah Tustarī and 'Amr." Ḥusayn said: " Oh, Shaykh, sobriety and intoxication are two attributes of man, and man is hidden from his Lord until his attributes are annihilated." " O son of Manṣūr," said Junayd, " you are in error concerning sobriety and intoxication. The former denotes soundness of one's spiritual state in relation to God, while the latter denotes excess of longing and extremity of love; neither of them can be fulfilled by human effort. Oh son of Manṣūr, in your words I see much folly and nonsense."[2]

'Amr al-Makkī said of Ḥallāj: " If I could meet him, I would kill him with my own hand." When asked the reason for his anger, he replied: " I was reading a verse from the Qur'ān and Ḥallāj said: ' I, too, can speak like that.' "[3] Ḥallāj's teachings were very similar to those of Junayd and the Ṣūfī School of Baghdād. He presented Junayd's doctrine of Unification, *Tawḥīd*, however, with such an excess of realism that it shocked many muslims. The doctrine which he put

[1] Cf. *Luma'*, pp. 395–406. *Talbīs Iblīs*, pp. 358–361.
[2] Hujwīrī, p. 189.
[3] *Tārīkh Baghdād*, v. 8, p. 121.

forth in his Kitāb *aṭ-Ṭawāsīn*, he summed up in the formula: " Ana'l Ḥaqq " (" I am God "), so it is not astonishing that, when Ḥallāj was arrested and prosecuted on the charge of heresy, many Shaykhs disavowed him.

Al-Khaṭīb gives us a very important quotation expressing the relation of Ḥallāj to the Baghdād School. The following words were written in a letter of Ḥallāj to one of his friends: " From the most gracious, most merciful (Al-Raḥmān, Al-Raḥīm) (which are the Qur'ānic attributes of God) to so and so." When this letter was placed before him, he said: " Yes, that is my handwriting and I have written this." He was questioned: " You have been proclaiming your prophetic power and now you proclaim your divinity? " To which Ḥallāj replied: " I am not proclaiming my divinity, but it is what we mystics call the complete Unification with the Divine Will ('ayn al-jam'). God is the Writer and I am only an instrument." When asked: " Are there others who hold these principles? " he said, " Yes—Ibn 'Aṭā, Abū Muḥammad al-Jurayrī and Abū Bakr al-Shiblī. Jurayrī and Shiblī keep their thoughts concealed, but not so Ibn 'Atā'." Jurayrī and Shiblī as witnesses were questioned, but they both denied Ḥallāj. Ibn 'Atā', however, declared his agreement with Ḥallāj's doctrine and in consequence was executed.[1]

Nicholson sums up the case of Ḥallāj in the following words: " Ḥallāj was so deeply in earnest, that it was impossible for him to compromise with his conscience. Against the public authority of the Muslim Church and State he sets up the personal authority immediately derived from God with whom the saint is one. And he was no theorist like Junayd; he was suspected of dealings with the Carmathians, he had preached his faith to believers and infidels alike, and, above all, sought to win converts by working ' evidentiary ' miracles. On these grounds he was justly condemned. His crime was not that, as later ṣūfīs put it, ' he divulged the mystery of the Divine Lordship,' but that in obedience to an inward call he proclaimed and actively asserted a truth which involves religious, political and social anarchy."[2] Ḥallāj was condemned to death and executed in

---

[1] *Tārīkh Baghdād*, v. 8, p. 127.
[2] The Legacy of Islam, p. 218.

Baghdād in 309 A.H. The research on the profound and historically significant teachings of Ḥallāj has become possible through recovery of documents and exhaustive studies of the scattered Ḥallājian fragments by Professor Massignon, of the University of Paris.[1]

Other well-known pupils of Junayd were Ja'far al-Khuldī and Abū Sa'id al-A'rābī, whom we have already mentioned; Abū 'Alī Aḥmad Muḥammad al-Rūdhabārī al-Baghdādī, who died in Egypt in 322 A.H.; Abu Bakr Muḥammad ibn al-Kittāni al-Baghdādī, who died in Mecca in 322 A.H.; Abū'l Ḥasan 'Alī ibn Muḥammad al-Muzayyin, who died in 328 A.H.; Abu Muḥammad 'Abdullah ibn Muḥammad al-Murta'ish, who died in 328 A.H.; Abū Ya'qūb Isḥāq ibn Muḥammad an-Nahrajūrī, who died in 330 A.H. We name these pupils of al-Junayd, but he had many others from Baghdād and a considerable number who came to him from distant places.

Baghdād at that time was the spiritual and cultural capital of the Islamic World, and in this setting the Ṣūfī School of Baghdād flourished and was truly representative as such. Its influence spread far and wide, to the western countries such as Syria, Egypt, Arabia and Africa, and to the east as far as Khurāsān. This school held in itself all the preceding and contemporary mystic thoughts belonging to and within the reach of the Moslem World.[2]

Makkī says: " When our Shaykh Abu Sa'id ibn al-A'rābī wrote his book *Ṭabaqāt al-Nussāk*, he described the first man who taught this knowledge and the others who came after him, men of Basra, Syrians and Khurāsānīs, and said that the last to come was the Baghdād School." He also said " that the last person to teach ṣūfism was al-Junayd; he had vision and truth and expression, and we hesitate to mention anyone after him."[3]

The circle of the Ṣūfī School of Baghdād was at the time very much in the centre of spiritual life in general, and as a central point of this spiritual circle of friends and students we find the personality of al-Junayd.

---

[1] See Massignon, *Kitāb at Tawāsīn.*

[2] Mecca, as the chief place of pilgrimage, has always played an important role in spreading Ṣūfī teaching in the outlying countries of the Islamic World.

[3] *Qūt al-Qulūb*, v. 2, p. 41.

Chapter IV

THE PERSONALITY OF AL-JUNAYD

We may assume from the various sources which we have examined that al-Junayd was a gifted and thoughtful boy. His brilliant talents showed themselves at an early age and were soon discovered by his uncle Saqaṭī, himself, as we have seen, a distinguished mystic and theological thinker and also an eminent educationist. Saqaṭī bestowed infinite care on the boy, developing and disciplining his talents, and restraining him from wasting himself before admiring audiences, as infant prodigies are apt to do.

Saqaṭī also ordered the lad not to mix with the people, but he himself developed Junayd's youthful mind by conversing and putting questions to him in a " Socratic " manner, and he allowed him to listen to the conversations of the distinguished Shaykhs who used to gather at his home. Under the influence of his uncle, Junayd, therefore, led a retired and reserved life at home in his early years, thus discovering for himself the mystical path—the path of the ṣūfī. He was rather a shy youth.

On attaining the age of a student, when he was about twelve, Junayd studied mainly law at the feet of Abū Thawr, and very soon it was obvious that the young man had the makings of a remarkable jurist, as he gave striking answers to complicated legal questions which occurred in the circle of Abu Thawr, his friends and students.

He seems to have shown and retained an originality of thought, a quick wit and a discerning intelligence, and a splendidly clear diction throughout his life as, for instance, is shown in the anecdote between himself and Ibn al-Karanbī.

In his attitude towards life, he appears to have fallen neither into the extreme of aesthetic luxury nor of hardy asceticism, both of which were prevalent amongst the ṣūfīs of his time.

Junayd was a silk merchant by trade and is stated to have

had considerable means, which he used moderately and judiciously for his own living, and which he utilized in the main in entertaining his numerous friends. His house in Baghdād seems to have been a centre for the ṣūfīs of the town and for those from other countries passing through the capital, a meeting place where they gathered and remained as guests. His money was also used to help many poor ṣūfīs who followed the ascetic way of life.

He was regarded by his colleagues as an excellent friend, understanding and loyal, and many of his friendships continued throughout his life, as is confirmed by these many stories and by his exchange of letters. No information exists to show whether or not Junayd had a wife and children. No sons of his are mentioned anywhere and, if he had a family of his own, they cannot have played a central role in his life.

In an age when travelling of ṣūfīs was a common feature, al-Junayd cannot have travelled much, as the only journey which has been recorded is his pilgrimage to Mecca. It would seem that Junayd was not in favour of making numerous pilgrimages to Mecca; he rather felt that pilgrimages to Mecca should be on a spiritual plane, and his attitude is illustrated by the following story:

" A certain man came to Junayd. Junayd asked him whence he came. He replied: ' I have been on the pilgrimage.' Junayd said: ' From the time when you first journeyed from your home have you also journeyed away from all sins? ' He said: ' No.' ' Then,' said Junayd, ' you have made no journey. At every stage where you halted for the night did you traverse a station on the way to God? ' He said: ' No.' ' Then,' said Junayd, ' you have not trodden the road stage by stage. When you put on the pilgrim's garb at the proper place did you discard the attributes of humanity as you cast off your ordinary clothes? ' ' No.' ' Then you have not put on the pilgrim's garb. When you stood on 'Arafāt did you stand one instant in contemplation of God? ' ' No.' ' Then you have not stood on 'Arafāt. When you went to Muzdalifa and achieved your desire did you renounce all sensual desires? ' ' No.' ' Then you have not gone to Muzdalifa. When you circumambulated the Temple did you behold the beauty of God in the abode of purification? '

'No.' 'Then you have not circumambulated the Temple. When you ran between Ṣafā and Marwa did you attain to the rank of purity (ṣafā') and virtue (muruwwat)?' 'No.' 'Then you have not run. When you came to Mina did all your wishes (munyatha) cease?' 'No.' 'Then you have not yet visited Mina. When you reached the slaughter-place and offered sacrifices did you sacrifice the objects of sensual desire?' 'No.' 'Then you have not sacrificed. When you threw the stones did you throw away whatever sensual thoughts were accompanying you?' 'No.' 'Then you have not yet thrown the stones and you have not yet performed the pilgrimage. Return and perform the pilgrimage in the manner which I have described in order that you may arrive at the station of Abraham.' "[1]

Obviously Junayd preferred to remain in Baghdād, which from year to year attracted travellers from distant lands and from all parts of the Moslem world, and which was a pre-eminent centre of commerce as well as of spiritual communication.

He had a loyal female servant named Zaitūna, who served him and two other Shaykhs, Nūrī and Abū Ḥamza.[2] A slave girl was once given him as a gift for a wife, but this girl he, in turn, presented to one of his companions.[3] Junayd was always industrious, was extremely modest in eating and drinking, and led a very regular life of prayer. As, however, he was physically stout and vigorous, some people are said to have doubted the genuineness of his ṣūfī asceticism.[4]

He disliked being involved in politics and, in order to allay the suspicions of the authorities, he did not teach in public. Neither did he mix with the Carmathians and others. At the time of the ṣūfī trials, he referred to himself as "nothing but a jurist" and remained in the background. He also held himself aloof from Ḥallāj and turned him away.

As a consequence of continual trials and prosecutions, the popularity of the ṣūfīs in the public life of Baghdād waned and Junayd, in his declining years, experienced a phase of dis-

---

[1] Hujwīrī, p. 328.
[2] *Tārīkh Baghdād*, v. 5, p. 134. Qushayrī, p. 171.
[3] *Rawḍat an-Nādhirīn*, p. 10, quoted from Mez Renaissance, p. 288.
[4] Ibid., p. 12, quoted by Mez, op. cit., p. 290.

appointment and resignation and seems to have withdrawn himself more and more from public life.

He was most considerate and cautious regarding what should and should not be taught to the multitude. It is said that, when his pupil Shiblī wrote him a daring mystical letter, Junayd returned the offending letter to the sender and on it wrote: " Oh, Abū Bakr, be careful with the people. Always we devise some means of camouflaging our words, splitting them and discussing them between ourselves, yet here you come along and tear away the veil! "[1]

Junayd was sceptical with regard to the profession of a judge. Many religious people of the time took the ḥadīth literally: " Two judges in hell and one in paradise." Two of his friends, Ruwaym and 'Amr al-Makkī, who were jurists, accepted posts as Qāḍis with the government. Al-Junayd strongly criticized them and separated from them on this account.

The following is another anecdote which demonstrates the cautious and diplomatic attitude adopted by Junayd, who, knowing the capacity and nature of the people, restrained himself from telling them more than they could fully grasp. His friend Nūrī is reported as saying: " I went to Junayd and found him seated in the professorial chair. I said to him: ' Oh, Abu'l Qāsim, thou hast concealed the truth from them and they have put you in the place of honour. I have told them the truth and they have pelted me with stones.' "[2]

On reading Junayd's letters to his friends, we find that he continually warns them to be cautious in their writings and to talk to the people carefully and with restraint.

Junayd was a non-radical and was considered in his attitude to orthodox theology. He held that ṣūfī teachings were based on the fundamentals of the tradition of Islām, and worked continuously to prove this. In this spirit he raised, as we have seen, ṣūfīsm to the level of orthodoxy, and thus made it acceptable to the orthodox representatives of Islām. As an educationist with a deep knowledge of the nature of human

---

[1] *Luma'*, pp. 233–4.
[2] Hujwīrī, p. 131.

beings and of human society, he was afraid to break with the orthodox accepted tradition of Islām. He always led a full and regular devotional life. It is said that he prayed many *rak'a* every day, recited the Qur'ān and fasted. He continued this devotional life of prayer and mortification even in his old age when he was very weak, right up to the day of his death.[1]

Junayd was an accomplished scholar—endowed with a subtle intellect of a wide scope. He was familiar with the various branches of learning of his time. He spoke with authority on jurisprudence, theology and *ethics*, yet, in spite of his learning, he was inwardly of a retiring and reticent disposition, and lived in a state of mystical awareness and self-concentration.

It is reported that, when someone asked Junayd about a certain mystical state of the mind, he would retire to his home, where he would concentrate in devotion, and later he would emerge and give the questioner an account of what had been his experience.[2]

Khuldī, a pupil of Junayd, is reported to have said: "We know no other Shaykh who has combined knowledge and experience but al-Junayd. Most Shaykhs have great knowledge but no experience, while others have experience but very little knowledge. Junayd, however, has deep experience and a very great and profound knowledge. On considering his knowledge, it could likewise be said it surpasses his experience."

We find in al-Junayd that deep feeling and profound intuition which is characteristic of many Persian classicists. Although of Persian descent, he at the same time possessed that discipline of thought and clarity of Islamic doctrine characteristic of a thinker of the Arabic school and training. He thus unites in himself, as many other remarkable personalities do, the virtue of a double heritage.

It may be assumed from what we have learned of Junayd that he was a harmonious personality. He was a teacher in the full sense of the word, and he was a true friend. We imagine that he was a man serene, unpretentious and of good cheer, radiating something of his inner life towards those who surrounded him.

---

[1] *Luma'*, p. 210. Hujwīrī, p. 303.
[2] *Tārīkh Baghdād*, v. 7.

Chapter V

THE WRITINGS OF AL-JUNAYD

JUNAYD'S MODE OF EXPRESSION

Junayd was not as prolific an author as was his teacher al-Muḥāsibī. Indeed his works are relatively small in number and actually only very few of them are in our possession. Ibn an Nadīm has attributed to him the following works:

Kitāb Amthāl al-Qur'ān.
Kitāb Rasā'il.[1]

Sarrāj, in his *Kitāb al-Luma'*, has mentioned some passage from al-Junayd's work "*Sharḥ Shaṭḥiyāt Abī Yazīd al-Bisṭāmī,*" and also refers to a book called "al-Munājāt" by Junayd.[2]

Hujwiri, in the *Kashf ul-Maḥjūb*, has spoken of another book by al-Junayd called "Tasḥiḥ al-Irāda."[3] Actually what has survived on Junayd's works is only his *Rasā'il*, which is preserved in Istanbul in the Sehit Ali MS. Nr. 1374, and his Risāla *Dawā' at Tafrīṭ* and a few other Rasā'il in *Ḥilyat al Awliyā'*. This can be explained by the fact that Junayd rarely used the medium of paper when teaching his pupils; instead he preferred to teach them by word of mouth, through his lectures and through his many conversations with those around him. These unwritten teachings have come down to us in considerable volume. They are preserved in many classical ṣūfī books, and one cannot raise any question of ṣūfī teaching without meeting Junayd's personal opinion quoted *in extenso* in the literature we still possess. This can be readily accounted for by considering Junayd's penetrating, perspicacious and original style of diction in teaching and in answering questions. It seems that Junayd did not intend that his writings should reach a wide public. Khaṭīb

---

[1] *Fiḥrist*, p. 264.
[2] *Luma'*, pp. 209, 280.
[3] Hujwīrī, p. 338.

relates that, when Junayd was dying, he requested that all his books should be buried with him.[1]

Characteristic of the colour and manner of al-Junayd's mystical expression are the following quotations:

" Once, when I was reciting my daily lection, I fell asleep and, when I was between sleeping and waking, I saw an angel descending from heaven. He cast his spirit into my heart and then prompted me, saying: ' Stand, Abu'l-Qāsim, and speak. The spirit is in you! ' and I fell to weeping."[2]

Someone asked Junayd regarding the speech of the ṣūfīs and he answered: " The ṣūfīs have no speech." Ibn Khafīf was questioned on this and his reply was: " What Abu'l-Qāsim has said is true . . . a ṣūfī is concerned with nothing but the invisible world . . . when his tongue is loosened and God allows him to speak, he will speak, otherwise he will remain silent. Eloquence if the prerogative of those who study the sources and learn them by heart."[3]

It is reported that al-Junayd, when asked to repeat what he had already said, replied that he could not. " God put those words into my mouth and made my tongue overflow, they are not from books or from learning, but only from the favour of God."[4]

On another occasion, on being asked to dictate what he had spoken, he replied: " If it came from my tongue I could dictate it to you."[5]

Thus we see that Junayd in his speech, as we should expect of a ṣūfī, was inspired. He did not express his ṣūfī convictions as a man of letters would, nor as a scholar would expand on a subject, but it is obvious that he opened his heart and poured forth what was in the innermost depths of his soul.

But these " unwritten teachings " preserved by the hearers and found in the classical literature are by no means the most profound, original or fundamental of his teachings. The most

---

[1] *Tārīkh Baghdād*, v. 7, p. 248.
[2] See Rasā'il, fol. 51a.
[3] See Rasā'il, fol. 66a.
[4] See p. 5, footnote 7.
[5] See p. 7, footnote 1.

original and fundamental of his thoughts al-Junayd entrusted to his writings, which were not intended to get into the hands of the public at large, and this explains why, whilst his sayings were so widely quoted, his writings were scarcely known to the generations after him.

It seems that even al-Ghazālī himself only read Junayd's teachings in quotation, and in his autobiography he refers to them as " scattered sayings " attributed to Junayd, Shiblī and Bistami (al-Aqwālu'l-Manthūra, 'an-al-Junayd wa'l-Shiblī, wa abī Yazīd al-Bisṭāmī,[1] which means that these writings of al-Junayd were not in the hands of the people in general, or even of all the learned ṣūfīs. Had they been circulated amongst the public, they might easily have been misjudged and misunderstood. Sarrāj, in the *Luma'*, has explained this matter, and mentioned several instances where the people accused the ṣūfī Shaykhs of being atheists, unbelievers and given to heterodoxy, owing to their hearing sayings which they were unable to understand.[2]

The Style of al-Junayd

Junayd in his speaking and writing was inspired and the nature of his utterances was such that they were shaped by unconscious insight. Moreover, his writings within the frame of ṣūfī literature have their own very special characteristics.

(a) His ideas concerning what he wished to say were always very clear and concentrated in his own mind. He placed and retained them in the forefront of his thoughts; thus they were before him from the beginning to the end, and never did he lose the thread of his subject. When he expounds a point, it is an experience which he is describing, and he himself was in the actual " state " of it. He does not talk about it " as of a theory," but rather as of something which has happened to him and which he has undergone. While speaking, he is full of his experience. It is said that, when asked something, he would not answer immediately, but would retire to be alone to experience the particular state; then he would emerge and give the answer.[3]

[1] Al-Munqidh, p. 123.
[2] See *Luma'*, p. 14.
[3] *Tārīkh Baghdād*, v. 7, p. 246. Cf. *Luma'*, p. 152.

In accordance with the custom of the Moslem scholars, Junayd always began with a foreword, praising God and the Prophet, and in this introduction he would immediately put forward his ideas wholly and concisely, and later unfold them in detail. On reaching the conclusion, he always linked this in a subtle and lucid way with his leading idea—UNIFICATION.[1] Such was his method.

(b) Thus we may say that Junayd's style of writing was systematic.

In his works we meet for the first time in Islamic literature writings in the highest mystical sphere and, at the same time, with a mature, adequate method, in a systematic order. This style and method was entirely his own. He has in this no fore-runner and teacher. Also, after him we find scarcely anyone who could be considered his equal and who could write on the highest mystical questions in an inspired condition and yet in a systematic manner as he does. In his writings can be traced his use of logic and reasoning. They have the shape of treatises which are addressed as letters to his friends.

In the process of his reasoning he sometimes comes to a point when he finds it is impossible for the intellect to grasp the idea and to go any further, as it is something beyond reason. We give here some examples:

Junayd said in one of his letters:

> " How can this be described, or the intellect perceive it, unless it be that God grants His control to the perception and His care to its secrets. Where are you when God has taken you entirely to Himself and has received before Him that of you which He desires? When He has granted you the indulgence of His communion and favoured you with the ability to answer Him? In this state you are spoken to and you speak; you are asked about yourself and you ask questions. The words communicated are as unique pearls, testimony upon testimony, a cloud of witnesses multiplying continually, harbingers of divine grace. They are as heavy rain from every side, generous donors to you of glory from God the glorious. Were it not for God's gift of grace and

[1] See as example—" *Kitāb al-Farq bain al-Ikhlāṣ was aṣ-Ṣidq.*"

His vouchsafing His Holy Spirit, then would man's mind be completely stupified before Him and his perception, in the presence of God, utterly shattered."[1]

Junayd also wrote in another letter:

"Here then is the perception of those that understand, shackled, and the learning of the learned, halted. This is the objective of the wisdom of the wise. (This is as far as words can take us.) What has been described is of the highest elevation and is as far as we can go since man's description of God is limited subjectively."[2]

(c) Junayd's style is full of intimations. The reason is that the idea proves inexpressible and incapable of being transmitted by mere words. As Junayd said in one of his letters:

"The foregoing is but an indication of what cannot be further explained. Moreover, this of its very nature, cannot be understood from indication, but only when you yourself are in the state which is described. I have wrapped up what is in it, but have not elaborated. Accept it then from its only source; if God wills, He will guide you to its comprehension."[3]

Another reason for his using these intimations and this veiled way of expressing himself is that it would be dangerous to attempt to express the meaning more explicitly, as the reader might be incapable of understanding and of grasping it in full, and so might be led astray. Thus Junayd said in another of his letters:

"One must be kind and careful of what one says to these people, and must talk to them in a matter they can understand."[4]

(d) For the reason mentioned al-Junayd's style is often enigmatic. As we have seen, he likes to hint at what he has to say. It seems that this style was the usual way of corresponding amongst the ṣūfīs of this time. They would use such a difficult and esoteric style in the exchange inside their circle. We quote the answer of al-Junayd to such a mystical letter he received from a friend of his:

---

[1] See Rasā'il, No. 1, p. 2.
[2] See Rasā'il, No. 3, p. 8.
[3] See Rasā'il, No. 6, p. 52.
[4] *Luma'*, p. 241.

"In what precedes, I have only indicated what can be described at great length, but in this essay there is no place for a full description. Oh, my brother—may God be pleased with you—I have received your letter which I was delighted both to read and interpret. I rejoiced in it from the beginning to the end. I was happy to discover the esoteric knowledge, fine wisdom, indications both clear and illuminating. That which you indicated was not concealed from me and I saw clearly that which was clearly described. All this reached my comprehension since I know in advance the object which you sought. It is clear to me whither the thought leads, the object of its train as well as its origin, where the thought begins and where it ends and what happens to him in whom God inspires this train of thought."[1]

It was extraordinarily fortunate that the great ṣūfī mystics of this time were not isolated individuals, as mystics often are, but that they were a group of friends who each somehow shared the religious experience of the other. They were able to exchange those religious experiences with one another in their letters in an adequate esoteric language.

(e) In these letters there appears the Islamic mystical terminology used genuinely in the right place, a language which certainly has its own unconscious artistic quality. In this exchange of letters between friends it developed and reached its maturity.

Thus, the Mystical School of Baghdād, and first of all Junayd, amongst his equal established the mystical terminology. This was a heritage enriching the language, ready as a medium for the later generations of Islamic mystical, theological and philosophical thinkers.

It would be a very valuable work to compare the terminology in the letters of al-Junayd with the terms of the mystics after him. Thus we might see how the mystical language terminology developed.

(f) We can also trace in the writings of al-Junayd the influence of his legal training. He would put his thought in the form of a question asking for an opinion, and thus arguing,

[1] Rasā'il, No. 3, p. 9.

would add the answer in the manner of a legal adviser, as we see in his eight questions on Unification. Even the title of this essay, *Mas'ala* (question), is a legal expression.

He sometimes uses a dialectic method, putting one part of his thought into the mouth of a scholar, and the other part into the mouth of a wise man, and developing a dialogue between the two. We can see this in his treatise on *Fanā'* and in his letter to Yayḥā ibn Mu'ādh.

(g) Finally, if we cannot count Junayd's works amongst Arabic Belles Lettres, his style is indeed very forceful, genuine, expressive and warm. It is passionate, enlightened and full of grace. It springs from the very heart and touches the heart. This is what we might call the eloquence of Junayd's style.

JUNAYD'S WRITINGS

Extant Works

The writings which have been preserved are, first of all, the " Rasā'il Junayd " in Ṣehit 'Ali MS. No. 1374. It contains the following of his writings:

(1) Risāla ila ba'ḍ ikhwānihi (fol. 3s/3b).

(2) Risāla ila Yaḥya b. Mu'ādh ar-Rāzī (3b).
This Risāla is not that one which as Sarrāj quotes is in the *Luma'* as stated in Brockl., Sup. I, 355.

(3) Risāla ila ba'ḍ ikhwānihi.
This Risāla quoted in *Luma'*. (See introductions (*Ṣudūr*) by Junayd, p. 242.)

(4) Risāla ila abī Bakr al-Kisā'ī ad-Dīnāwarī (4a).
In our manuscript we have only the end of this Risāla. Sarrāj has quoted it completely, pp. 239–241. Between folios 4a and 33a in the manuscript is Kitāb aṣ-Ṣidq of Kharrāz.

(5) Risāla of al-Junayd without title (33a–34a).
Brockelmann has not given this Risāla.

(6) Risāla ila 'Amr b. 'Uthmān al-Makkī (34a–42b).
This Risāla is not complete. In folio 43a a part of another Risāla has nothing to do with al-Makkī, as he

calls the receiver Abū 'Abd Allāh, which is not the Kunya of al-Makkī.

(7) Risāla ila Yūsuf b. al-Ḥusayn ar-Rāzī (43a–44b).
This Risāla is also not complete. In folio 45a we find chapters about *Sukr* and *Ifāqā*, which are different in script and not by Junayd, as we shall see. In folio 51a we find sayings and poetry of Junayd. In 51b sayings not by Junayd.

(8) Dawā'al-arwāḥ (52a–54a).
The same in Kairo I, VII, 109, 27, 298. (See Brocklemann, Sup. I, 554.) Professor Arberry has published it with translation. (JRAS, 1937, 219–231.) This Risāla is also quoted in *Ḥilyat al-Awliyā'*, v. 10, pp. 103–107. Junayd has attributed it to al-Ḥārith al-Muḥāsibī. That seems impossible for the style is Junayd's style and not that of al-Muḥāsibī; maybe Junayd has used what Muḥāsibī said in a discussion with him, putting it down in his own words.

(9) Kitāb al-Fanā' (54b–57b).

(10) Kitāb al-Mīthāq (58a–59b).

(11) Kitāb fi'l-Ulūhiyya (59b–60b).

(12) Kitāb fi'l-Farq bain al-Ikhlāṣ waṣ-ṣidq.

(13) Bāb ākhar fi'l-Tawḥīd (63a–63b).

(14) Mas'ala Ukhra (in Tawḥīd) (63b–63a).

(15) Mas'ala Ukhra (in Tawḥīd) (64a).
This one is quoted by Quahayrī.

(16) Mas'ala Ukhra (in Tawḥīd) (64a–64b).

(17) Mas'ala Ukhra (in Tawḥīd) (64a).

(18) Mas'ala Ukhra (in Tawḥīd) (64b–65a).

(19) Mas'ala Ukhra (in Tawḥīd) (65a–65b).

(20) Ākhir Mas'ala (in Tawḥīd) (65b–66a).

(21) Adab al-Muftaqir ila 'llāh (66b–60b).

From his writings which also have been preserved:

(22) Kitāb Dawā' at-Tafrīṭ.
Mingana Arabic (Islamic) (Selly Oak Library). No. 905, folios 109–119, Birmingham.

The majority of this Risāla is quoted in *Ḥilyat al-Awliyā'*, v. 10, p. 262, line 9, p. 271, line 10.

From the letters of Junayd, we possess also the following quoted by Abu Nu'aym:

(23) Risāla ila ba'ḍ ikhwānihi.
Ḥilyat al-Awliyā', v. 10, pp. 260–261.

(24) Kitāb al-Junayd to Abū'l 'Abbās ad-Dīnawārī.
Ibid., p. 263.

(25) Kitāb al-Junayd to Abū Isḥāq al-Māristānī.
Ibid., p. 276.

(26) Risāla ila ba'ḍ ikhwānihi.
Ibid., p. 279.

(27) Risāla ila ba'ḍ ikhwānihi.

As-Sarrāj, in the *Luma'*, quotes also considerable passages of Junayd's introduction to his letters (see *Luma'*, p. 241, ff.) and the following writings:

(28) Part of a letter from Junayd to Yaḥya ibn Mu'ādh.
Luma', p. 356.

(29) Sharh Shaṭḥiyāt Abī Yazīd al-Bisṭāmī.
Luma', pp. 380–385.

The writings mentioned above are, without doubt, Junayd's. They are written in the same style which we know as Junayd's, and there is no difference in manner or matter, so that we have to accept them as his.

There is another work of Junayd mentioned in Brockelmann, Sup. I, which we have not had an opportunity to examine.

(30) Qaṣīda Ṣūfīya.
Berl. 7542.

Lost Works

There are also works of Junayd named and quoted by various authors which appear to be lost.

(1) Amthāl al-Qur'ān.
Ibn an-Nadīm, *Fihrist*, p. 264.

(2) Taṣḥīh al-Irāda.
Hujwīrī, Kashf al Maḥjūb, p. 338.

(3) Kitāb al-Munājāt.
Sarrāj, *Luma'*, p. 259.

(4) Muntakhab al-asrār fī ṣifat as Ṣiddīqīn wa 'l-Abrār.
Ibn 'Arabī, Mawaqi', p. 30, 16.

Brockelmann has mentioned two more, but these actually cannot be from the works of Junayd:

(1) Ḥikāyāt.
Sakhawī, A'lām, 41, 16.
This book seems to be a work of al-Khuldī (see Introduction).

(2) Al-Mutafarriqāt al-Ma'thūra'an al-Junayd wa 'sh-shiblī wa Abī Yazīd al-Bisṭāmī.
Ghazāli, Munqidh, p. 123.
This also is not a work of Junayd; it is merely the scattered sayings of the Shaykhs in the various ṣūfī books.

Works Wrongly Attributed to al-Junayd

(1) Risāla of Abū'l Qāsim al-Junayd to Yūsuf ibn al-Ḥusayn, attributed to Junayd by Brockelmann, Sup. I, p. 354.
Arberry, JRAS, July 1935, pp. 499–507.

This Risāla is given as the first one in our Istanbul manuscript, Shit Ali 1374, as the answer (Jawāb) of Yusūf ibn al-Ḥusayn to the following Risāla of Junayd (folios 43a–44b), mentioned above as No. 7.

The word answer (Jawāb) is not very distinctly written in the manuscript. Moreover, we have some passages from this Risāla quoted as a work of Yūsuf ibn al-Ḥusayn in the Ḥilyat al-Awliyā', vol. 10, pp. 240–241, and the Risāla of Qushayrī, p. 22. At any rate, the style of this Risāla is very refined and elaborate and altogether different from the style of Junayd. Further, the author of this Risāla has named some of his teachers and these Shaykhs, Dhū'n-Nūn and Abū'l Ḥawārī, are not the teachers of Junayd, but of Yūsuf.

(2) Risāla Fi'l-Sukr and Risāla Fi'l fāqah (folio).

These two letters are attributed to Junayd by Massignon and Brockelmann, while Professor Arberry says: "They are in reality the product of a later pen, as is proved by the fact that in folio 496 there are references to Junayd himself among other ṣūfīs." See JRAS, 1935, p. 499.

(3) Kitāb al-Qaṣd ila 'llah, MS. Lucknow and Asaf, I, p. 390.

Attributed to Junayd by Ḥājjī Khalīfa, Vol. II, p. 1806, see Brockelmann, Sup. I, p. 355. Nicholson has studied this work and has come to the conclusion that it cannot possibly have been written by Junayd, since a passage in it is dated later, 395 A.H. See Islamica II, 401–15.

(4) Ma'ālī al-Himam, in the same MS.

Also attributed to Junayd by Ḥajjī Khalīfa (ibidem). Nicholson in Islamica (ibidem) does not give this attribution verification. Arberry in *Islamic Culture*, 1937, p. 95, says: " This attribution to al-Junayd is, of course, completely false, as is evidenced by the fact that not only are persons quoted in this tract who lived long after the death of al-Junayd, but also Junayd himself is mentioned in a passage." This is according to Arberry, the book of Abū'l-Qāsim al-'Ārif.

(5) As-Sirr fī Anfās as-Sufiyya, Cairo, I, II, 87, 2, I, p. 316 (anon.).

Also attributed to Junayd (see Brockelmann, Sup. I, p. 354). A. J. Arberry, in Journal of the Bombay Branch, JRAS, MS., vol. 15 (1937), p. 1, has examined this work and found it to be certainly not by Junayd.

PART II

THE DOCTRINE OF AL-JUNAYD

INTRODUCTION

The starting point of the religious feeling of the ṣūfī is the sense of the tremendous distance between man and God. This fundamental feeling prevails throughout the consciousness of the ṣūfī. Sometimes it seems as if this fundamental consciousness were a distinct dualism and, even if it is not dualism, there always remains the feeling of the gulf between the powerless human being and the omnipotent God.

The ṣūfīs are always aware of this, and the positive supplement of this feeling is their longing to bridge the gap by striving to transcend the gulf.

If we ask what is the means whereby the ṣūfīs can overcome the distance realized by them between man and God, we will first of all receive the answer: It is *Taṣawwuf* (Mysticism). They may differ in their definitions of *Taṣawwuf*, in ways of life, in expressions, in the emphasis they may put on this or that, and thus they may vary and come to different conclusions. But the fundamental feeling and the aim are the same.

If we now endeavour to trace and follow up al-Junayd's teaching, we ought first of all to give his definition of *Taṣawwuf*, which will open to us the door to what is in his mind and which will allow us to see his ultimate aim.

Many of his definitions of *Taṣawwuf* have come down to us,[1] such as the following two:

> " *Taṣawwuf* is to be with God without attachment to ought else."[2]
>
> " *Taṣawwuf* is an attempt wherein man abides." Al-Junayd was asked: " Is it an attribute of God or of man? "

---

[1] See Nicholson, " The Origin and Development of Ṣūfīsm," JRAS (1906), p. 331, ff. Cf. Subki, *Tabaqat*, v. 3, p. 239.

[2] Qushayri, p. 127.

and his reply was: "In essence it is an attribute of God, but by image it is an attribute of man."[1]

The first definition means that to bridge the gulf is to detach oneself from everything else and to be with God.

The second definition means: in the state where the gulf is bridged, the ṣūfī realizes that his own attributes are in reality attributes of God, and so his own attributes vanish. He realizes that all attributes of man are only attributes in image—in a secondary and derived sense—but that they are in reality attributes of God. Or, in other words, as Hujwīrī explains this definition of al-Junayd: "In real Unification (*Tawḥīd*) there are, correctly speaking, no human attributes at all, because human attributes are not constant but are only in image and imprint (*rasm*), having no permanence, for God is the agent. Therefore, they are really the attributes of God.[2]

This state of the ṣūfī which Junayd means is described by him in one of his letters as follows:

> "In this state of absolute purity he has lost his personal attributes; by this loss he is wholly present (in God). By being wholly present in God, he is wholly lost to himself. And thus he is present before God while absent in himself; absent and present at the same time. He is where he is now, and he is not where he is."[3]

To define it in one word—the state described in this letter is *Tawḥīd*. The Muwaḥḥid, the man who has reached Unification, could not fully realize that God is One, except by losing himself in the Oneness of God.

Thus we meet here the Doctrine of *Tawḥīd*, Divine Unification, which is the centre of al-Junayd's experience and teachings. This experience of his carried him probably far beyond the frame given by traditional religion. Facing the fundamental Moslem dogma, which by the will of God places the believer in the midst of the community, he was well aware of the very danger of this state experienced and taught by him.

His experience, as we find, carried him to a further state which he describes in a second doctrine. He continues in the same letter:

---

[1] Hujwīrī, p. 36.
[2] Ibid.
[3] Risāla, No. 10.

"Then, after he has not been, he is where he had been (sc. before creation). He is himself, after he has not been really himself. He is present in himself and in God, after having been present in God and absent in himself. This is because he has left the intoxication of God's overwhelming, *Ghalaba*, and come to the clarity of sobriety, *Ṣaḥw*, and contemplation is once more restored to him, so that he can put everything in its right place and assess it correctly."[1]

Thus we meet al-Junayd's essential doctrine of Sobriety, which the majority of ṣūfīs at this time accepted. The Qur'ān and Sunna were proclaimed to be the standard to which not only speculation, but also spiritual feelings and states must conform.[2] Al-Junayd's moral personality was able to save him from the dangers into which some of his successors fell.[3]

These two doctrines—the "Doctrine of Divine Unity," *Tawḥīd*, and the "Doctrine of Sobriety," *Ṣaḥw*—are the two main pillars which support the structure of al-Junayd's mysticism, of which we shall now try to give a fuller survey and interpretation.

---

[1] Risāla, No. 10.

[2] See Nicholson, ibid., p. 328. Cf. Qushayri, Introduction of ar-Risāla.

[3] Cf. Qushayrī, p. 137.

CHAPTER VI

THE DOCTRINE OF UNIFICATION

During al-Junayd's lifetime, in the third century A.H., the Doctrine of the Unity of God was particularly discussed by all religious groups, especially by the Mu'tazila, who had great authority at this time. They were, in fact, called the " People of *Tawḥīd* "—they treated this question and approached the Oneness of God through the means of reason, and arrived at conclusions of a complex nature.

The ṣūfīs, on the other hand, being dissatisfied with reason and its results, strove to experience the Unity of God by way of feeling and revelation. Thus Ibn al-Kātib, a ṣūfī of the fourth century, says: " The Mu'tazila have practised the *tanzīh*, the remotio of God from attributing to Him any imperfect qualities, by reason (*'aql*), and have gone with this the wrong way. The ṣufīs have practised it through *'ilm*, revealed knowledge, and have hit the right way."[1] Ibn al-Kātib compared in this way the method of the ṣūfīs with the method of the Mu'tazila and shed light on their respective views on the Unity of God. So we see that the ṣūfīs, amongst whom al-Junayd stands out as a central figure, were in complete harmony with the spirit of the age in dealing with the same essential problem, as the others.

The ṣūfīs maintain that the Unity of God is indefinable. Al-Junayd says: " The noblest saying referring to *Tawḥīd* is the word of Abū Bakr: ' Praise be to God, Who has vouchsafed to His creatures no other means of obtaining Knowledge of Him except through their impotence to attain Knowledge of Him.' "[2] This certainly shows that, according to al-Junayd, *Tawḥīd* is far beyond the sphere of any intellectual cognition. The same is probably the meaning of these words of al-Junayd: " *Tawḥīd* is a reality in which the traces disappear and the signs

[1] Qushayri, p. 27.
[2] Hujwiri, p. 284; similar saying in *Luma'*, p. 124.

fade away, and God is as He always was."[1] More clearly he expresses the same thing in other words: "If the understanding of understanding has ended in the *Tawḥīd*, it ends in fixity."[2] On an occasion when he attempted to speak of the *Tawḥīd*, he merely expressed it by several descriptions illustrating certain characteristics of it, because, as he stated when he was asked for an explanation: "It is an idea (*mā'na*) the definition of which cannot be defined, despite the vast and complete knowledge contained therein."[3] In fact, all ṣūfīs are aware of this and realize their own incapacity to put *Tawḥīd* into words and explain it in speaking, and the impossibility of fathoming it by reason.[4]

If we seek now to explore the essence of *Tawḥīd* according to the ṣūfīs more closely, we find the result is somewhat meagre. We first give the summing-up of al-Qushayrī:

"*Tawḥīd* has a threefold meaning:

(1) '*Tawḥīd* of God as subject with regard to God as object in His knowledge that He is unique and His assertion of Himself that He is One.'

(2) '*Tawḥīd* of God as subject with regard to man as object in His assertion that man is a confessor of Unity and His creating the power of confession of Unity in man.'

(3) '*Tawḥīd* of the created being as subject with regard to God as object, is the knowledge of man that God is unique and his judgment and assertion about Him that He is unique.' "[5]

If this were the whole *Tawḥīd* of the ṣūfīs, one would not really know much about the distinctive ṣūfī element in it. Dhu'n Nūn al-Miṣrī defines *Tawḥīd* as follows: "*Tawḥīd* is that you know that God's omnipotence in the calling into being of anything does not result necessarily from a natural power,

---

[1] Qushayrī, p. 135.

[2] Ibid.

[3] Ibid.

[4] This resembles closely the descriptions of *Tawḥīd* given by the later writers, e.g. Ibn Khaldūn, who says: "The trouble is only caused by the weakness in our language which does not lend itself to the expression of abstract realities, and by the deficiency of the words for rendering the truth in and by them."
Muqaddima, v. 3, p. 76 (edition Quatremere).

[5] Qushayrī, p. 135.

and that His creation goes on without instrument; that the cause of all things is His creation which has no cause and that everything of which you, yourself, may form a conception is a thing, so that God is different from it."[1] This signifies purely dogmatic confession of Unity with an anti-Mu'tazilite colouring.

Both these definitions are clear and truthful, but they lack the particular ṣūfī approach.

Only al-Junayd seems to have had a capacity for a more intimate approach to the conception of *Tawḥīd* in its specific significance for the ṣūfī.

He has expressed the " Unification " (*Tawḥīd*) in his famous phrase: " Unification is the separation of that which has from that which was originated in Time." " *Ifrād al-Qadīm 'an al-muḥdath*."

That means:

(1) To separate the *Eternal Essence* from the originated essence, i.e. to fix or hold fast to this Essence of God and to disprove or reject all others.

(2) To separate the *Attributes* contained therein from all other attributes, i.e. to fix or hold fast to the Attributes of God and to disprove or refute all others.

(3) To separate *Actions*, i.e. to separate the actions of God and to disprove and refute all others.

All of these, His Attributes and His Actions, are so completely absorbed in His Essence that he who is in the state to comprehend this Unification sees that the Essence, Attributes and Actions are all completely absorbed in the Essence of God. He comes to this as he himself in this state is absorbed in God.

The early and the later ṣūfī writers were extremely impressed and attracted by this phrase of al-Junayd, and considered it the most brief and comprehensive of all the ṣūfī sayings on Unification; each ṣūfī has interpreted it in the light of his own particular approach.

For instance, Sarrāj, after having mentioned the definition of Unification according to the sense which the Moslems

---

[1] Ibid.

generally attach to it, and according to the sense which the ṣufīs attach to it, commented on a saying of Shiblī to the effect that: " The Unity of God is utterly inexpressible and indefinable," and quoted the brief sentence of al-Junayd as a justification of this statement.[1]

Al-Hujwiri commenced with this sentence of al-Junayd when he considered the indications which the Shaykhs had given on this subject, and has interpreted it in this manner: " You must not regard the eternal as a place of phenomena, or phenomena as a place of the eternal; and you must know that God is eternal and that you are phenomena, and that nothing of your genus is connected with Him, and that nothing of His Attributes is mingled in you, and that there is no homogeneity between the eternal and the phenomenal."[2]

Al-Qushayrī began Chapter I of his *Risāla* on the dogma of the ṣūfīs with this saying of al-Junayd, as being the foundation of their faith, and mentions it again in the chapter on Unification, saying: " Al-Junayd said: ' Unification is the separation of the Eternal from that which was originated in Time, and departure from familiar haunts and separation from brethren and forgetfulness of what is known and unknown, and God only in place of All.' "[3]

The later writers, too, have put stress on this sentence; for instance, Tahanawi, in his definition of Unification by the ṣūfīs, said: " The result of all the hints and signs is in brief that ' Unification is the separation of the Eternal, etc.' "[4]

Ibn Taymīya, who was an extreme Sunni, quotes this phrase of al-Junayd, stresses and praises it. He says: " What Junayd has said about the difference between the Eternal and the originated, is something to safeguard many of the mystics from the danger of following the wrong path." Some of them have scolded Junayd for this phrase, like Ibn 'Arabī in his book, " *Al-Isrā ila Maqām al-Asrā*," in which he says: " O Junayd, who could distinguish between two things, except if he is neither the one nor the other." And Ibn Taymīya argues against

---

[1] *Luma'*, p. 30.
[2] *Kashf al-Maḥjūb*, p. 281.
[3] Qushayrī, Risāla, v. 3, p. 136.
[4] Tahānau'ī, *Kashshāf Iṣtilāḥāt al-funūn*, v. 2, p. 1468.

Ibn 'Arabī proving that he is wrong and that al-Junayd is right.[1]

At any rate, the meaning of *ifrād al-qidam*, separation of the Eternal, or we may also say the Absolute, is not only a separation (*remotio*) carried out theoretically, by reason, but a practical experiencing of the Infinite with the extinction of everything finite. This will become clearer as we proceed with other definitions of al-Junayd.

Al-Junayd has illustrated *Tawḥīd* in its various aspects in many of his letters. He made it especially clear when he classified the stages of the *Muwuḥḥidūn* and described in detail their respective features. He says in one of his letters:

> "Know that *Tawḥīd* is found in four stages in people. The first is the *Tawḥīd* of the ordinary people; the second is the *Tawḥīd* of those who are well versed in formal religious knowledge. The third and fourth stages are experienced by the elect who have esoteric knowledge (ma'rifa)."[2]

The theologians do not agree with this classification of those who possess *Tawḥīd*, saying that this word *Tawḥīd* could not be classified neither from the viewpoint of God nor from the viewpoint of man. *Tawḥīd*, they say, is only a right way between two wrong extremes and nothing more. And so that majority of theologians hold that the faith in each and all of the believers is one and the same, and they differ only in the manner of approach.

Al-Ghazzālī solves this difficulty by saying that the classification of *Tawḥīd* means that everyone is in a special state different from any other.[3]

Certainly al-Junayd, in his endeavour after classification, has in mind that state of every individual. They all believe in God, but are in various stages according to their kind of belief.

This question of the degree of belief takes up a large proportion of the discussion between the theologians.[4] But al-Junayd analyses this question in another way than the theologians.

---

[1] *Minhāj as-Sunna*, v. 3, p. 85, ff. Massignon, " Essai sur les origines du lexique tecnique," p. 277, footnote 2.

[2] Risāla, No. 16.

[3] *Al-Imlā' 'ala ishkālāt al-Iḥyā'*, p. 98.

[4] See as example *Bukhari in Kitāb al-Imān* (*Saḥīḥ al-Bukhārī*).

He approaches it in a psychological and ethical way, describing the effect and result in the person of the believer. So his distinction is not speculative, but through a mature experience and fine human understanding, an approach which we meet for the first time in Islamic thought.

He describes the *Tawḥīd* of ordinary people as follows:

> " As for the *Tawḥīd* of ordinary people, it consists in the assertion of the Unity of God, in the discarding of any conception of gods, companions, opposites, equals, likenesses to God, but with the retention of hopes and fears in forces other than God. This type of *Tawḥīd* possesses a measure of efficacy since the assertion persists."[1]

This simple *Tawḥīd* is what Islām demands of every believer as a basis of faith in God. Such a muwaḥḥid has not the complete awareness of God, because while these two things, hope and fear, in forces other than God, are still existent in the consciousness of the believers, they prevent the complete realization of God. If one possesses the complete power of *Tawḥīd*, these things will certainly disappear just as, when the sun shines, the stars disappear.[2]

Then Junayd describes the second stage as follows:

> " As for the *Tawḥīd* of those who are well versed in formal religious knowledge, it consists in the assertion of the Unity of God, in the discarding of any conception of gods, companions, opposites, equals, likenesses to God, combined with the performance of the positive commands and the avoidance of that which is forbidden so far as external action is concerned, all that being a result of their hopes, fears and desires; this type of *Tawḥīd* has a measure of efficacy since the assertion of the Unity of God is being publicly proved."[3]

The difference between these two states is that, while the man who lives in the first state may not be able to master life and to reach the standard of decency, balance of mind, reason, truthfulness and goodness in society, and the state of perform-

---

[1] Risāla, No. 16.
[2] *Luma'*, p. 31.
[3] Risāla, No. 16.

ance of the commands of Religion and avoidance of what is forbidden, a man in the second state possesses all these virtues, and thus he will prove through his virtue, his whole life and actions in society, the Unity of God. Yet his motive for being good may still be partly rooted in his hopes, fears and desires.

These two stages are not the highest stage of awareness of God which man can reach. So al-Junayd goes further to the next state:

> " As for the first type of esoteric *Tawḥīd*, it consists in the assertion of the Unity of God, the discarding of the conception of the things referred to, combined with the performance of God's command externally and internally, and the cessation of hopes and fears in forces other than God, all this resulting from the ideas which tally with the awareness of God's presence with him, with God's call to him, and his answer to God."[1]

This muwaḥḥid still preserves his individuality. This state is not the complete Unification which the muwahhid can reach as he is still aware of something other than God, namely, himself. Yet higher still for Junayd is that other experience, the last stage of Unification, which he describes as follows:

> " The second type of esoteric *Tawḥīd* consists in existence without individuality (*shabaḥ*) before God with no third person as intermediary between them, a figure over which His decrees pass as He in His Omnipotence determines, and that he should be sunk in the flooding seas of His Unity, completely obliterated both from himself and from God's call to him and his answer to God. It is a state where the devotee has achieved the true realization of the Oneness of God in true proximity to Him. He is lost to sense and action because God fulfils in him what He hath willed of him."[2]

That is, he is in the Will of God and has no more a will of his own. This is not the absolute subjection of will and personal desire to the Eternal Will of God, as the foregoing state. It is more than mere resignation to God's Will. It means that the individual will become none other than the very Will of God,

---

[1] Ibid.
[2] Ibid.

who wills and works, lives and creates, through our will, so that there is but one Will.

This saying of al-Junayd indicates that, according to Hujwīrī, " the muwaḥḥid has no regard to himself so that he becomes like an atom, as he was in the eternal past, when the Covenant of Unification was made. It means, as the same time, the annihilation of the individual when he is overpowered by the revelation of His majesty, so that he becomes a passive instrument and a subtle substance that feels nothing, and his body is a repository for the mysteries of God to Whom his speech and actions are to be attributed."[1]

This highest stage of Unification, as Junayd witnesses it, is based on two theories of his system:

(1) The theory of *Mīthāq*, which means the relation between God the Creator and the human creature, and realization by man of his place before God.

(2) The theory of *Fanā'*, Obliteration, which means that man fulfils the Unity of God through losing his individuality and being present only in God.

We proceed to analyse this last state through an explanation of these two complementary theories.

---

[1] Kashf al-Maḥjūb, p. 28.

Chapter VII

THE THEORY OF MĪTHĀQ

Junayd continues his description of the final stage of *Tawḥīd*:

"This implies that in his final stage the worshipper returns to his first state, that he is as he was before he existed."[1]

Junayd holds the belief that the worshipper before his corporal existence had another existence. He proves this from the verse of the Qur'ān:

"When thy Lord had brought forth their descendants from the loins of the Sons of Adam and made them to witness concerning themselves, 'Am I not,' said He, 'your Lord?' They said: 'Yes! we do so testify.'"[2]

He interprets this verse as follows:

"In this verse God tells you that He spoke to them at a time when they did not exist, except so far as they existed in Him. This existence is not the same type of existence as is usually attributed to God's creatures; it is a type of existence which only God knows and only He is aware of. God knows their existence; embracing them he sees them in the beginning when they are non-existent and unaware of their future existence in this world. The existence of these is timeless."[3]

And also:

"When He called them and they answered quickly, their answer was a gracious and generous gift from Him; it was His answer on their behalf when He granted them their being, their function being that of interlocutors. He gave them knowledge of Him when they were only concepts which He had conceived. He then wished it, and made them

[1] Risāla, No. 16.

[2] Qur'ān 7, v. 166, 167.

[3] Risāla.

like seeds which He transformed at His Will into human seeds, and put them in the loins of Adam. . . . In this verse Allah has stated that He spoke to them when they had no formal existence. This is possible because Allah perceives them in their spiritual existence. This spiritual existence connotes their knowledge of God's spirituality without in any way postulating their being aware of their own individuality."[1]

So, according to Junayd, there are two types of existence: the one being divine existence (existence in Him), which is timeless and which we have before our coming here, and the other being existence in this created world. He described the first as follows:

> "This then is a divine existence and a God-like conception which becomes only Him."[2]

And further:

> "This type of existence is without doubt the most perfect and penetrating. It is the most significant, dominant, and is more adequately described as conquering, victorious and truly overwhelming, than the normal existence of which the worshipper is aware, because in the Divine existence his individuality is entirely obliterated and his worldly existence departs from him. This is because no human quality survives nor does normal human existence persist, as we have made clear in describing the Divine qualities of God's Truth and God's Victory."[3]

And also:

> "Whereas their first existence is completely real, is better, higher, and more conducive to God's conquest and victory, and to their complete absorption in Him by means of that which He has granted them."[4]

But al-Junayd refrains from giving a detailed description of this type of existence. He says:

---

[1] Risāla.
[2] Risāla, No. 6.
[3] Risāla, No. 6.
[4] Risāla, No. 7.

> "It is a type of existence which only God knows and only He is cognisant of."[1]

And also:

> "It follows then that, at this stage (of his), God has existence of a sort which is known only to Him and recognized only by Him."[2]

On the other hand, he tells us who existed and how. He says:

> "Who existed, and how could he have existed before he had existence? Did anyone answer to God's question other than the pure, fine and holy souls in accordance with God's Omnipotence and Perfect Will?"[3]

This idea of al-Junayd of a pre-existence of the soul, real existence before our becoming here, and existence different from our "secondary," derived existence as created beings, seems to echo Neo-platonic ideas and is similar to what Plotinus says in the Enneads:

> "Before we had our becoming here, we existed There, men other than now; we were pure souls. Intelligence inbound with the entire of reality, not fenced off, integral to that All. . . . Then it was as if One voice sounded. One word was uttered and from every side an ear attended and received and there was an effective hearing; now we are become a dual thing, no longer that which we were at first, dormant, and in a sense no longer present."[4]

About our secondary existence as created beings Plotinus says:

> "By this non-being of course we are not to understand something that does not exist, but only something of an utterly different form from Authentic-Being; the non-being we are thinking of is, rather, an image of Being or perhaps something still more removed than even an image."[5]

This differentiation reminds us of the differentiation which al-Junayd makes between real existence and our secondary, not real, existence. He has already made this differentiation in his

---

[1] Risāla, No. 6.
[2] Risāla, No. 7.
[3] Risāla, No. 14.
[4] Enneads, V 1, 4. 14. (See "The Essence of Plotinus," compiled by J. H. Turnbull.)
[5] Enneads, V 1, 8. 3.

definition of Taṣawwuf, where he says: " Taṣawwuf in essence; is an attribute of God, but by image, it is an attribute of man." (See p. 87.) This means that, inasmuch as our being is conceived by God, it is real. In our opinion Junayd interpreted the Qu'rān verse on the Mīthāq through the Neo-platonic doctrine of the pre-existence of the soul. In his mind there was a deep harmony between the verse of the Qu'rān and the teachings of mystical philosophy.

If we try to sum up this theory and to describe this highest state of Unification which the worshipper can attain, we find that the worshipper returns to his primordial state where he has been before he was created. That is, he departs from his worldly existence, his normal human existence does not continue, and hence he exists in God and is completely absorbed in Him. It is thus that the muwaḥḥid can attain the real *Tawḥīd*. As long as he preserves his individuality he cannot attain this full state of *Tawḥīd*, as the continued persistence of his individuality means that something other than God is still present.

Junayd seems to aim at that stage when he says:

> " In this state He has full possession of them and has destroyed their individuality and has removed their characteristics as we perceive it.
>
> " This is because Existence, after complete suppression of person is not the same as normal existence. The ultimate Truth of God is now refulgent and His Victory is complete."[1]

And also:

> " It is for this reason that we said, that when God granted existence to His worshippers, He caused, as it were, His desire to flow over them according to His Will."[2]

This means that, according to Junayd, God, when He creates a human being, has already the intention to overwhelm him and to make him fully One with Himself again. Even in this world, if He chooses him and if man lives up to His choice, He will obliterate his individuality and make him realize the Oneness of God. Thus Junayd continues:

> " In view of the foregoing we said that God has obliterated what appears to the worshipper, and when He has

[1] Risāla, No. 6.
[2] Risāla, No. 6.

overwhelmed him, God shows Himself as the most overpowering, the perfect conqueror, the completely victorious."[1]

In this state, God is the direct actor according to His perfection, and what man does and wills in this state is nothing but the Will and Action of God.

This state is not something which the worshipper attains unaided, but it is a gift of God to the worshipper whom He chooses. Junayd proves this from the *Ḥadīth*:

" My servant draws nigh unto me by works of supererogation and I love him; and when I love him I am his ear, so that he hears by Me, and his eye, so that he sees by Me."[2]

Junayd comments on this Ḥadīth, explaining that this should not be understood literally. The meaning can be only:

" That it is God who strengthens him; who enables him to achieve this; who guides him and who gives the vision of what He wishes in the manner He wishes, so that he achieves rightness and is in accord with Truth. This, then, is the act of God in him; the gift of God to him and only to him. It is not to be attributed positively to the worshipper, since it does not originate from him. Nay, it comes over him from elsewhere and must, therefore, be attributed to another source. This, then, is a possible interpretation of the secret and independent state of the nature described above."[3]

This whole state is what Junayd meant by his definition of Taṣawwuf: " Taṣawwuf is that God should make you die from yourself and should make you live in Him."[4]

He further says:

" The living man in the one for whom life founds itself on the life of his Creator, not the one who founds his life on the subsistence of his bodily form (*haykal*), so that the reality of his life will be his death, as his death in the access to the stage of his primordial Life."[5]

How can the worshipper die in himself and live in God—how can he achieve and fulfil this state? Junayd explains this in his theory of *Fanā'*.

---

[1] Risāla, No. 6.
[2] Risāla, No. 6.
[3] Risāla, No. 6.
[4] Qushayrī, p. 126.
[5] Baqlī, v. 11, p. 173. Quoted by Massignon: " Essai sur les origines du lexique technique," p. 277.

Chapter VIII

THE THEORY OF FANĀ'

Both al-Junayd's theory of *Mīthāq* (Covenant) and his theory of *Fanā'* (Oblivion) show us the road to the same end, the highest state of Unification. Both Mīthāq and Fanā' are different approaches to *Tawḥīd*, the former explaining the state of Return to God, the latter describing the way, method, training and successive steps to attain this state. Thus, for the *muwaḥḥid* to reach this state of his divine existence, he will have to lose his human existence, which is a secondary one, so that he may realize his divine existence in the Oneness with God, which is the primary one. So, in fact, the two theories are mutually complementary.

Junayd recognizes three stages of Fanā' (oblivion, obliteration), which he defines and expounds as follows:

> First: " The obliteration of attributes, characteristics and natural qualities in your motives when you carry out your religious duties, making great efforts and doing the opposite of what you may desire, and compelling yourself to do the things which you do not wish to do."
>
> Second: " The obliteration of your pursuit after pleasures and even the sensation of pleasure in obedience to God's behests—so that you are exclusively His, without any intermediary means of contact."
>
> Third: " The obliteration of the consciousness of having attained the vision of God at the final stage of ecstasy when God's victory over you is complete. At this stage you are obliterated and have eternal life with God, and you exist only in the existence of God because you have been obliterated. Your physical being continues but your individuality has departed."[1]

The first stage is concerned with man's active life, his *vita*

[1] Risāla.

activa. Man has to put behind himself his personal affections and impulses, his calculations and passions—this is what al-Junayd describes as the "attributes and qualities of his aiming"—while carrying out his duties as a Moslem. He will need a continued moral training, a conscious ascetic way of life in order to fulfil this task, and will often have to act against the wishes and desires of his own soul which disturb and entangle the purity of his aiming. This state of *Fanā'* is of a moral and objective order.

The second stage implies that the worshipper should cut himself off from all the worldly pleasures of his senses and even from the enjoyment of his own good deeds in fulfilling the religious injunctions of God, thus remaining without any intermediary object which might serve man to put himself into indirect contact with God. This stage of *Fanā'* is of a mental and subjective order.

The third stage implies that man loses even the consciousness of his having reached the vision of God. Facing God, his consciousness of himself becomes extinct. This is the state of which we have heard previously, when the worshipper is entirely overwhelmed and engulfed by God—the complete victory of God over him. At this stage the individuality of the worshipper is quite obliterated—though for his fellow men he still has his physical body and appearance. In himself he has now no separate existence any more. His former being is, so to speak, dead. He has returned to eternal life—he lives with and in God only.

This state—the final state of *Fanā'* includes *Baqā'*, the abiding and continuing in God. *Fanā'* and *Baqā'* mean the same state from a different aspect. When one has reached the complete *Fanā'* of one's individuality in God, one, at the same time, is remaining and perpetuated in God. *Fanā'* is not merely the cessation of Self, like the Buddhist Nirvāna, but, as we have seen, it includes the continuation of the worshipper's self in God.[1]

At this point we gain a very important insight into al-Junayd's conception of God. Though *Fanā'* might lead to Pantheism if it were an end in itself, this, as we see it, is not the case with the

[1] *Luma'*, p. 214. Cf. Nicholson, "Mystics of Islām," p. 149.

Fanā' of al-Junayd. His *Fanā'*, as we see it, is consistent only with the *Baqā'* in God. The personal character of God remains even in this state and there remains—in God—the eternal self of the worshipper. This is so, even in the state of *Fanā'*—before the worshipper returns to himself (state of Sobriety).[1]

We have to keep in our mind that even in this highest state the Worshipper cannot comprehend the full Reality of God, though he is " taken up by God " and lives in Him. Al-Junayd says:

> " Even so, in this divine state, it is not possible for him to approach the Ultimate Reality which now possesses him. It is only in this state that God can be seen in His exalted Nature, and His Beatific Names be appreciated."[2]

Thus, even in this state, the worshipper cannot be identical with God (Ittiḥād). Al-Junayd insists on this point in all his teaching. He says:

> " At this stage, then, when God has complete possession of them, *Balā* overtakes them because of their human qualities which still persist, because of their enjoyment of physical pleasures. This, then, is the veil between them and God, which God has placed between them and Him, so that they can still retain a measure of their individuality and use both their physical and spiritual faculties in this environment of glory, in this consequence of praise (dhikr) in the victory of God's conquest. How can this be known to you if none but the elect know it, and only they can discover it, and only they are capable of this knowledge? Can you comprehend how it is that they should seek God and yet not reach Him though they are helped by God's revelation to them, and are aided by the help of God's Truths? It is because God has made them cognisant of an aspect of His existence and given them complete conviction of His hidden secrets which are the path to Him when the human qualities are obliterated and human needs are nullified."[3]

Fanā', as al-Junayd experienced it, is thus not the passing

[1] Nicholson, who is well aware of this theological meaning of Junayd's *Baqa'*, yet sees this preservation of Self only in the following state of Sobriety. Cf. " The Ideal of Personality," p. 14.

[2] Risāla, No. 6.

[3] Risāla, No. 6.

away of man's being in God's being . . ." since they are wholly separate from His and lose their own eyes, God being firmly established in His Power and Glory," but it is the passing away of man's will in God's Will, as we have seen before.

This point is very important in Junayd's mystic teaching on *Fanā'* and it has been misunderstood by later interpreters. Sarrāj was aware of this error, for he says: " Some mystics of Baghdād have erred in their doctrine that, when they pass away from their qualities, they enter into the qualities of God. This involves incarnation (*ḥulūl*) or leads to the Christian belief concerning Jesus. The doctrine in question has been attributed to some of the ancients, but its true meaning is this: that, when a man goes forth from his own qualities and enters into the qualities of God, he goes forth from his own will, which is a gift to him from God, and enters into the Will of God, knowing that his will has been given to him by God, and that by virtue of this gift he can stop seeing himself and become entirely devoted to God; and this is one of the stages of those that seek *Tawḥīd* (Unification with God). Those who have erred in this doctrine have failed to observe that the qualities of God are not God. To make God identical with His qualities is to be guilty of infidelity, because God does not descend into the heart, but that which descends into the heart is faith in God and belief in His unity and reverence for the thought of Him."[1]

Sarrāj also says: " Some have abstained from food and drink, fancying that when a man's body is weakened it is possible that he may lose his humanity and be invested with the attributes of divinity. The ignorant persons who hold this erroneous doctrine cannot distinguish between humanity and the inborn qualities (*akhkāq*) of humanity. Humanity does not depart from man any more than blackness departs from that which is black or whiteness from that which is white, but the inborn qualities of humanity are changed and transmuted by the all-powerful radiance that is shed upon them from the Divine Realities. The attributes of humanity are not the essence of humanity. Those who speak of the doctrine of *Fanā'* mean the passing away of regarding one's own actions and works of

---

[1] *Luma'*, p. 432.

devotion through continuously regarding God as the doer of these actions on behalf of His servant."[1]

In this highest state of *Fanā*, according to al-Junayd, where the worshipper has lost his worldly individuality, he yet is still separate from God. Many veils have been removed, but a veil still persists between God and man. This condition, as Junayd experienced it, is indeed full of longing—and pain. It is a state of suspense, of anguish and of thirst for God. To bear it, is thus a test to the soul, *Balā*. God will help him and sustain him in this test of having given up his wordly individuality and yet not being able to merge in the Absolute. Yet the soul may derive spiritual pleasure from its *Balā'*, this test and ordeal in facing God. Junayd says:

> "They are consumed with longing for Him who has brought them *Balā'*, and moan constantly in this *second* loss of their individuality. This loss has been a grievous wound to them, their new state has depressed them. They grieve, suffering deeply as they seek after God. They are overcome by a thirst which is all-consuming and constantly increasing. The pursuit of knowledge of God is now the constant preoccupation of the soul, it is entirely devoted to submerging its individuality in the attainment of intimacy with God. This thirst for God is an anguish even more intense than the mourning for a beloved one. God makes of every external form a sign. He gives to the soul the taste of poverty and renews for the soul knowledge of the experience of spiritual effort.
>
> "The soul accepts the spiritual burden with its implication of suffering, seeks for its cure, and is preoccupied with that divine revelation vouchsafed to it. Consequently, it is able to look on the remote with the eye of propinquity, to be closer to God because a veil has been removed and it is no longer completely concealed. Though the soul has *Balā'*, it is not rejected. How can it be hidden from God by a veil when it is, as it were, a captive bound before Him? God has allowed the suppression of the individuality when man has *Balā'*. The soul no longer arrogates a degree of import-

[1] *Luma'*, p. 426.

ance to its individuality but is amply satisfied with God's love and nearness.

" Such, then, is the infinite duration of this newly found spiritual life and the intensity of the stage of *Balā'* that the suppression of the individuality is completely submerged by the lightning flesh of God's regard.

" As a result, the soul derives spiritual pleasures from *Balā'* and is delighted with its *Balā'* with God, because it can enjoy propinquity with God and the wound of *Balā'* is soothed. The soul is not bent down under the burden of *Balā'* nor does it chafe at its spiritual load. Their experience makes heroes of them—because of the secrets revealed to them they stay conquered by God, awaiting His commands, that Allah may designate what shall be done."[1]

We come to the conclusion that al-Junayd, who has experienced as well as analysed the highest state of Unification (*Tawḥīd*) and who has clearly described the *Mīthāq* and the *Fanā'*, has yet neither been swept into the sea of Pantheism, which would be losing consciousness of God and man and acknowledging one existence only, nor has he made himself, the worshipper, equal with God, deifying man (Ittiḥād). But he has experienced and described Unification as losing his will, which characterizes the worldly individuality, being possessed by God and returning into the life of his eternal self in God. Thus he would be unified with God, to the extent that this is granted by God to His creatures.

We may count al-Junayd as the classical witness, the teacher and interpreter of *Tawḥīd* in its most profound, aware and disciplined form. This is his place in the development of Islamic Mysticism. He was not the first who spoke of *Tawḥīd*. His teacher, Sarī' as-Saqaṭī and, before him, Mar'ūf al-Karkhī, have done so, teachers to whom al-Junayd always felt indebted. But al-Junayd has put the *Tawḥīd* into the centre of the system of ṣūfīsm and has left to us a clear and explicit doctrine of *Tawḥīd* in his works. This doctrine, he taught, as we have seen, in his oral teachings as well as letters in his small esoteric circle to those who could understand. Yet some of his pupils and later

[1] Risāla, No. 6.

mystics were not able to grasp the meaning of this doctrine as a whole, in its integrity, but have picked out this or that part of it, thus sometimes being led into exaggeration and error.

Rightly understood and fully comprehended, al-Junayd is a sound and lucid guide to ṣūfīsm. His teaching on *Tawḥīd* is basic, and is echoed in the doctrine of most ṣūfī orders right up to modern times.[1]

[1] Cf. The literature of the Shadiliya Order, especially the books of Ibn 'Aṭā al-Sikandarī'.

Chapter IX

THE DOCTRINE OF SOBRIETY, ṢAḤW

All those who have reached the state of *Tawḥīd*, having lost their individuality, having passed away from their human existence to live in God, all those who have been overwhelmed, and are entirely in the possession of their conqueror, their Lord, are without a will of their own, in the Will of God. It is not possible for them to think of doing or aiming at anything in this world. In this state the laws and standards which normally apply are without significance or meaning since for them everything is God's Will, whose instrument they are. The distinction between good and evil has become meaningless—since everything coming from God is good.

This situation may logically lead the ṣūfī to an attitude by which he puts himself outside the laws and order of society. In fact, some of the ṣūfīs came to ignore all the injunctions of the religious law, all the religious precepts and duties; " the performance of the positive commands and the avoidance of that which is forbidden," saying, that if one is in the Will of God, one need not follow the orders given by Him to men in their worldly state. These laws, they maintain, are intended by Him for the benefit of the common people, but they are superfluous for those who live in union with God.[1]

This complete indifference to the laws of religion and the established customs of society may lead the ṣūfī to a special kind of libertinism, as the history of ṣūfīsm has shown repeatedly.

We find in many ṣūfīs a completely negative attitude to religious works. We can see this in the story which is reported of al-Junayd. A man said to al-Junayd: " Amongst the men of God (ṣūfīs), there are those who hold that the keeping away

[1] Ibn Qayyim al-Jawzī, Madārij as-Sālikīn, v. 1, pp. 135, 138, 143. Cf. Ibn Ḥazm Fiṣal, v. 4, pp. 188, 226.

from activity belongs to piety and fear of God." Al-Junayd answered: "That is the doctrine of people who treat religious works as of no worth, which I hold to be a grievous sin. Even the man who steals or commits adultery is still in a better condition than he who holds that view. In fact, those who know God receive the works of God and in return render them back to God. And, if I were to live a thousand years, I should not like to be found lacking in the works of piety even as much as a single grain of dust."

So we come to the ethical theory of al-Junayd, his theory of Sobriety (Ṣaḥw) which, with *Tawḥīd*, is the basis of his whole system of Mysticism. Hujwīrī said of this doctrine of al-Junayd: "It is the best known and most celebrated of all doctrines and all Shaykhs have adopted it, notwithstanding that there is considerable difference in their statements of the ethics of ṣūfīsm."[2]

Al-Junayd recognized and experienced that the highest stage of Unification already referred to, the stage of *Fanā'*, when man has given up his will in the Will of God, is not the last stage, nor the final goal. This state of *Fanā'* may be vitiated, according to al-Junayd, by ecstatic drunkenness. It cannot be the exclusive aim of the saint who also has a responsibility to his fellow men, because it involves the disturbance of his balance, the loss of his sanity and self-control.

God does not wish to keep His worshipper in isolation for ever. Al-Junayd says:

> "In this stage of companionship, the range of his movements is limited; he can only go from God to God, for God and in God. He has *Fanā'*, and this too is obliterated because he persists in *Baqā'* only through complete obliteration. God desires to return His worshipper to the community and does so, making clear the evidence of His grace to him, so that the lights of His gifts in the return of his individual characteristics scintillate and attract the community to him who appreciate him."[3]

Al-Junayd says further:

[1] Qushayrī, p. 19.
Ḥilyat al-Awliyā', v. 10, p. 278.
[2] Hujwīrī, p. 189.
[3] Risāla, No. 11.

"He is himself, after he has not been truly himself. He is present in himself and in God after having been present in God and absent in himself. This is because he has left the intoxication of God's overwhelming *ghalaba* (victory), and comes to the clarity of sobriety, and contemplation is once more restored to him so that he can put everything in its right place and assess it correctly. Once more he assumes his individual attributes, after *Fanā'*. His personal qualities persist in him, and his actions in this world, when he has reached the zenith of spiritual achievement vouchsafed by God, become a pattern for his fellow men."[1]

Thus, no one can be a true Shaykh and teacher whom God will make a model to others, whom God trusts with a message to his fellow men, and whose life will be beneficial to men around him, except that, after being with God and absorbed in God, he returns unto himself and so will be one of the community, acting as they should, and accepting the law and order which God has established amongst them.

But when the ṣūfī comes to this state of Sobriety and thus returns to the community, he still does not quite get away from the state of *Fanā'* which he has experienced. But he keeps this experience like a secret treasure concealed within himself, inside his new state. In a manner of speaking, it radiates through him when he lives, speaks and works amidst the community. He lives, as it were, at the same time in God and in the community.

These two states are only two facets of the same crystal. Al-Junayd says:

"After their union with Him, He separates them from Himself (and grants them their individuality again). Then He makes them absent (from this world) when they are in union with Him, and makes them present (in this world) when He has separated them from Himself (and granted them their individuality again). Thus it is that their absence from this world is but a facet of their presence with God and their presence in this world is a necessary cause of their absence from God."[2]

---

[1] Risāla, No. 8.
[2] Risāla, No. 5.

In this state of Sobriety which al-Junayd experienced and described, the ṣūfī is, so to speak, released to return to the community and to serve God's creatures. He will be able to spread the gifts he has from God to his fellow men, to each according to his degree of capacity; he will support the simple people through his piety; he will help those who have embarked on theological study as a theologian; he will lead and teach the young; and he will be a companion to the initiated, to his fellow mystics, and will share with them his most sublime experience. Thus, in his state of perfection, he will not be isolated, but with what he has received from God, he will be able to help others.

The combination of these two states, the state of *Fanā'* and the state of *Sobriety*, in one and the same person, is difficult to achieve and uphold. It will be possible only to those whom God grants His continued grace. To be present and absent at the same time means a continual strain on the self. Al-Junayd says in a short poem:

" I have realized that which is within me.
And my tongue has conversed with Thee in secret.
And we are united in one respect,
But we are separated in another.
Although awe has hidden Thee from the glances of mine eye,
Ecstasy has made Thee near to my inmost parts."[1]

In this state al-Junayd experienced various waves of feeling. In one of his letters he says that he felt the sadness and grief of his soul longing back to God. It feels as if it were banished from the presence of God and the accomplished living in Him. He says:

> " But when God brings the spirit back to its normal state, he re-establishes it and gives it back to its own nature. Thus the experience with God and from God is hidden, the soul grieves, and becomes used to its normal state, because it has lost its first perfection and highest favour. It has been brought back to the bounds of reason and perception. Its regret is profound and its anguish for what it has lost continues in its conscious existence and present reality.

---

[1] *Luma'*, p. 212.

This, then, is the reason for the soul's longing, its needs have returned to it; how should it not suffer for being banished from God? The soul was satisfied and now thirsts anew."[1]

Al-Junayd says that it is characteristic of this state that the soul will seek for sights of beauty and aesthetic accomplishment in this world—a longing which is well known to many mystics and which is the source of many of the most beautiful pages in classical Persian poetry—it springs from the spiritual refinement of the soul of the mystic and its longing for the beautiful. For the mystic the beautiful in this world is an echo of his experience before God. But all these things of beauty and accomplishment which he may see in this world are a source of pain to the soul of the mystic, as they remind him that perfection is unobtainable here—they remind him of the lost Beloved for Whom he is always homesick. This deep nostalgy of all mystics.

Al-Junayd says further:

" Thus it is that the souls of those who have known God seek after the green meadows, the beautiful vistas, the fresh green gardens—but all those other things which they long for, echoing their experience before God, are a source of pain for them, because they serve only to remind them that they are unattainable, and recall the Lost Beloved. Sad indeed is their lot! "[2]

On the other hand, the mystic in this state of release will often feel at liberty; he will neither care nor worry; whether he is alone or amidst the multitude will be a matter of indifference to him; he will not be impressed by outside currents and influences; he will be independent of the things of this world and will enjoy an otherwise inconceivable state of liberty.

Al-Junayd, on looking at his earlier and his present life, said:

" For a time I was such that the inhabitants of heaven and earth wept over my bewilderment. Then again I became such that I wept over their absence. And now my state is such that I have no knowledge either of them or of myself."[3]

---

[1] Risāla, No. 4.
[2] Risāla, No. 4.
[3] Hujwīrī, p. 255.

The state of Sobriety is sometimes termed by the mystics " The Second Separation " (*al-farq al-thānī*), since they call the state before *Fanā'* " The First Separation " (*al-farq al-awwal*). They also sometimes call the state of Sobriety " The Natural Separation " (*al-farq al-ṭabī'ī*), or they call it " Union of Union " (*jam' al jam'*), while calling the state of *Fanā'* itself " Union" (*jam'*).

Of those two states of the mystic, the one being Intoxication or Ecstatic Drunkenness, which is one aspect of being overwhelmed by God, the other being Sobriety, al-Junayd puts a strong stress on Sobriety. He is opposed to the school of Abū Yazīd al-Bisṭāmī, who puts the main stress on Intoxication.

Hujwīrī, whose book we have to consider as an essential source for ṣūfī schools in general, and for al-Junayd's teachings in particular, gives an account of the two attitudes. He says of Abū Yazīd's school: " Abū Yazīd and his followers prefer Intoxication to Sobriety. They say that Sobriety involves the fixity and equilibrium of human attributes which are the greatest veil between God and man, whereas Intoxication involves the destruction of human attributes like foresight and choice and the annihilation of a man's self-control in God, so that only those faculties survive in him that do not belong to the human genus, and they are the most complete and perfect."

Concerning al-Junayd and his school, he says: " Al-Junayd and his followers prefer Sobriety to Intoxication. They say that Intoxication is evil, because it involves the disturbance of one's normal state and the loss of sanity and self-control; and, inasmuch as the principle of all things is sought, either by way of annihilation or subsistence, of effacement or affirmation, the principle of verification cannot be attained unless the seeker is sane. Blindness will never release anyone from the bondage and corruption of the phenomena. The fact that people remain in the phenomena and forget God is due to their not seeing things as they really are. For, if they saw, they would avoid falling into this error.

" Seeing is of two kinds. He who looks at anything sees it either with the eye of subsistence (*Baqā'*) or with the eye of annihilation (*Fanā'*). If he does so with the eye of subsistence, he will perceive that the whole universe is imperfect in comparison with his own subsistence (in God), for he does not regard the phenomena as self-subsistent, and if he looks with the eye of annihilation (in God), he will perceive that all created things are non-existent beside the subsistence of God. In either case, he turns away from created things. On this account the Apostle said in his prayer: 'O God, show us things as they are, because whoever thus sees them, finds rest.'

"Now such vision cannot be properly attained except in the state of Sobriety and the intoxicated have no knowledge thereof."[1]

In this issue, Hujwīrī chooses to follow the school of al-Junayd. He says: "My teacher, who followed the doctrine of al-Junayd, used to say that Intoxication is the playing-ground of children, but Sobriety is the battle-field of struggle and death of men. I say, in agreement with my teacher, that the perfection of the state of the man who has been intoxicated is Sobriety."[2]

If we survey al-Junayd's doctrine of Sobriety, we come to the conclusion that his attitude to it and this teaching of his are something unique. In the history of mysticism in general, we are accustomed to find mystics who speak of their experience of unification with God and of being overwhelmed by God. There is always the danger that a man who is distinguished by God with such a degree of grace might remain isolated and be lost to the community. Some mystics, it is true, have returned to the community as preachers and teachers and sometimes as founders of orders. But it is very rare that a mystic, a man who has undergone all the stages of mystical experience, can so far distance himself from his own experience as al-Junayd does, and gives us a clear theory of his state of accomplished Unification, and his following state of return into himself and into the world. This return of the mystic, as an altered and more perfect being, into the human community—with a special mission from God to his fellow men—is what al-Junayd's theory of Sobriety means. This attitude of a mystic is by no means negative towards human civilization.

---

[1] Hujwīrī, p. 185.
[2] Ibid.

That men with such a high and rare religious experience and such an intimate personal approach to God as were given to al-Junayd would, following in his footsteps, return to the community, in order to work for the benefit of their fellow men, was, as we feel, of significance for all the wider fields of human activity. Such men would be able to face at the same time the mystery of God and the tasks of the world in what al-Junayd describes as the stage of Sobriety. We mainly think of the field of teaching to which al-Junayd himself was devoted. It is not the place here to measure the degree of influence which this attitude—at the same time mystic, clear and active—may have had in the fields of Philosophy, of Art and Literature, and at times even of beneficent statesmanship.

The part played by ṣūfīsm in spreading and integrating Islām and Islāmic civilization throughout many lands, from this early age through the centuries—to the present, is, to a large degree, an outcome of this attitude. That al-Junayd has been a guide to this attitude should not be forgotten.

Chapter X

THE KNOWLEDGE OF GOD (*MA'RIFA*)

The ṣūfīs, in general, hold that the knowledge of God cannot be acquired by means of reason (*'aql*), as this knowledge is beyond the ken of reason. The sphere of reason is limited by its very nature to objects which are finite.

God is not only immaterial, but also beyond the reach of logical comprehension. The knowledge of God, according to the ṣūfīs, can only be acquired by a state of the mind of man, which would allow God to grant him the gift of illumination and inspiration; it can only be reached by revelation.

In this tenet they differ from the theologians by rejecting rational knowledge (*'ilm*) as irrelevant. Instead of rational knowledge (*'ilm*) which, according to them, is insufficient for acquiring a comprehension of God, they use the term *ma'rifa*, which is exactly like and possibly derived from the gnosis of Hellenistic theosophy—direct intuitive knowledge of God based on Revelation and Vision. They see in *ma'rifa* (gnosis) the goal of the mystic, and they call the one who achieves this goal *'ārif* (gnostic). They therefore value *ma'rifa* higher than *'ilm*.

Al-Qushayri says: " According to the ṣūfīs, *ma'rifa* is the attitude of the man who acknowledges God in His names and attributes; who is further sincere in his actions, who frees himself from the blameworthy traits of character and from weaknesses, who at all times stands at the gate and continuously lets his heart dwell with God, so that God would grant him friendly reception, and who in all his conditions is sincere and free from the influence of his self, and who in his heart does not listen to any influence which calls him in a direction other than that to God. When thus he has become alien to creature, free from the frailties of self, liberated from the bonds of human contacts and mental distractions, when in his innermost being he is in continuous communion with God, and at each moment truly comes back to God, when he has knowledge of God by receiving His secrets concerning the operating of His decrees; then he will be called *'ārif* and his condition will be called *ma'rifa*.[1]

The theologians (mutakallimūn—the schoolmen), on the other hand, in their conception of the knowledge of God, do not make a distinction between direct and indirect knowledge of God; they hold that knowledge of God is based on evidence and on reason; they may make a distinction between *'ilm* and *ma'rifa*, but both are to them, in any case, of a rational nature and are the same in value.[2]

Now we come to the place of al-Junayd in this controversy. Al-Junayd holds that the nature of knowledge of God is always essentially the same because the object is the same. But it has degrees, a different degree for the ordinary man and for the saint. A different degree for the beginner, for the advanced and for the one who reaches the highest stage. But none of them can attain to the complete knowledge of God on account of the limited nature of the human mind and the infinite nature of God.

Thus al-Junayd, like the theologians, and unlike most of the ṣūfīs, uses the words *'ilm* and *ma'rifa* for knowledge of God equally. He does put great stress on it that the knowledge of God in every case is essentially the same and differs only in degrees. He explains this in a very clear and explicit statement, and this is what he says:

> " I was asked about Knowledge of God (*ma'rifa*) and how to acquire it, and I answered that, since the object of this knowledge is one, knowledge of God, both by saints and by ordinary men, is of the same nature. However, it differs in degree. Clearly the saint has more profound knowledge, but complete knowledge is impossible, because of the infinite nature of God. Knowledge of God cannot be complete, since the instrument of knowledge is the intellect, and both mind and imagination are limited by their very nature.
>
> " Those of His creatures who know most about Him

---

[1] Qushayrī, p. 142.
[2] See Tahanawī, *Kashshāf*, v. 2, p. 994.
Ibn Qayyim, Madārij, v. 3, p. 215.

are the first to say that they are unable either fully to comprehend His greatness or to reveal His nature to their fellow human beings. They know that they are unable to comprehend Him, to whom nothing is like, because He is the everlasting and others are created, and He is the eternal and the others are appearances, and He is the Godhead and the others are subservient to Him, and He is Almighty, being Himself the source of His own strength, and every strong being is strong through His strength, and He knows all without being informed. He needs not to have recourse to others, and every being who has knowledge has his knowledge from God. Praise be to God—the First without beginning, the Everlasting without end. No one but He can be so described and to Him only is this description fitting.

" It follows, then, that His saints have a higher degree of knowledge of Him, even though this knowledge is imperfect, whereas the ordinary man, albeit he is devout, has a lesser degree of that knowledge. But, since this knowledge exists in varying degrees in both types of man, it is possible to investigate the nature of the phenomena of this knowledge as they occur in these men. In its first and simplest stages, knowledge of God expresses itself in the proclamation of His Unity, the affirmation of absolute monotheism, belief in His existence, acceptance of the Qu'rān and the ordinances contained therein. In its higher stages this knowledge is expressed in righteousness, the fear of God at all times, the recognition of God in all His creatures, the observance of a high moral standard and the avoidance of what is forbidden.

" Now, the higher degree of knowledge of God enjoyed by those who are privileged exceeds that of the ordinary man in intensity. This intensity depends on their perception of His Majesty, His Glory, His Omnipotence, His all-embracing Knowledge, His never-failing Generosity, His Nobility and His Superiority in all those attributes. In the measure of their perception they become aware of His Exaltedness, the elevation of His Majesty, the reverence due to Him, His Omnipotence, the efficacy and thoroughness of

His punishments, the richness of His rewards; His Generosity and unfailing Kindness in Paradise, His compassionate Nature, the multitude of His Gifts, His Graciousness, and His Good Actions, His Generosity and His Mercy. The more intense their perception of these qualities becomes, the more they extol Him, revere Him and love Him. They become humble before God, they fear Him and they hope in Him. They observe His ordinances and do not do that which is forbidden. They dedicate both mind and body entirely to God, and are impelled in this course by the intensity of their knowledge of God, their appreciation of His Exaltedness, the richness of His reward and the efficacy of His punishment. These are the privileged people and they are His saints.

" It is, therefore, that people say of someone: ' 'Arif bi Allah ' or ' 'Alim bi Allah.' Among Moslems, when a man is seen to extol God, to revere Him, to fear Him, to hope in God, to seek Him, to yearn for Him, to practice righteousness and godly conduct, to weep and be grieved for his iniquities, to approach God with meekness and humility; this man is recognized as one whose knowledge of God is of a higher degree than that of an ordinary man.

" They are described in the Qur'ān in the following verse:

' Of his worshippers God esteems
highest those that know Him.' "[1]

We see clearly from al-Junayd's words that the instrument for acquiring knowledge of God is the intellect (*'aql*), but this rational approach will be in degrees. The knowledge of the ordinary man will be less than the knowledge of one whose intellect is clearer and who has reached a clearer and surer insight. But even the latter will not have the complete knowledge of God as the instrument is limited by its very nature, and God, by His very nature, is infinite. It is possible, according to al-Junayd, to inquire into the nature of the phenomena of this knowledge as it occurs in these different men.

Al-Junayd finds two types of knowledge of God which he calls the " first knowledge " and the " second knowledge." The

[1] Ḥilyat al Awliya, v. 10, pp. 257–259.

one is discursive knowledge and the other intuitive knowledge. He says in one of his letters:

> " A man who has acquired knowledge genuinely, who performs what this religious knowledge demands punctiliously, who is completely devoted to it, will find that the exigencies of that knowledge will not be one with his instinctive mental desires. He will then return to God, humble, modest, poor and with little, and ask Him to carry his burden of the knowledge of truth. At this stage he becomes able to carry out the exigencies of the second type of knowledge by the dominance of his intuitive spiritual desires over his actions, and is no longer positively aware of his knowledge of truth of the first type which bound him to the conditions laid down in its laws."[1]

It seems that Ibn Khaldūn in his *Muqaddima* (prologomena) shares this view of al-Junayd. He gives exactly the same theory in the same terms.[2]

The rational attitude in acquiring the knowledge of God, according to al-Junayd, will lead a part of the way, but not all the way, to the goal. The goal for al-Junayd is still the Unification with God, the *Tawḥīd* in which the worshipper has lost his individuality and his individual reason. He thus says further:

> " At this stage he comes to the stage of the obliteration of his individual instinctive desire for pleasure and also to the disappearance of his critical distinction with regard to the purification of his instincts through the disappearance of his desire for pleasure. Then he is able fully to comprehend the true indications towards God from the nature of events, the changes in things, without need for any media of understanding, since now his faculty of distinction coincides with a purified intuition."[3]

So we see that human reason (*'aql*) and the work of the human intellect has its tasks and directs the seeker in the first stage of acquiring knowledge (*'ilm, ma'rifa*). This knowledge will be either discursive or, on a higher level, intuitive. But after that, in the state of *Tawḥīd*, the muwaḥḥid is completely

---

[1] Risāla, No. 9.
[2] See Ibn Khaldūn, *Muqaddima*, v. 3, pp. 32, 33.
[3] Risāla, No. 9.

possessed by God and has lost his individuality, and here the human intellect, which, according to al-Junayd, is the instrument of knowledge (*'ilm* and *ma'rifa*), has no place. He says:

> " When the worshipper has reached this stage he can no longer be described in rational terms. In fact, the promptings of his reason to the worshipper who has realized to the full the special *Tawḥīd* are now nothing but evil whispers which he has to overcome. It is reason which formerly directed the worshipper in his worship when he worshipped God as an individual, but when he is completely possessed by God, his individuality is suppressed. He is, as it were, transmuted. His external characteristics remain the same, but his individuality has vanished. Thus he is at once present and absent."[1]

Al-Junayd experienced and witnesses that, when the seeker has reached that high stage of intense knowledge, he will quite naturally have left his individuality behind, and with it his human knowledge, and God's integral Knowledge will appear before him. Al-Junayd says in one of his letters:

> " When the Knowledge of God has become intense and has raised you to a high degree, when your heart is full of this Knowledge, and you are pleased to serve Him and your mind becomes clear by mentioning His Name, and your understanding depends on Him, then your human existence is gone, your self-will have vanished, and your knowledge shall be enlightened because it comes from God, and God's Knowledge (*'Ilm al-Ḥaqq*) shall appear before you."[2]

This highest state of enlightenment is what al-Junayd calls, as we have seen, *Tawḥīd*—Unification; yet in this state a new kind of knowledge—*ma'rifa*—is revealed to him. This revealed knowledge is not additional knowledge about God, but a part of God's Knowledge which He gives to the muwaḥḥid.

Al-Junayd experiences that the knowledge of the Unity of God may be reached by the seeker and he still may not be in the state of Unification. If and when he reaches the state of Unifica-

---

[1] Risāla, No. 7.
[2] *Ḥilyat al-Awliyā'*, v. 10, p. 281. *Luma'*, p. 225.

tion, he will do so entirely without knowledge. Al-Junayd says further:

> " The knowledge of Unity of God is different from the finding and feeling of Unification itself, and the finding and feeling of Unification is different from the knowledge of Unity."[1]

Ibn Qayyim interprets this as follows:

> " That means, one may, without any doubt comprehend the Unity of God and feel its intensity, but under circumstances which may be changed the worshipper may still be liable to be changed himself, because he is not yet in the state of Unification. This man is referred to as having the knowledge of the Unity of God, but still has not found Unification. Others feel Unification in their hearts and are *overwhelmed* in seeing the Unity of God, but what they find and feel is quite different from the knowledge of God; they *are* in a state of Unification."[2]

In al-Junayd's terminology—different from the terminology of some other ṣūfīs who take *ma'rifa* as the last goal—the last goal is quite clearly: *Tawḥīd*, Unification. Yet in Unification he himself has experienced a new thing, a vision and revelation from God for which he has no word: so that for lack of a term he calls it *ma'rifa*. Yet it has nothing to do with that knowledge, *ma'rifa*, of the striving seeker before that last stage which al-Junayd has described. It is essentially different, that is to say, it is not any more knowledge of God but a share in God's Knowledge.

What we have seen may explain to us why al-Junayd uses the term *ma'rifa* in two quite different senses, and why he sometimes uses the word *'ārif* for the one who has reached the state of *Tawḥīd*. He says, for instance: " The *'ārif* could not be an *'ārif* until he is like earth upon which the pious and impious walk; and like the clouds that are spread over everything; and like the rains that descend upon all places quite without any likes and dislikes."[3] Once, when he was asked about the *'ārif*, he replied: " The colour of his vessel is the colour of water."[4]

---

[1] Qushayrī, p. 136.
[2] Madārij as-Sālikīn, v. 3, p. 150.
[3] Qushayrī 142, also 127.
[4] Ibid.

Or: " The *'ārif* is a son of the time being,"[1] meaning that he looks not to the past nor to the future. Al-Junayd, when asked about the saying of Dhu 'n-Nūn about the *'ārif*: " He has been here and has gone away," gave the explanation: " The *'ārif* does not restrict himself to any state which would prevent his entering another state, nor does he restrict himself to a station which would prevent his moving to another station. He behaves just like the people in whichever state they may be, whom he meets. He shares their feelings and speaks with people whatever their spiritual condition, so that they may understand and benefit from his words."[2]

By expression *'ārif*, when applied in this way, al-Junayd, as we clearly see, does not mean the one who still seeks the knowledge of God—a seeking which, according to him, works by the means of the intellect—but he quite clearly means the *muwaḥḥid* whom God inspired and to whom God in His grace has revealed Himself.

Now, after having reached this stage for which he left his individuality and all that goes with individuality, passions, will and reason behind, he will have to return to his normal state as an individual in which his reason and individuality and all that will be restored to him. Yet he will be a new individual with human qualities, carrying at the same time his experiences of God within him. Thus he will be at once present and absent, absent and present.

[1] Qushayrī, 143.
[2] Ibid.

Chapter XI

AL-JUNAYD AND PLOTINUS

The influence of Neo-platonic philosophy on the mystical teaching of Islām has been proved definitely for the later Islāmic period. It has been clearly traced in Ibn 'Arabī, Sahrawardi, and others. But for the earlier period, from lack of material, this question has remained in doubt.

The letters of al-Junayd, which we have endeavoured to interpret in this study, have shed a new light on this problem and give a firm basis for considering it.

In al-Junayd's letters we meet, as we have indicated above,[1] numerous traces of Neo-platonic philosophy which cannot be put down to the chance of similar thinking and parallel experience only, but which must be based on some positive contact. Moreover, we find that these Neo-platonic elements in al-Junayd are in no way tinted by the Christian mystical thought, itself largely of Neo-platonic inspiration, which flourished before and at that time in the Near East. What we find appears to be a sum of pure and classical Neo-platonic ideas, not blended with any other elements so characteristic for the later evolution of Neo-platonism in Eastern Christian thought.

As the Neo-platonic literary tradition is very complex and scattered, we think it the best way to go back to the originator of this whole vast and profoundly influential school, to Plotinus himself (A.C. 205–270). The philosophy of Plotinus of Alexandria, which bases itself on the system of Plato and integrates much of the Aristotelic and Stoic thoughts, is preserved to us in full in the six books of the Enneads which contain the teachings of the great thinkers, in his inimitable personal style, written down by the hand of his nearest disciple, Porphyry. We thus propose to give a brief survey of Plotinus' general philosophy and of his mystical approach. This will convey to

---

[1] Pg. 18.

us a wide view of the problem and will allow us to make a comparison.

Al-Junayd's writings seem to indicate that he has not had in his hand any Neo-platonic systematic work. We find no signs that he made a study of the whole general system of the Neo-platonics with its characteristic cosmology, astronomical theory, physics and aesthetics. The influence is only in the range of mysticism which is al-Junayd's personal concern. We thus assume that this current of ideas must have reached him through his teachers or other contemporaries unknown to us, by word of mouth. He seems not to have been conscious of "philosophising," but to have absorbed and integrated these thoughts, as they reached him, into his own seeking and thinking.

SUMMARY OF PLOTINUS' GENERAL PHILOSOPHY

We try to give a brief, sketchy survey of Plotinus' system and of his mystical thought.[1]

Plotinus starts from two facts, which he takes as accepted by those who are his students: the higher Reality or intelligible World other than the ordinary world around us, and the soul sharing in this higher world.[2]

In the centre of his system stands what we may call the Plotinian trinity.

(a) The primary for him is the One which he traces in his deductions as *the Origin*, *the First*, *the Good.* He is shy to give It or Him any name, and stresses that each of these terms is insufficient. One ought to call it neither that nor this. He states that the One is even beyond being. He is but one, not composite, quite Himself, supermundane; neither is He thought, nor thinkable, non-active, nor Himself thinking. "He needs nothing," being utterly self-sufficient. Thus he cannot, according to Plotinus, be imagined as the creator of the existing all which still originates from Him. Plotinus uses the comparison with the Light itself which is eternally, and with diffused light

---

[1] We base our survey particularly on the 9th Book of the VIth Ennead, *On the Good and the One*, which concludes the whole work. Our translations are from the original Greek. Plotinus Enneades, ed. Fr. Dübner, Didot, Paris 1896.—The author is grateful for Greek scholarship and translations to Ruth Gaevernitz, Ph.D.

[2] VIth Ennead, 9, 5, pg. 532, 533, Didot.

which derives from it " without any streaming out and thus without making the source, the Light, any less."[1]

(b) Thus Plotinus comes to the second principle of his trinity: the *Nous*, *Mind*, which, according to him, is the primary being. The Nous is all-knowing, perpetually thinking, seeing. His is wisdom (*sophia*) and power (*dynamis*). He is creating and upholding all that there is. He comprises—creating and thinking in the same process—all existence, the whole intelligible world and visible universe, the ideas or original forms, the divine beings whether invisible or those visible ones, the stars and planets and the earth, the human beings endowed with thinking souls, and the other creatures of nature. " The Nous sees as well the First, the One, as also the World. He is similar to the One, yet not the One, still composite, at the same time many-and-one, all-embracing, swinging eternally in himself in a tranquil spherical movement."[2]

(c) The third principle of Plotinus' trinity is *Soul*, Psyche. Soul is the creation of Nous, " the daughter of Nous." She is with and near to him. Yet she longs! She is bold enough to " separate " from Nous, craving for what is not Nous—not spiritual—the dark, low and heavy; that which is dangerously luring her away—*matter*. Thus, " running away like a naughty child, she descends to the material world " and " embraces matter."[3] She branches off into individual souls which will combine with matter, by this act imprinting the spiritual, the formative ideas on the material, thus bringing forth individual intermediate beings that possess soul in all ranges of creation, and particularly that double-natured being, *man*.

Her separation from her origin is a self-willed act which Plotinus feels to be a kind of going astray. She now feels unhappy, homesick, longing to go back to her origin, her abode

---

[1] VI 9, 2, p. 530. " Generally speaking, the One is first, while the Mind and the ideas and the being are not first."
VI 9, 3, p. 531. " *It* has not even an intelligible form. The nature of the One is the originating source of all things that are, yet is nothing of them all. One ought to call it neither that nor this, but we, like soaring around It, long to express what we suffer, now getting near, now falling off . . ."
VI 9, 9, p. 537. " . . . just as when the Sun remains, the light remains."

[2] VI 9, 3, p. 531; 9, 5, p. 533.

[3] VI 9, 8, 5. " Soul is from mind and shares in reason with him and thus has virtue."

in the eternal. She is ever longing to return to her father.[1] In most men, the soul is, as it were, submerged in the material existence, but in the best men—the pious, the philosophers, the soul rises above the material. Such a man is not like ordinary creatures, men as well as animals, " submerged under the surface of the water," but he may be likened to someone " who has his feet in the water while his figure stands erect in the bright daylight."[2]

The soul longing to go back to her origin, may break her fetters. She feels she has suffered violence by the body and " like an unhappy bride she flees from her mate and runs away to her Father's house and finds comfort in the arms of her Father."[3]

The soul, according to Plotinus, may even be able to soar beyond Nous and reach the First, the One.

In Plotinus' system Soul, as we have seen, is primarily Universal Soul—individual souls are thus to say loans from this All-Soul. When Eustochius, his disciple and physician, came into the room when Plotinus was on his deathbed, Plotinus said: " For you I wait. I am just trying to give back what is spirit in me to the World Spirit."[4]

Far from these three principles, the One, the Mind, and Soul, there is for Plotinus the utterly formless and soul-less, the *not-being:* matter. Thus creation is thought of in three stages, starting from the highest, lower and lower, sharing less and less in the spiritual, " a descending scale of perfection, the diminution continuing until it fades into not-being, like light into the darkness."[5]

PLOTINUS' MYSTICAL APPROACH

The soul, according to Plotinus, cannot return to her origin without becoming light and no more heavy. The seeker has to put behind himself the cravings of the senses, the moods of feeling, the promptings of the will and even the activity of reason. He has to leave behind even the ideas, making *It, God,*

---

[1] VI 9, 8.
[2] VI 9, 8.
[3] VI 9, 8.
[4] Porphyry. Life of Plotinus, Ch. 2., Brehier, Plotin, Paris 1924.
[5] Zeller, Outlines of the History of Greek Philosophy, reprinted 1948, p. 294.

the sole object of his search. (He will perceive the ideas again later after his return " from the secret innermost chamber of the temple.") The seeker will finally lose even his self-consciousness. " He should get empty of feelings—and even of ideas—he shall even *ignore himself* as being now inside of It and living together with It and having communication with It." (VI 9. 7.)

Plotinus warns the mystic not to give access to any optical " visions." " The soul must be without any images, and there should remain in her nothing hindering from getting filled up and lit up with the First Nature." (VI 9. 7.)

The soul thus will become, as Plotinus teaches, quite herself: not any more composed or combined with anything alien, but quite *one*. (VI 9. 3; 4, pp. 531, 532.)

Concentrated on her goal, the soul will not any more move astray, but like in a circle she will be moving around *Him*, as a member of sacred choir moves around the leader of the choir and looks at him only, thus dancing right and singing in tune. Finally, the soul, from being a swinging point of the periphery of the circle, will fall back into the centre of the circle, " like an image stepping back into its original." (VI 9. 11, pp. 539, 540.)

The philosopher warns his disciples not to be misled by such comparisons. " These circles and this centre are *not* in space like the circles of the mathematicians."

Plotinus makes it quite clear that God and the soul are not in space; we must not think in terms of space. *The contact with Him is not in any other way but through similarity, through being of the same kind—kindred to Him. Separation is through difference, through being different.* (VI 9. 4.)

Plotinus accepts, as we have seen above, an original state of the soul with God, before she became united to the body by birth. " This is," according to Plotinus, " her origin as well as her goal; her origin because she comes from there, her goal because the good is there. Living here, amongst these things in this world, means a falling-out and a flight and a loosing of her wings. *Being there, she becomes what she was.*" (VI 9. 9.) Or, in another word of Plotinus: " When he is as he was when he came from Him, then he will be able to see Him, because He by nature can be seen." (VI 9. 4.)

As we see, Plotinus trusts and witnesses that the soul of a human being living as yet in this world, may be graced to return to the state " in which she was One, before she came into this world," thus to say anticipating, as far as humanly possible now, her final return.

God is called by Plotinus—in the language going back to Plato—the *True Light*, and the blessed man is the one who is able to " receive the *True Light*, and to let his soul be lit up entirely in having drawn near." (VI 9. 4.) He also compares God with the ever-vivifying air (in the original sense of the word pneuma, spirit = breath). " *We breath Him—and safe.*" (VI 9. 9.)

The Union is, according to Plotinus, experienced through an utter sensitiveness by virtue of similarity. " He is like all-feeling, touching It, as it were, with subtle fingertips throughout, fitting in and harmonized throughout, and thus to say all-embraced." (VI 9. 9, p. 532; cf. VI 9. 4.)

The experience of that splendour of light there, blissful as it is, means at the same time a suffering, an undergoing, like a lover's. " If he suffers nothing, and has not in himself like a suffering of love through that seeing, like a lover who found rest in the beloved . . . he will not yet have been carried to the One." (VI 9. 4.) The soul in this world may, Plotinus says, smile like a courtezan at ever so many of its passing features. Yet she loves God with her only true love. (VI 9. 9, p. 537.)

Plotinus ascribes a relative value to the longing for the beautiful in this world—to love and friendship between two mortals—" love of images " he calls it—as transient reflections of the Love of the One.[1]

Plotinus impresses upon his disciples the difficulties of the progress " from knowledges, through knowledge, to view . . ." and he equally witnesses the difficulty, yea impossibility, for the soul to remain in the state of Union. She is liable of getting tired. She will get heavy again and sink and be separated—like birds, he says, who, flying over the shining surface of the sea, will feel tired out and will come down on firm ground for a rest. (VI 9. 3, p. 530.)

[1] Cf. Ennead I, Book VI, On the Beautiful.

Again and again Plotinus stresses the difficulty of telling. The mystic is at a loss how to render account of his experience " because there was neither a seeing nor a seen—but One." Neither subject nor object remained. He quotes Plato's word: " One can neither say nor write it. And yet—we will ever try to do so."

Plotinus has the attitude of a teacher. It is possible, he says, to guide your disciple on the path of discipline and to induce him, through higher and higher argument of reason, to faith: " Part of the way the teacher may guide you. But *then* you will be quite left to yourself, quite alone, depending on your own firm will and innermost power . . ." (VI 9. 4.) " Take those notions, though inadequate: the First—the Origin—the Good—the One, and starting from thence—*see* . . ." (VI 9. 7.)

He urges that it is neither right nor pious to impart this knowledge to anyone who has nothing of this experience and longing in himself. He mentions the decree of contemporary mystery cults: " Don't Divulge Anything to the Uninitiated." Doing so might, according to Plotinus, cause grievous misunderstanding and misuse. This was already the attitude of Plato, who urged the recipient of his second Letter with its theological passages to burn the Letter after carefully reading it, so that it might not fall into wrong hands, and who, in his seventh Letter, says: " I have never written these things, nor will I." Young King Alexander reprimanded his teacher Aristotle, in a letter, for publishing his Metaphysics : " In what will we still differ from the crowds ? " he wrote. Aristotle wrote him, not to worry: " Those who read it, will read it and not understand it, if they are not of those who possess the knowledge."[1]

We may follow Plotinus further and hear what he gives as his experience as to the state after the mystical Union. It is a positive, not a merely negative state. In this enlightened state after the Union, when the soul finds herself ordered and lit throughout, the mystic, led by the *memory* of his experience, may be able to do good deeds for others in the earthly society of men. " This," Plotinus says, " is probably what the ancient Greek poets meant when they called King Minos of Crete a

[1] Platon. 2nd Letter, 114 b.c. and 7th Letter, 341 c., 342 a. Plutarch, Life of Alexander, 7.

'companion of God.' He may have put down his celebrated laws for his people like shadows and memories from his experience." (VI 9. 7.)

On the other hand, Plotinus witnesses that the soul, when she has fallen out of the Union and finds herself remote and isolated, will be filled with deep longing and sorrow. But, he says, she may yet repeat her experience, " she may become light again, and ascend again . . ."

We can do no better than to give Plotinus' own words, the last sentences of the Enneads, which conclude the whole work. (VI 9. 11.)

" But soaring upwards, the soul will come into nothing other than into herself . . . to be in herself alone, and not in anything that is, means to be in Him: For He Himself is not being, but beyond being, there where she communicates.

" Could someone see himself become such, he would have himself as a likeness of Him. And if he now would step beyond himself like an image into the original, then he would have reached the end of his journey.

" Yet should he fall out of the vision, he will again awaken the virtue which is in him and will find himself well ordered throughout—and he will again, through virtue, become light and rise to the Mind (Nous), and further, through wisdom, to *It*. And such is the life of gods and of godly and blessed men: a life turning away from all other things here and not enjoying things here, a flight of the only to the Only."

COMPARISON BETWEEN PLOTINUS' AND AL-JUNAYD'S MYSTICAL TEACHINGS

This brief sketch of the doctrine of Plotinus, which does not claim to be detailed or complete, yet allows us to compare the mystical teachings of Plotinus with those of al-Junayd.

Both Plotinus and al-Junayd hold that there is a highest Reality, and for both there is a gap between this Reality and the world of phenomena we live in.

According to both, the soul derives from that yonder. She has descended and finds herself in this lower world into which she came by birth. She is now a compound, complex creature, soul, reason, will, senses, held by the physical body. She *longs* to return to her origin and, through continuous striving and labour, she may be able to become quite herself—quite one again, and thus ascend towards her original state.

Yet here we find a significant difference. According to Plotinus, the soul has separated from her Origin, having been drawn, through a kind of curiosity, down to the lower world into the embrace of the body. She makes a straying step, which leads to separation. For Junayd, while he also uses the term of separation, the descent of the soul into this lower world, and her being linked with the body by birth, is by no means caused by a volition of the soul, but simply by an act of God.

There is a very strong similarity between Plotinus and al-Junayd in this doctrine of the pre-existence and post-existence of the soul in the Divine Origin before and after this life. Al-Junayd interprets the verses of the Qu'rān, VII, 166 and 167, in this sense, as we have shown above in our chapter on the Covenant, " Mīthāq."[1]

Both Plotinus and al-Junayd hold that by her nature the soul may ascend to her Origin, as God, by His nature, can be *seen* " through force of inner vision " (mushāhada).

The stages of this mystical path are indicated to their disciples in a very similar way by Plotinus and al-Junayd. The soul can only return to her goal through the hard method of discipline; by " becoming light and no more heavy," not any more composed, quite simple and *one* again in an unwavering quest for the One. She has to leave behind the craving of the senses, the promptings of the will, even reason and all those thoughts with which her reason provides her continuously, and even the ideas. Finally, she will leave behind even her consciousness of self in order to sink and lose herself in the One.

Plotinus, as well as al-Junayd, calls this final mystical stage " *oblivion* " (*lētē, fanā'*). Both Plotinus and al-Junayd describe the struggle of the soul to abide in this union with her interfering weakness, which makes her apt to be separated again, as a painful *trial* (*agōn, balā'*).

---

[1] P. 76, 77.

The contact and Union, according to both Plotinus and al-Junayd, is not through approach in space, but through similarity; separation is through difference. The soul, according to both, is liable to get tired, and she will find herself separated again. Both thinkers stress the utter difficulty to give an account of the experience, because subject and object were no more while there was One.

The mystic thus will speak in comparisons. Both Plotinus and al-Junayd use the metaphor of Light. Plotinus also has similes for mathematics: " it is like a point in the periphery of a circle falling back into its centre," while such mathematical comparisons are not in al-Junayd—though they may be found in later Muslim thinkers. Plotinus' metaphor of the lover and the beloved is known to al-Junayd, and it plays an even more essential part in later Ṣūfīsm.—Both thinkers value the state after the Union positively, not merely negatively. In this state, according to both, the soul will find herself " well ordered and lit up throughout." The soul may well hold memories of her unique experience, *principia* which will allow the mystic in this state to be active for the best of his fellow men. Al-Junayd calls this state the State of Sobriety. This expression does not occur in Plotinus, and seems original to al-Junayd.

Both Plotinus and al-Junayd witness that in this state after the mystical Union the soul often will be homesick and in pain, and will long for what she lost. Al-Junayd and Plotinus feel that, when the mystic sees something beautiful in this world, his longing will be awakened and he will feel both joy and sadness. It may happen, for instance, says al-Junayd, when he looks at a beautiful landscape. The soul, according to both, may be able to rise again and reach the state of Union once more.

Both Plotinus and al-Junayd consider the mystical gift to be a special grace granted to only a few elect ones. Such men can be led, according to both, by a good teacher and guide on the path. Yet the teacher can lead the disciple only a certain length of the way. Then the disciple will be left to himself and will have to reach his goal alone.

What in fact makes the mystic try to tell of an experience beyond words is his deep concern for his close friends and fellow seekers. The relation between teacher and disciple,

Shaykh and murīd, becomes of high importance, just as for Plato and Plotinus, so also to the Moslem ṣūfīs. To this relation between teacher and disciple we owe the whole mystical esoteric teaching and discipline among the Greeks and in Islām.

After having surveyed the numerous common elements and related notions in Plotinus and al-Junayd regarding the mystical path of the soul, we raise our minds to what is bound to be the first and last for the thinker and for the mystic, the idea of God. In al-Junayd's religious experience, as we have seen throughout his letters, God is all-present, all-seeing, all-active, all-creating. He is victorious, overwhelming. He is close by. He draws his worshipper near and engulfs him in His Presence. He personally elects His worshipper and endows him with super-human force to reach Him. He Himself acts in him to bring difference to nought and to bridge the gap.

For Plotinus, on the other hand, God was utterly remote, *beyond being*, beyond thinking, beyond acting, beyond creating—a conception of utter Oneness which caused Plotinus to accept the idea of a mediator, a creator who, thinking and active, " comprises the Universe in his creative thought," the Mind or Nous. Here the difference is fundamental indeed.

This is what we find: Al-Junayd's idea of God shows no influence whatever of the Greek philosophy. His faith in God is purely Islāmic: God all-present, creating, preserving, active, victorious, ever near to man, is the idea of God of the Qur'ān. God, electing his worshipper, drawing him nigh on the path of the seeker, finally engulfing and overwhelming him and merging him into His Presence—this shows the development of Islāmic religious experience from the Qur'ān to the early ṣūfī mystics. No external philosophical influence can be assumed as an explanation for this development.

We may well feel that no sublimated gnostic theology, no remote Deity such as Plotinus had taught, could influence the strong Muslim conviction alive in al-Junayd.

In realizing this fundamental difference, it becomes more evident that in the doctrine of the Soul and the mystical path the Plotinian influence on al-Junayd seems indeed deep and significant.

We may pause for a moment to consider the question: What

attracted the early Muslim mystics to this Neo-platonic philosophy so that they opened their minds to it and became widely and deeply interested? It may have been, as we feel, this: That there came within their reach a comprehensive and enlightened system of thought, which based itself on the Oneness of God, and which, from this central point, comprised and deduced all spheres of knowledge about the Deity, the Universe and Man. The mystic in primitive Islām had been at first an isolated, groping individual. Then there may have been groups. Some among these early Muslim mystics will have been attracted particularly by the fact that in this sum of Greek knowledge they found a theory of the nature and potentialities of the soul and of the conditions and stages of the mystical path—in one word: A mystical system. Acquaintance with this was like a confirmation of their own quest at a time when they were often misunderstood by their contemporaries. It encouraged them to make conscious to themselves their own mystical experiences, to "speak and write about it," and prudently to teach it to their nearest friends. They would penetrate deeply into those thoughts, pondering, selecting, and together discussing them. The contact of the early muslim mystics with Neo-platonic philosophy made possible the development of a mystical system in Islām, with its discipline and its terminology, thus giving the opportunity for the emergence of mystical schools around the personalities of the early and later ṣūfī thinkers.

It is known that Greek philosophy, through translations into Arabic, and it may be also through personal contacts, reached Baghdād under the auspices of Khālifs al-Ma'mūn and al-Mu'tazim. With regard to Neo-platonism, its influence on later Muslim thinkers and mystics has been established already.[1] The new fact which emerges from our study is that it influenced muslim mystics so essentially at such an early date as we have traced in the thought of al-Junayd.

This brings us back to our comparison between Plotinus and al-Junayd, both of whom were born teachers of men. Plotinus is, first of all, the philosopher who left a comprehensive system of thought on the Universe and man to posterity. He

[1] See p. 13, 14, 15.

was himself a mystic, and this enabled him to make the mystical experience the crowning feature of his general philosophy.

Al-Junayd, on the other hand, was first of all a mystic who, with his mature experience, became a guide to his close circle of friends—seekers like himself. His teaching is thus always aphoristic, not systematic. His contact with philosophy may have helped him to develop that deep and subtle knowledge of himself and his fellow men which is characteristic of him, as it is of Socrates. It may have enabled him to communicate in lucid words his own spiritual life to those who trusted him as a guide and friend. Plotinus' philosophy may have helped him in his endeavours to speak of the mystical experience in its essence and in its stages as clearly as is humanly possible. The clarity of the thinker and teacher, and the sublime, intimate experience of the ṣūfī, are happily integrated in al-Junayd's personality.

BIBLIOGRAPHY

Arabic Books

Abū Nu'aym ... ... *Ḥilyat al Awliyā'*. Cairo 1938.

Al-'Arūsi ... ... *Natā'ij al Afkār al Qudsiyya*. (Commentary on Ar Risāla al-Qushayrīya.) Cairo 1290.

Abū Ṭālib al-Makkī ... *Qūt al Qulūb*. Cairo 1351.

Ghazzālī ... ... *Al-Iḥyā'*. Cairo 1939.
Al-Munqidh. Damascus 1939.
Al-Imlā' 'alā Mushkilāt al-Iḥyā' (margin Iḥyā').
Mishkāt al Anwār. Cairo 1322.

Hujwīrī ... ... *Kashf al Maḥjūb*. (Trans. Nicholson.) London 1926.

Ḥājjī Khalīfa ... ... *Kashf az ẓunūn*. Istanbul 1943.

Ibn Al-Jawzī ... ... *Talbīs Iblīs*. Cairo 1928.
Muntaẓam. Hyderabad 1357.

Ibn Kathīr ... ... *Al Bidāya wa an-Nihāya*. Cairo 1932.

Ibn Khallikān... ... *Wafayāt al-A'yān*. Cairo 1299.

Ibn Khaldūn ... ... *Muqaddima*. (Ed. Quatremere.) Paris 1847.

Ibn an-Nadīm... ... *Fihrist*. Cairo 1929/1939.
MS. Cheater Beatty.

Ibn Qayyim ... ... *Madārij as Sālikīn*. Cairo 1333.
Tarīq al Hijratayn. Cairo 1357.

Ibn Taghrī-Bardī ... *An-Nujūm az Zāhira*. Cairo.

Ibn Taymīya ... ... *Minhāj as Sunna*. Cairo 1321.
Al-Rasā'il al Kubra. Cairo 1323.
Majmu'āt al Rasā'il wa'l Masa'il. Cairo 1349.

Al-Junayd ... ... *Rasā'il Junayd.* MS. Schi. Ali 1374.
Kitāb Dawā' at Tafrīṭ. Selly Oak Library 905.
Rasā'il Junayd in Ḥilyat al Awliyā'.

Al Kalābādhī ... ... *Kitāb at Ta'arruf.* (Ed. Arberry.) Cairo.

Al Kharrāz ... ... *Kitāb as Ṣidq.* (Ed. Arberry.) Calcutta, 1937.

Al Khaṭīb ... ... *Ta'rīkh Baghdād.* Cairo 1931.

Al Qushayrī ... ... *Risāla.* Cairo 1346.

Sam'ānī ... ... *Al Ansāb.* (Ed. Margeliouth.) Gibb Series 10. Leyden 1912.

Sarrāj ... ... *Kitāb al Luma'.* (Ed. Nicholson.) Gibb Series 12. Leyden 1914.
Page from *Kitāb al Luma'.* (Ed. Arberry.) London 1947.

Subkī ... ... *Ṭabaqāt ash-Shafi'iyya al Kubra.* Cairo 1324.

Sulamī ... ... *Ṭabaqāt aṣ Ṣūfiyya.* MS. British Museum. Add. 18520.

Tahanawi ... ... *Kashshāf Iṣṭilahāt al Funūn.* Calcutta 1862.

Yāfi'ī ... ... *Mirat al janān.* Hyderabad A.H. 1338.

Non-arabic Books

Arberry ... ... An Introduction to the History of Sufism. London 1942.
The Book of the Cure of Souls. JRAS. 1937.
Al-Djunaid. Handwoerterbuch des Islam, p. 116. Leyden 1941.
Junayd. JRAS. 1935.

T. W. Arnold and A. Guillaume (Editors) The Legacy of Islam. Oxford 1931.

A. Brockelmann ... Geschichte der Arabichen Litteratur. Weimar 1898–1902.
Supplement 1937–1942.

E. G. Browne... ... A Literary History of Persia. 4 vols. Cambridge 1928.

Goldziher ... ... Vorlesungen ueber den Islam. Heidelberg 1910.
Die Richtungen der Islamischen. Koranauslegungen. Leyden 1920.

R. Hartmann ... ... Al-Kuschairi's Darstellung des Sufitums. Berlin 1914.
Die Frage nach der Herkunft und der Anfaenge des Sufitums. Der Islam. Vol. 6.

A. von Kremer ... Geschichte der herrschenden Ideen des Islams. Leipzig 1868.

A. E. Krimsky ... A Sketch of the Development of Ṣūfīsm up to the End of the Third Century of the Hijra (in Russian). Moscow 1895.

B. B. Macdonald ... The Religious Attitude and Life in Islam. Chicago 1912.

L. Massignon ... ... Essai sur les origines du lexique technique de la Mystique Mussulmane. Paris 1922.
Texts indits. Paris 1929.

Metz. ... ... The Renaissance of Islam. London 1937.

R. A. Nicholson ... The Idea of Personality in Ṣūfīsm. Cambridge 1923.
The Mystics of Islam. London 1914.
Studies in Islamic Mysticism. Cambridge 1921.
The Origin and Development of Ṣūfīsm. JRAS. 1906.
The Goal of Muhammadan Mysticism. JRAS. 1913.
Selected Poems from the Duvani-Shamai Tibrizi. Cambridge 1898.

Ritter ... ... Cunayd. Islam Ansiklopedisi Cilt 3, p. 241. Istanbul 1944.

Margaret Smith ... An Early Mystic of Baghdad. London 1935.

TRANSLATION

CONTENTS

PART III

THE RASA'IL OF AL-JUNAYD

Another Letter by ABU'L QĀSIM AL-JUNAYD *to* ONE OF HIS FELLOW MYSTICS[1]

May the beauty of that which God, the Magnificent, the Resplendent, has granted you, shine before you undimmed. May He grant you the clear perception of that which He has specially chosen for you and vouchsafed to you. May God reveal to you the true nature of your creation. May God prefer you by that gift which is not granted to others but is kept specially for you. May He bring you near unto Him, close to Him before Him, may He bring you nigh unto Him. May He grant you the jous of familiarity in proximity to Him, and may He commune with you. May He choose for you His beauteous behests and be your intimate! May God grant you His aid in those significant stations, the state of proximity to Him, through His gifts of strength, assurance, quietness, acquiescence and composure. May God grant all this to you so that the ideas which occur to you and the revelations which reach you are not too much for you! When God first became your intimate it is so overpowering that amazement and astonishment overwhelm you in your ineffable discovery.

How can this be described, or the intellect perceive it, unless it be that God grants His control to the perception and His care to its secrets? Where are you when God has taken you entirely to Himself and has received before Him that of you which He desires? When He has granted you the indulgence of His communion and favoured you with the ability to answer Him? In this state you are spoken to and you speak; you are asked about yourself and you ask questions. The words communicated are as unique pearls, testimony upon testimony, a cloud of witnesses multiplying continually, harbingers of divine grace. They are as heavy rain from every side, generous donors to you of glory from God the glorious. Were it not for God's gift of grace and His vouchsafing His holy spirit then would man's mind be completely stupefied before Him and his perception, in the presence of God, utterly shattered. For God, may His praise be exalted and His holy name be sanctified, is the generous benefactor of him who puts his trust in Him and cossets him to whom He has granted the gift of companionship.

[1] For the preceding letter *see* p. 62.

God carries for them that burden which He has undertaken and they bear that which He desires them to carry. To them has He granted the privilege of perceiving Him.

May God grant us and you the station of the elect nigh unto Him!

Verily my Lord hearkens unto prayer and is nigh unto His worshippers.

The Letter of ABU'L QĀSIM AL-JUNAYD IBN MUḤAMMAD *to* YAḤYA IBN MU'ĀDH OF RAYY—*May God have mercy on them both*

May you not be absent from Him who sees you by the barrier of yourself, and may that barrier not prevent Him from seeing you!

May you not change when God translates you from your present state, and may your state remain essentially constant when God translates you from your normal self!

May you not be far removed from the true perception of God's revelation to you and may God's revelation to you not be far removed by the absence of revelation to you!

May you continue in timelessness to apprehend timelessness when you too are in your eternal state. May the Eternal always be your support for that of you which persists eternally!

Thus, then, you are in your pristine state, in the state before you had existence, in union with God but separate, and in that unity supported by God with no witness to see you.

May you not lose your spiritual individuality when you are absent from your temporal individuality as a result of the unknown when you are absent! In this state " where? " has no special significance since the concept of whereness is meaningless for the omnipresent. (If we say) God destroys (whereness) the destruction is itself destroyed in the eternity (implicit) in God, who brings all things to an end.

The union of that which has been separated and the separation of that which was in union with Him, are both ideas of Separation implicit in perfect union with God. Thus it is that union takes place through itself and for itself. It is union with God which God has made.

Another Letter by ABU'L QĀSIM AL-JUNAYD *to* ONE OF HIS FELLOW MYSTICS

May you continue, O created being, to remain at the gate of God, by His help and through His grace directed towards Him, seeking that which is of God's love in you. May you continue to enjoy those aspects of God and His extraordinary revelation which He vouchsafes, that love of God in you, which God's love grants to you, and whereby He brings you near unto Him.

God has chosen that in you which He desires in order that He may select you for that special gift which He has chosen for you. First God chooses you, then He causes to appear before you that with which He intends to endow you: with this He overwhelms you in the magnificence of His revelation, elevating you high above the vision of your fellow men, concealing your true nature from them. He withholds from them the knowledge of your (high) status and in His graciousness to you, He reveals to you the essence of the secrets of your status.

In this state you are in a place which its creator has buried away and hidden, He has concealed all traces of it from the perception of him who would perceive it. Thus, in this state, you are in the unseen world of whose true nature there can be neither doubt nor denial.

These are truths which can be apprehended with certainty, though direct vision of them is (by their very nature) denied to physical perception. Over and above these truths are to be found the Unity of God, the dominion of His divinity, His separateness from the beginning and for ever, the perpetuity of His eternal continuance. Here, then, is the perception of those that understand shackled and the learning of the learned halted. This is the objective of the wisdom of the wise. (This is as far as words can take us.) What has been described is of the highest elevation and is as far as we can go since man's description of God is limited subjectively.

This, then (the limitation by man's perceptual range), is the gulf which divides the spiritual from the material until the day of resurrection. On this day, after humanity has passed a time in that gulf, when they have been brought back from the dead, they will know and recognize the gift of life and the donor of it. Their life is eternal and persists for ever by God's decree.

In what preceeds, I have only indicated what can be described at great length, but in this essay there is no place for a full description.

O! my Brother—may God be pleased with you—I have received your letter which I was delighted both to read and interpret. I rejoiced in it from the beginning to the end. I was happy to discover the esoteric knowledge, fine wisdom, indications both clear and illuminating. That which you indicated was not concealed from me and I saw clearly that which was clearly described. All this reached my comprehension since I knew in advance the object which you sought. It is clear to me whether the thought leads, the object of its train as well as its origin, where the thought begins and where it ends and what happens to him in whom God inspires this train of thought. May you never lack the closest bonds with God, their continued existence through Him with Him. The conquering victories have prevailed, the clear manifestations have appeared and lead to the strength of their dominion, a dominion which is maintained by that constant victory resulting therefrom. These victories multiply and remain hidden, although in fact they are revealed in strength. These victories prevail against every onslaught, gloriously conquering without " where " and without " whether " essentially without progress to an objective and not leading to a limited destination which can be defined. These victories are completely overwhelming and universal.

Aha! and what can come after this? God has made them a target for *Balā'* and the object of His trial and banishment. He has brought upon them trials which were pre-ordained, He gives them unadulterated death for a potion and causes to happen to them that which He wills. Some there are who try to hold off the decree, who are pertinacious but are conquered, others accept without a struggle. Neither the one who accepts escapes through his resignation, nor does he who struggles get freedom from *Balā'* through his pertinacity. Their life's break is imprisoned by its very nature. At the height of *Balā'* they are restrained. They choke as they drink that bitter and deadly draught, they are face to face with death. If the spirit man can be said to pass away, perhaps that is its rest, but in death, the very pain of the taste of death imprisons. The soul and the hope of ultimate salvation after death is gone. But before death, their only course is *Balā'*.

O! my Brother, I have been able but to describe a few aspects of these people. I would not lengthen my discourse with a further description of their state. There are some who have heard an account of what these men have undergone, and before what ultimate realities they have come. These onlookers conceive the ambition of seeking after that elevated aim before they have passed through the state of reality (which precedes it). They are confused in their appreciation since the incorrect states appear to them like the correct states while the height of complete proximity to God is concealed from them. What happens to them is what would be expected for them, and error is continuous throughout their days. For themselves, they thought that they were of the elect, but in fact they were not. They were convinced that they had achieved a high state, a false conviction which goes with their present state.

Alas, alas! How far indeed are they from achieving that eminence! How grievous their error of judgment of their own attainment! May God protect us and you, my brother, from being in a state which is not compatible with genuine reality, and not closely associated with that which God has established. In spite of what I have said about this state and what appertains to it, it is none the less an intermediate stage between two states. When it is revealed it shows itself to be a separate state between two stages. God's intention with regard to it was not in itself, but when truly achieved, it reveals in its turn, the next stage. It is only after this stage has been traversed that it is possible to have the knowledge of the great, the stages of the noble, the place of the wise, and the true exposition of the understanding of the learned. This final stage is one which, when a man thinks of it, and tries to describe it, or has the intention of explaining some of it, then " their faces are downcast before the Living, the Existing, they are undone by their burden of iniquity."

O! my Brother! May I not miss the point of that which you indicate which God has revealed to you! May I always have happiness from you when you reach the goal which God has revealed to you. You are indeed one of my close companions, you share in my longings and are one of the leaders of my fellowship. You are of the friends of the heart for whom my devotion is sincere. Are you not one of those that remain of our brotherhood, one of us who has been singled out? Are you not the recipient of that Grace of God who benefits us all?

O! my Brother! Please continue your grace, your condescension, your good deeds, your writing to us and your communicating with us. We derive great joy from your good news and are delighted that you continue alive. We rejoice in the greatness of God's gift to you! Should you consider us worthy please continue to enlighten us as your duty, but if you cannot find us worthy, please continue to enlighten us out of the goodness of your heart, a gracious gift from you to us.

To you, then, be the peace of God and His mercy, and on all our brotherhood.

A Copy of the Letter (Kitāb) by AL-JUNAYD *to* 'AMR IBN 'UTHMĀN AL-MAKKĪ—*May God grant (this) mercy to both*

May you reach the highest peak of acquired knowledge and inborn wisdom, may you achieve the highest possible state of confident knowledge! May God bring you into His intimate companionship and may you be of those who are nearest to Him! May God grant you familiarity with the finest of His revelations so that you have complete comprehension of them! So that you have this knowledge with confidence and comprehension. May you achieve the highest pinnacle of its perfection and have that clear and dominant view which comes from the comprehensive knowledge which you have achieved, which God may grant you abundantly. Once you have achieved this confident knowledge you will no longer need to seek after God because by means of this knowledge you will see the Truth directly. Moreover, where opinions differ in the realm of scientific knowledge, you, for your part, possess perfect certainty.

Thus, then, does God make of you one who helps his brethren to achieve the object of knowledge by his explanation and comment. The true and satisfying conclusions are revealed to them by the means of his discourse. His status is a happy source of pride both to those who can be with him when he teaches and also to those who are absent. Surely God has made you a light whose brilliance fills the universe, whose brightness rises and illuminates all heaven and earth. Thus all creatures can achieve their perfect happiness, felicity, and attain that noble, all-embracing aim they seek (and these then) are the manifest signs within which the chosen teacher is clothed, the external appearances in which he is dressed. When this is seen (it must be realized that) restraint in its appearance happens, it is withheld, barred and hidden so as not to appear. This is a secret which so bewilders the mind that it cannot explain it. Such inspiration is granted to few, it is withheld and reined and kept back from most. This is a secret which intellect alone cannot perceive, which understanding (academically) cannot achieve. Alas, alas! the most learned are sealed off from this knowledge, the comprehension of the greatest doctors cannot attain it. For God is unique, is single and exalted and removes the nature of His existence in the sight of man by denying him His vision. How many an aspirant in God in his mind, and how many that would show their inspiration, when they try to prove the bounty that is theirs, when they try to describe their privilege, can only babble and show their perplexity and are so bewildered that they cannot explain it. In spite of their thoughts their words require interpretation.

When the ignorant man hears the discourse of the learned, he thinks he understands his point, but in reality (the learned man is also) in utter darkness and does not fully appreciate the subject of his discourse. In the midst of his discourse he is impelled by the essential truth of his subject and draws the listeners' attention to attempting to understand the words he uses and to follow out the verbal positive commands and observe the prohibitions. But this is only part of knowledge. When you are yourself satisfied that you have certain knowledge, this knowledge is part of you before you have imparted to others what this knowledge demands. Of necessity its advantage and its light through its mark is clearly apparent to you. This is the verdict of knowledge against you when its mark is clearly apparent in you. Therefore, beware O thou who hast donned the garb of learning, whom his fellow men point out as a scholar, but who falls short of knowledge in its pure reality. Be aware of what I have said and be wary of public fame. This is but the bitter death of the type of scholar I have described, and God's verdict against him.

When the scholar hears the discourse pronounced by the wise man, when he actually has heard the exposition which he expounds to him, he bows his head lost in thought and then after concentration he sobs and his tears last a long time, his sobbing is intense. He is most deeply distressed. At that point the wise man approaches him and says: "Now (that you realize your shortcomings), when the sun of wisdom rises it will shine on you, the rays of its light will reach you. And then the darkness of your ignorance within the sphere of your knowledge will be illuminated, those things which you have overlooked and which bar your way to full comprehension will be removed. And I hope that thereby, that the things you have spoilt will be set right, that which you *have lost from your keeping will be restored to you.*"

Now when the scholar hears this approach to him by the wise man his distress is assuaged and he ceases from his bitter tears. Then he turns to the wise man and says: "Give me more of this medicine because it has cured my wound, and my hope and desire to answer my problem is now intensified. And save me by your kindly treatment and your gentle wisdom from the confusion which you know so well to be hidden in my secret soul, from those evil desires concealed within me. In the past up till now there was concealed from me those hidden things within me (which were denied to me). You have revealed them to me by your excellent description of them. You have enabled me to perceive by your kindly gentleness that which was concealed." The wise man then said to him: "First you must praise God always for granting you the revelation of this and for his putting you in a position to perceive that which you lacked. Stand abased and humble before Him. Approach Him with quietness and humility, and pray to Him. Surely, then, your communing will not be concealed from Him and He will hear your prayer. When you have reached this stage you have obtained thereby an intercessor with Him.

For surely you must realize that the speech of the wise is void except when it is permitted by God. When the wise speaks he who listens profits. This aspect of the grace of God to His creatures is like the rain from the heavens which God sends down to revive the dead earth. You surely know the verse in the Qur'ān: ' Look, then, at the signs of the Mercy of God, how He revives the earth after it has died. God surely revives the dead. He can do all things.' In the same way God will give new life by means of the speech of the wise to that faculty of perception in the hearts of those who had been heedless which they had slain by turning away from Him."

The scholar said to the wise man: " Yes, indeed, your description fits him perfectly. I now can hope from what you have said in your wisdom and in your exceedingly generous kindness that you will liberate me by your guidance from the sorry plight of my ineptitude, that you will extricate me from the depression brought on by my lack of progress by means of the opportunity of meeting you. Now I realize that my object is to discover what it was in me which led to that sorry plight when I did not practise what I knew, when I failed to keep up with the demands of my knowledge, to discover that which was hidden in my own soul, that which was concealed and overlaid within my innermost secret consciousness. This is an object which I have not yet attained nor is my knowledge sufficient to enable me to reach it. Now, in so far as God has helped me through you, I see more clearly. God has granted me this that His revelation to me by you shows me something of that which I seek. And with the limited knowledge at my disposal I realize how very much more there is to be known which I have not attained. There are recondite and hidden mysteries which I have neither seen nor known. So, O wise man, reveal to me my present spiritual state which you know better than I do. For surely the physician knows more about the ailment of the sick man than the sick man himself, and is in a better position to diagnose the cause of the illness and prescribe the treatment to cure him."

The wise man said to him: " Knowledge begins to dawn on you which will enable you to understand what is due from you and to you in this matter. The first glimmer of spiritual awareness lights the way to your perception and you are now rousing yourself to move towards that which is concealed in your innermost soul. You must realize that the spirit is heir to greater ills than the body can sustain. The diseases of the limbs and the organs are easier to cure than the illness of hearts and minds. For the diseases of religion and the afflictions to which faith is liable are a cause of destructions and lead their victims to Hellfire and expose them to the anger of the Almighty. Indeed the illnesses which afflict the spirit are in quite a different category from the illnesses and diseases which happen to the physical body, which are afflictions for whose cure there is hope, whose ill effects can be overcome. In any event you may still hope for God's reward.

" You must realize that the learned physician who is experienced and the wise and educated man who gives counsel are in a better position to understand the illnesses of the body and the diseases which occur affecting faith. The reason is that when they give an opinion it is the fruit of their personal experience, whereas the person who is himself afflicted is unable to describe his illness accurately. The diagnosis made by the informed, experienced and perspicacious physician reveals to those who are ill what they themselves have suffered and indicates to them those features which they have missed. So that what is described in words is as vivid as if it were before their eyes.

" And now I shall describe to you, in this manner, certain features which will give you encouragement and grant you all that which you seek in your question. May God grant us the necessary strength."

Know, then, a scholar concerned with knowledge, that when you wake up you will realize in what intoxicated perplexity you were, when you come to become aware of your overwhelming ignorance. When you remember exactly what you thought you will realize the harm of your forgetfulness. When all is well, and you are recovered, you will be able to appreciate how ill you were.

Know that all this is a preoccupation which, when present, prevents you from having true knowledge of God, is hurtful to those who have it in so far as they become clothed—as it were—in perplexity. Yet this knowledge of the state of being clothed in confusion and lost in darkness is one which God brings about in the worshipper and makes a fixed stage in his ṣūfī experience, a valid argument on the day of judgment. So do not worry about this you who are so concerned, who are so anxious quickly to get rid of it, nor should you worry about the confusion of intoxication, of being overwhelmed, of being in a state of forgetfulness and perplexity when you come to practise through what I am about to describe to you, when you hasten towards the goal towards which I encourage you, when you seek early to achieve that which I indicate to you. For surely the purity of *Sidq*, and the completeness of your devotion to your object, will lead you to that place which is at once the entrance gate to that which you love and the exit from that which you dislike. Nor will it bar your way from achieving that which you desire—for in God is surely the source of all strength—unless you lack perseverance in your efforts, which God requires. So beware and then again beware lest you should be found in any way lacking, lest I should meet you and find you lax and your efforts slackened. For it is your sincerity in maintaining absolute purity in your perseverance on which you ride the course to your desired objective. Thus, then, I have placed you on the right path, or on the first step of the ascent and you are now well on the road.

Now know, O you who are cautious, devoted and assiduous, that the circumstance which prevents you and those in your state from achieving your goal after you have acquired the necessary intellectual appreciation through constant long hours of study and protracted meditation in collating your knowledge and increasing its field, is your inclination towards indirect sophistical interpretation and your predilection for worldly standards of which you yourself are unaware. Now there are many types of those devoted to indirect interpretation. There is the type who is aware of his own failings and recognizes his hidden fallibilities, but none the less continues to interpret indirectly, to rely on fallible knowledge and from time to time forgets the inherent weakness in his method of deducing knowledge. There is also the type that favours indirect interpretation with the objective of clear and proven truth in his deduction. But in this process he cannot escape his own unwitting prejudice which must influence him in his aim. As a result he has an overweening trust in the conclusions which he achieves and relies on them exclusively. Such, then, is his position. The conclusion then to which his indirect interpretation has led him is in accordance with our first description and he appreciates what is concealed within himself, what is hidden in his soul, since he has used knowledge as an instrument, and a means thereto. He has donned the raiment of knowledge, put on its clothes and reveals in his indirect interpretation the traces of his knowledge. He calls the attention of the world to his interpretation, gives his name to the views he holds and expounds them to the people. Now when his position becomes known, when his fame spreads abroad and people come to him he is personally delighted with his following and flattered by the praise of the ignorant—praise which he scarcely deserves. This public approval breeds confidence in his method of interpretation and he claims for himself a position he does not rightly deserve. His head is turned by the continued chorus of applause, the deepness of their respect for him, the awe with which they speak of his findings and he has credit for that which God knows to be the very reverse of that which is concealed deep within him. When he has established his reputation with the common people and the ignorant, and the multitude who praise him wrongly and in error, he looks to a reward for publishing his knowledge and is pleased with his immediate reward for his knowledge. He has become a vendor of knowledge at a cheap price, of little account. He accepts the ephemeral in exchange for the eternal, in exchange for the garments which God bestows as a reward for right action. He becomes of the number of those whom God reprimands in the Qur'ān about whom He has told us through the tongue of Muḥammad. The verse runs: "Moreover, when God entered into a covenant with those to whom the book was given that they should expound it to their fellow men, and not conceal it, they cast it behind their backs and sold it for a sorry price. How bad was the transaction!" And again we have the verse: "And they have had successors to succeed them, they have inherited the Book and taken the ephemeral good things of this world saying the while 'ultimately we shall surely be forgiven,' but still they continue to seize on the ephemeral attractions as they did before." But God holds their action to be wrong and states His view explicitly in the Qur'ān. He stresses this point for those of his worshippers who understand. The responsibility that goes with knowledge is made abundantly clear beyond all later possibility of debate or pretext however specious. Moreover, God continues to give us the stories of the prophets—on whom be peace!—and describes for us their qualities. He tells us of His covenant with them, that they should give over the things of this world and devote themselves with all their might to the external things of the spirit. This they do without the condition of a price, without the desire for a reward.

For surely the prerogative of knowledge which carries with it the responsibility of instructing the laity is of its very nature without worldly reward, but carries with it the raiments of God and a home in that garden of paradise which He has made a home for those that trust in Him and obey Him. God says to Muḥammad: " Say: I ask no wage of you for this, nor am I one of the specious pretenders," and elsewhere He says: " Say: I ask no wage of you for this except that you should love your relatives." Similarly in the stories of the prophets recounted in the Qur'ān we read that Noah said: " I ask of you no reward for this, nor do I desire to." There is another verse: " My reward cometh only from Him who created me." And there are many such verses in the Qur'ān. Such, then, was the conduct of the prophets among the nations and the manner of life of the learned among the people that they took no price for the knowledge which they imparted, and asked for no reward for their teaching. For surely a reward which the learned take for imparting knowledge is an unlawful profit, as is that reward which the Rabbis and the Jewish wise men took though they had specifically forbidden it. In support of this we read in the Qur'ān: " Had not their Rabbis and sages forbidden them from saying lies and consuming unlawful profits, surely that which they had done would be Evil! " There are indeed many stories about the forbidding of the acceptance of this type of reward. An exhaustive argument of this point would be extremely long, but what has been explained is sufficient and adequate, " God is the guide." And as for that section of the learned community which expounds and is of the opinion that its exposition is the truth exclusively, they have come to the wrong conclusion, because knowledge of the truth escapes them. The doubts and difficulties which they experience are that aspect of their error which shows up only after they have become involved in that error and confused in its evil implications. These people are they who have based their guidance on the exposition of men whose counsel though sincere is wanting, men whose fate it is not to light on the ultimate truth which they seek. They aver: " Mankind has the greatest need for our knowledge. The purpose of our knowledge is the establishment of righteousness for all mankind, by which is meant respect of the leaders, consultation with them and modelling our lives after theirs. So also should we respect the princes and the chiefs and the aristocracy." Therefore, they seek out and co-operate with the caliphs, the princes, the learned and the aristocracy.

This action they suppose to be for God's sake and they hope that it will have its reward. They reckon it to be one of the loftiest actions of the very highest degree and carrying the richest reward. It is, however, to the mighty that they bring their knowledge and by means of it they knock at their gates. They seek strenuously to pass on their knowledge to those who have neither asked them for it nor asked them to come to them nor respect them for it. To begin with, they must have the humility of the suppliant and ask of the chamberlains permission to suter; they must suffer the humiliation of long waiting at the door, whereafter some are permitted entry and others rejected. Those that are rejected are humiliated, punished, mortified and return to their homes made low and mean. In this wise they continue the labour of going and returning, going and returning—this is the cause of their ruin and destruction—till finally they achieve that after which they sought. But they have forgotten God whom they worshipped originally and it is this forgetfulness and neglect which carry in their train the paths of death. They are overwhelmed by the afflictions and diseases of the soul. Their perception and their minds are seduced by the wealth which the mighty have acquired in this temporal world and they come to prefer the things of this world to the next because of their tinsel-shine, their fresh charm, the magic of their perfume.

And know, O seeker after the preference and glory which knowledge inspires, O searcher for intimacy with God by means of good works exclusively for God, that the feet of the people have strayed from the right paths and that their hearts are not evenly balanced in their search after their real objective. They have turned aside and follow subconscious motives distracted by superficial beauty and misted by the ambition of fame, the desire of public respect and honour which is the due of that knowledge which they seek. We see them delighting in the concourse gathered before them to hear their wisdom, delighting in public recognition and reference to them as authorities, scholars whose views are decisive and whose dicta are final. Their ambition has become overweening and their appetite for praise unsated. If they do not receive this recognition they are dissatisfied, if they do not achieve what they delight in, they are angry. Do not dare to ask them about the excess of their anger or station, they blame all who would oppose their capricious desires. It would be possible to describe their extreme emotionalism in all they do at considerable length, but I have contented myself with what springs to my lips. I trust that the flow of my description and account is an ample sufficiency for you!

And therefore put on now the garments of caution, don the clothes of fear and take unto yourself the shield of reverence. Stand before God in constant servitude, examine your heart constantly, weigh your actions deliberately, energetically pursue the performance of good actions and be completely sincere in seeking your aim. And all this while let your spiritual and inner aim go hand in hand with a constant awareness of God and complete concentration of Him. Be then one who devotes to God that complete energy and devotion which is due to Him, one whom God praises of the number of His sincere worshippers who will receive His glorious promise and His rich reward. We read in the Qur'ān (29.69): "These who have striven towards us shall we surely lead on our paths for God is always with the righteous" and again (4.62): "Had they done that to which they had been exhorted, it would gave gone better with them and their faith more firmly founded." Now these two verses give the key to the attainment of goodness and the achievement of correct and straight guidance. So take unto yourself as much as you can of what these verses teach and persist in God's teaching which is revealed in them. And be particularly careful in the light of what has gone before in your handling of exgesis of holy texts. Beware of misunderstandings which may well invalidate the whole of your religious practice and lead to nothing but chagrin.

The scholar then said to him: " O, wise man, you have spoken of the very matter which was in my mind and attained to the uttermost doubts which exercised me. What is more, you have described things whose value I perceived but dimly. This I regard as both grace and mercy from God to me. Surely, God has made you the means of bringing to my notice essential matters the gift of which is God's grace to me through your agency. Were it not for this gift I should have been lacking in understanding and like those whom you have described. By means of your sincere teaching you have enabled me to avoid their errors and misunderstanding. That which God has endowed me with through you is a gracious gift. He has raised my appreciation of the teaching for which He has found you a fit and worthy channel. I refer to that part of your teaching which explains and expounds the three types of schoolwear and reveals what is wrong in their approach, where they deviate from the right path in religious practice, where they have strayed from the road. I was in sore need that you should describe to me the nature of those whose worship of God is based on true knowledge, those who fulfill their religious obligations as they should, those for whom to know the right is to do the right. Those who fulfill their obligation to pass on their knowledge and who are praised when they spread that knowledge abroad and make it known to their fellow men. Their purpose in giving this instruction is a religious one, altruistic, piously directed and of good name. These are men who are not influenced by greed nor deceived by a show of tinsel, who are not the prey of desire, nor slaves to their appetites, nor led astray by the world. They err not nor do they sin and are abundantly aware of what they are about."

Then spake the wise man and said: " Rejoice in that God has

opened for you the gate of questioning and enabled you to couch your questions clearly. This will surely—God willing—lead you to carry out good works, to give virtue the substance of action and, as is my pious hope, will lead you by smooth paths to full sincerity of worship. Seek then the Lord wholeheartedly and in the acquisition of wisdom and devotion to that branch of it which attracts you, beware lest your inmost self becomes a victim of those ills which will deny you true wisdom. Learn to control your innermost perceptions for verily wisdom for those who desire its comprehension and those who hotly seek its acquisition can be more loving, more affectionate, and more devoted than the most tender of mothers and gentle of fathers."

And now I see learning like heavy clouds wide spread above you, rich with the promise of life-giving water, their deep shadows foretelling imminent rain and your hopes high for it. Seek, then, the rain which is in these clouds and wait patiently where it will fall. And make you plea to God who brings on the rain, who spreads wide the clouds, who removes famine, who gives freedom to the bound.

And know that God gives life to the dead desert places by a drop of her merciful rain which he causes to fall upon them. Seek out these places which require and receive the life-giving rain and you, too, will be well watered. For surely the first light showers from these clouds will cure your ills and the steady rain which follows will wash away from your innermost being the leaning towards the things of this world. When this rain pours on your body it will wash away from you all your spiritual afflictions and when you taste it its exquisite flavour will kill all passion within your soul.

And know that when the Almighty likes one of His worshippers He makes his path to God easy and clears this road of obstacles. He makes the time of his journey short and brings him to the glorious home and vouchsafes to him an exceeding reward.

I hope that God who has inspired you to ask such pointful questions and endowed you with such clarity of purpose in this conversation we have had will grant you by His grace and mercy the status of those selected by Him from the number of

His saints and familiars who themselves have been chosen by God from among His worshippers.

And now—if God will—I shall describe to you the nature of those who know the truth (AHL-UL-ḤAQĀ'IQ) among the learned who practise their learning and whose devotion to it is complete, whose every effort is devoted to fulfilling the obligations implicit in their learning, who seek learning without any ulterior motive, and who, in their seeking, are not deceived into following earthly appetites nor so influenced thereby that they do not achieve the essence of that knowledge. Nor do the wily distractions of this world touch them. " These are the truly godly who shall flourish." Know, then, that the genuine scholar, prior to starting his searches for God, must in the first place have the right attitude and the correct objective. He must constantly observe what is taking place within his soul, and keep close watch on his desire to seek God as it emerges. Nor will these genuine scholars permit their feet to take a step forward or any of their limbs to make any movement at all before their decision has been, in their own view, adjudged to be a valid point of departure. They then undertake their search for God in the light of what learning has taught them basically and they continue in this wise and in accordance with the testimonies of learning. Now the nature of that which God gives them in the beginning makes their hearts sensitive, cautious and fearful, all three qualities being present together and restraining their physical movements, controlling their inward thoughts, and staying silent for long periods. None the less, they fear that they may have fallen short of that which God expects of them by way of effort in their seeking after knowledge and they redouble their efforts and, in seeking after knowledge, they achieve that state wherein the name of God is on their lips and their minds constantly upon God. This will protect them from familiarity with the company of those who seek after knowledge, that accompany them on the road. Thus it is that they themselves are in a state which is quite different from that of those who are with them. Whenever any folly issues from this company they turn aside, whenever there comes from them any sinful neglect or diversion they become fearful and attentive. Whenever a disturbance arises from company they concentrate on maintaining their own attitude and redouble their hold on themselves. They pray to God for His guidance for those in their company and hope for their good and that they should stay on the right path. They bring no harm to their fellow men nor do they speak evil of them, they do not malign them nor blame them, but if they should see evil in them they have pity for them and pray for them when they become aware of their deficiencies. They recognize what is evil, reject it and avoid it, they recognize what is good, approve it and practise it. They do not despise those that have deficiencies because they recognize such weaknesses as universal. Nor do they detract from the laudable virtues which are possessed by those who are inferior to them, on the contrary they acknowledge these qualities to the full. That which God has implanted in their fellow men is abundantly clear to them. They know, through their true knowledge, how to assess the validity or invalidity of the claims of their fellow men, how to retain their equanimity at all times whenever they perceive that which is reprehensible in their fellow men. In all that they do they are led by pity for their fellow men and complete trust in God and they are devoted to seeking true knowledge. While they study true knowledge their tongues pronounce praise of their God, their hearts hasten to put into practice that which they learn, their ears listen and are fully receptive, and their bodies press on to the service of God—may He be exalted! When they gather true knowledge their conduct is fine and when they understand it they acknowledge that this is a grace of God's to them. Nor do they cease to be assiduous in their seeking after knowledge and extreme devotion to it and they are constantly in the company of him who has true knowledge until they themselves have obtained the fullest part of it, the greatest share of it. When they have achieved that which they sought for as aid and the object which they required, when they have achieved that state of knowledge in the light of whose truths they can act at all times, then do they return to the reconsideration of what they have written and the reassessment of the aim to which they directed their writing. It is this state which withdraws them from contact with the community and which causes them to dwell in seclusion worshipping God. Then the need of the people for them is real and their status as those fully devoted to the search after the true knowledge of God is recognized and the level of their attainment in that knowledge is known.

Their superiority is recognized and respected universally, their status—as it were—sallies forth into the world where it is accepted on all sides. Some are completely devoted to their studies, ignoring the mass of humanity in their preoccupation with the worship of God, giving preference to those holy works which God reveals to them by means of the knowledge they acquire and refusing any substitute for the worship of God, rejecting any change from that isolation revealed to them by God. And others are inclined to spread their knowledge, have the urge to teach it, and find in teaching their greatest virtue. They therefore are happy to spread their knowledge for God's sake, and are completely devoted therein. They seek to obtain God's greatest regard and hope for a blessed return to Him in the hereafter. In this they are never without God's right guidance. As a result, whatever they may say is by virtue of their knowledge and their silence, is deference to their maturity. When they seek to give an explanation it is well within the comprehension of their audience and when many people gather round them they are happy to serve them, and when they are about to leave they give them their counsel. They pass on such knowledge as they have acquired in simple language soundly expounded, their counsel comes from the heart and their words are exact. They are patient with the uninitiated and do not hold error against those that err and have missed the point. None the less they never pretend to agree with anyone who is wrong. They forgive those that do them wrong and give to those who have withheld from them, they requite good for evil, they overlook those that trespass against them, they do not seek for their actions a reward from man, nor are they concerned either with praise or commendation. All their energies are concentrated on God in all their actions and with complete sincerity. With their good works they seek God. They do not accept world things from those who offer them out of their generosity, nor do they long for free-will offerings. They see the world in that perspective ordained by God and are content with the portion with which God has provided them. They do not occupy themselves with what is not lasting nor do they toil with what is ephemeral. He turns his desire away from the trapping of this world and turns his back on the beckoning of its bright fascination. A little, provided that it is pure, satisfies him, he is content with what is sound and upright, he abstains from anything doubtful and he turns his back on complex matters even to the extent that he does not take advantage of certain things which are explicitly lawful and is chary in his approach to what is indispensable. Of all that the world can offer and all that is therein he prefers abstinence and adherence to constant and active worship of God. He has pity for those who are taken up with the things of this world and is sorry for those whose attitude to the world is demanding. He does not consider this world to be an adequate portion for those that seek it nor a fair price in return for the effort of those that devote themselves to it. He looks on this world fully conscious of its transience and aware of its imminent disintegration. This is the limited significance of the world in his opinion and its status so far as his knowledge is concerned. And this person, over and above what I have already described, is always alone and much in retirement, continually devoted to his worship of God. He finds spiritual satisfaction, happiness and inner content in confirming his good works in the direction of his Master and his hope for reward is fixed on his return to God in the next world. When he comes out of retirement to appear before those who have come to him to seek that perfected knowledge which he has, he does so with complete concentration and genuine good will. He regards this as a pious and good work. Moreover, he is always in a state of concentration on the main objective, when he is in retirement he is completely occupied with the worship of God, making every effort to approach closer to Him. Thus it is, that this state of consciousness of purpose to come nigh unto God is also realized when he comes before his fellow men to spread abroad the learning he has, and to be a teacher of that which God has taught him. At all times he is afraid of God and hears him, a cautious and respectful awareness of God and ever present with him. He does that which his knowledge demands and is just both in advice and in his decisions. He is one of the experts in religious law, and in what is permitted and what is forbidden and of the best informed in all matters pertaining to Islām. He walks in the footsteps of the prophets and follows the way of life of the saints and the righteous, he does not stray after those innovations (which, through contrary to tradition, have gained a measure of currency in Islām), nor does he refrain from accepting the agreed tradition of Islām. In learning he is expert, well grounded and strong and his attitude is clear, explicit and balanced. He does not side with any sect and is meticulous in adopting only the most valuable view. He has no leaning towards scholastic theology, never does it occur to him to consider it, he does not attack authority nor say evil of it, but he would like to see civil authority upright in every sphere. He holds the view that authority must be obeyed, nor will he separate himself from the community. He holds that rebellion against authority is an action of the ignorant who are not righteous, of those who have gone astray and are in error, those who seek rebellion and are enamoured of corruption in this world. These are they who are hostile criminals, who do wrong, who are in error, these are they who follow a path which is not that of right guidance, they are associated with error and distraction and in their rebellion against authority they turn their attention to worldly things. Now God has raised the status of the learned above these things and has made them leaders in the right path, good counsellors both pious and trusting in God, sincere, exceptional and outstanding, fine gentlemen, great, merciful, generous and saintly. God has made them unfurled flags of truth, lighthouses erected for guidance, made up paths for humanity. These are indeed the scholars among the Muslims, the truly trusting among the faithful, the noblest of those who are pious. They are those who guide in the crises of religion, and theirs is the light which leads in the darkness of ignorance, the brilliance of their knowledge shines through darkness. God has made them the symbol of His mercy for His creatures, and a blessing for those of humanity who so choose. They are the instruments whereby He instructs the ignorant, reminds the negligent, guides the seeker aright, grants to those who have through them are good works increased, and the noble state in religion reached, the traveller on the road of religion is encouraged by them and those whose religion is strong and complete are made firm by them. These are they who have filled and beautified their lives with consciousness of God (text, *dhikr li'llāh*, an allusion to the practice of *dhikr*). They pass their lives in good and fine works and thus they leave behind them for their fellow men a praiseworthy memory and the brilliance of their light shines clearly for their fellow creatures. He who makes a choice from the brilliance of their light is illuminated thereby, he who follows in their footsteps is guided on the right path, he who follows their mode of life will be happy and never depressed. God has granted them everlasting life and the fulfilment of a peaceful death and they find that their good works performed during their lifetime accompany them to the next world and give them pleasure. God has made the completion of their lives their best moment and their spiritual state at death most elevated.

And now, you who have asked me about the quality of the genuinely learned who act according to their knowledge during their lifetime; I have described for you something of their nature and given you a considerable description of their fine actions. Had it been my wish to give you an exhaustive description of them and the account of them which they merit, my letter would have been very long and my answer far larger. What God has inspired me to mention on this subject is sufficient for one who is on the right path and adequate means to attain the ultimate good for him who performs that which is preferable.

The learned man said to the wise man: " O, gentle and merciful teacher, instructor of good counsel and of wisdom, your description of these people has made my heart worry and you have filled my breast with fear. By your description I know my status and my rank and I fear that my knowledge which I now have may be beyond my endurance, because of what you have made clear about the extremity of my incompetence and the persistence of my being left behind. When I became aware of what you say I deposed myself, and became convinced of my misfortune and inadequacy. How, then, can I find a way out of the baseness of being backward, a road of departure from the blameworthy qualities which I have, a point of entry to initiation on to the path of the initiated. For in my view to withhold myself from this step is a sin, and to remain in the state in which I am now is a complete loss."

The wise man said to him: "You must realize that you asked about an exalted matter, an elevated and enormous subject. It is easy for those who practise its virtues to overcome fearful obstacles in their search for it, to carry great burdens and to bear exile from their native land and to dispense with property. Few indeed are they whose love for God is so strong that God has made it easy for them to give up their bodies and their very lives, for whom the achievement of their desire overrides everything. O, questioner about the status of the elect, about the ranks of the learned and the states of the great leaders, those that follow in the footsteps of the prophets, set about giving up everything which might divert you from the path of the initiated, which might hold you back from God's guidance and from righteousness. Be zealous towards God and in that which will bring you nigh unto Him. Know that your devoted attention to anything in this world, whether it be small or great, is a barrier between you and the next world, a means of obscuring your vision when it should be clear. Stop your consciousness from giving its attention to that which when perceived will make you lacking and inadequate. Purify your consciousness, make clean your inward thoughts by exclusive concentration on the main purpose, by complete and exclusive devotion, being of single purpose, zealous to achieve your objective. When you are cured of what was hidden in your secret thoughts, your external appearance, which is known and seen, will be vindicated.

"Beware lest you deviate towards anything, though its significance be trifling it will lead you away from that which is clearly virtue; surely he has the worst of the bargain at all times who sells much of permanent value for little of what does not last, who is occupied with worldly matters at the cost of neglecting the next world.

"O, you that seek the ideal in state and path to God, your prime undertaking which brings you nigh to your God, is the practice of denying the world and turning away from all things towards which the appetites of your soul may lean, be they small or large. For even the small things to which you lean must take something from you in her perception, preoccupy your heart and distract your mind. And it is in proportion to the strength or weakness of that small desire for the world that the strength or weakness of your preoccupation will vary. It is in accordance with the incidence of this distraction that the understanding of that which you seek will be obscured. For your actions will be effective and your hearts will be preserved in purity only when the distractions of the world are cut from both of them.

" If it should happen that something distracts, even though it be small, it becomes at once your labour and the object of your labour, and makes distant from you your awareness and comprehension. It will hold you back from achieving that perfect state. Be wary of what will incline you to worldly things and turn you in their direction even though its power may be trifling. In becoming completely free from all this you will exclusively achieve a fully balanced state, perfection of action and speech."

The scholar said to him: "I submit to your guidance unreservedly, and concentrate entirely upon it. I have no other occupation for my heart than it and recognize in it my right course of action. My hopes that through the righteousness of your guidance and through the rightness of your preaching and through the veracity of your counsel to me that God will bring me to all that for which I hope and the fulfilment of what I seek. I have seen the very springs of wisdom flowing from the deep, enclosed secret of yourself out upon your tongue and reaching me and imparting to me some measure of what you intended for me and I tasted of its water what I could assimilate and it brought me new life and proof of your desire to be of use to me. So give me more of that whereby life becomes stronger, and which brings me back from death, which was my past state, to that future so fraught with change. For, surely, the only thing left to me on account of which I can turn to God on your behalf is to entreat Him to vouchsafe to you a fine reward for what you have done for me, that this recompense to you should be in keeping of what is worthy of Him and His companionship to the faithful.

" O, wise man, since you have woken me from the slumber of error, and roused me from the dreams and the dozing of forgetfulness, it has become possible for me to apprehend your purpose. That which I found has compelled me to do certain things, and I found that the discovery of my own inadequacies impelled me to overcome them and achieve a clear judgment and certain knowledge."

Now in what concerns what God has made easy of inspiration and what knowledge itself requires by way of further extension . . .

A Letter of ABU'L QĀSIM AL-JUNAYD *to* ABŪ YA'QŪB YŪSUF IBN AL-ḤUSAYN AR-RĀZĪ—*May Allah have mercy on them both*

May God reveal to you the true nature of His revelation, and grant you the greatness of His favour and graciousness. May He contain you by embracing you yourself in the fullness of His beneficences which, when they reach you, are the grace of His raising you and exalting you. Then will you be where no other is a mediator between you and Him, but you will be in a relationship with God based on that which God has given you. That which God has given you is something chosen only for the chosen among the elect. He gives you a place, after selection, among those whom He has specially for His saints. He chooses you by His choice of the great ones whom He loves. These are they whom He has marked out by this preferment for the height of His companionship.

Their first steps directly towards Him on the paths which lead to Him are to remove all other than God on their way to Him. By God's aid they reach Him first of all others that seek Him, their footsteps are elevated up to Him alone when they have left behind all great desires. Then do the lights of revelation shine upon them generously, God's companionship flows over them like the rising flood, with all the generosity of an exuberant flow. Its downpour is overwhelming, like that of heavy, continuous rain, like the rich milk of steady piety. It utterly overwhelms and stupefies the human perception of those whom God marks out by piety. God dazzles those whom He wishes by the brightness of His sudden appearance.

Now to what extent and by what means is this stage of piety entered? I refer to this stage of piety which is achieved in the hearts of those who are thereby honoured by God. And how and in what degree can the intellect of him who approaches that stage of piety hold him back from it? Surely this cannot take place solely by the deed of the subject, even though he be the object of God's honour. Nor can he perceive this state of piety, the secret of the saint, even though the subject be firm and established. It is only God who can put this on, on behalf of His companions and friends, in the same way as it is He with His strength and power who imbues it into those who carry His throne. It is God who protects those whom He has chosen to be His personal companions.

In view of what has preceded, it is clear that, when God desires to create this state of piety in a man, He calls upon him to concentrate with all his being on God and He approaches nigh unto the individual whom He has selected. He takes unto Himself permanently the individual whom He has chosen as the recipient of the gift of His secret. Thus God's complete gift becomes the possession of those who are brought near unto Him and abide with Him. After these come those who are brought near to God, and after these come the saints of all types. Now all these have noble gifts which God has generously given them, which He has bestowed upon them by way of His gifts and His graciousness.

This is their favour and their fortune from God, their everlasting and eternal gift. Now all this, though it is of overwhelming value and a mark of special favour which God reserves for his elect, though it is the most precious of His gifts to His pious, is none the less of the nature of a veil which obscures the divine vision from all except the selected few whom God has specifically indicated. It, therefore, follows from this state of affairs that we have been describing the conditions of the beginning of the knowledge of God by the chosen few who have been specifically selected by God for this knowledge. Nor can this ever be achieved by any individual in whom anything earthy still survives, in whom the potentiality of an inclination to sin still exists.

O, my brother, may it be God's will that you and I join the companionship of God in this fuller sense, the company of those whom God has taken completely unto Himself!

And now to the body of my letter to you, O, my brother.

As you may know, the paths of righteousness go smoothly, the ways or uprightness are clear and well prepared and smooth for the steps of those who travel by them, they are wide enough for the journey of those who seek to travel by them and brightly illuminated and pleasant for the hearts of those that desire them. And yet how few are they that seek them? How few are righteous enough to travel on them? The paths are without travellers and lonely as a sequestered rutting camel. They are like the desolate, deserted places without inhabitants to tend them though God has made these places potentially habitable and promised any residents or travellers the finest of garments. Of all God's creatures none desires this elevated station.

I find that knowledge, in spite of the many who claim to possess it, and in spite of the universality of those who seek after it, is none the less bereft of human possessors. It is a rare quality beyond the capacity of the multitude, both solitary and distant. And this is because those that seek after it do not do so with all their might unreservedly,[1] do not show the necessary pertinacity in their search. I find that most people are ignorant though they claim to have knowledge. It is abundantly clear that many who, in their own eyes, perform that which is required of them, none the less lack that special knowledge. For, alas, most men's attention grips tight on the material world as they seek what their hands can hold. They prefer present profit and concentrate the whole of their perception in their devotion to worldly virtue. Surely their longing is limited by so little an object in the spiritual universe. And so, reluctantly, I find that which they seek is unworthy, is even reprehensible, for surely these are not works for the after life, they are utterly perplexed and cannot appreciate what this world brings upon them. There is none to wake them from their stupor. And yet if you

---

[1] صدق is used hereby Junayd in the sense of "sincerely," "entirely" much in the same way as it is used in the essay on *Ṣidq* and *Ikhl.āṣ* While صدق in early Arabic seems to describe the correct relationship between the worshipper and God which soon becomes what we should term " righteousness." There is reason to believe that Junayd by ṣūfī extension used صدق in the sense of sincerity as a quasi-technical term.

tell him of his plight he will deny it. Here, then, do we see the complete victory of evanescent earthly deception and complete perplexity and lack of comprehension of the things of the world to come.

And so, my brother, since humanity is so constituted, how great is their need for the gentle scholar, the sympathetic counsel of the teacher, the right guidance of the preacher! And you, my brother—may God be pleased with you!—are one of the few left of those who have passed on; you are one of the scholars universally recognized, one of the greatest of the wise. And you—may God be pleased with you!—know that God has made a covenant with those who know Him, who have knowledge of Him, those whom He has chosen in the Qur'ān, those to whom He has granted comprehension of Him, those whom He has specially selected and endowed with the ability to interpret the Qur'ān to the masses, to whom He has given the fullness of His faith. It is with these that He has made His covenant, that, in return for this knowledge of God, they should impart it to their fellow men and not withhold it. As we read in the Qur'ān:

> " The Rabbis and Jewish scholars in that to them was entrusted the care of God's book ",[1] and " Why do their Rabbis and scholars not forbid them from uttering sinful words and eating that which is forbidden? Their works are surely evil."[2]

Now you, my brother, are one of those still left to whom the Book of God is entrusted, to whom its interpretation and decisions are known and, as I see it, it is incumbent on you to expound to your fellow men that which God has granted you and to make public the grace which God has vouchsafed to you.

So—may God have mercy on you—turn to your disciples and give them your full attention, face them and concentrate on them, give them of the knowledge which has been vouchsafed to you, grant them your kindness, and privilege them with your guidance, with that fine teaching which leads them to God. Be generous to them with that of your knowledge which will help them, and show them the confidence of your understanding.

[1] Qur'ān 5, 47.
[2] Qur'ān 5. 66.

Be with them both by night and by day and give them that special cognisance of your experience.

This surely is the right which the people have over you, their prerogative. You will remember the verse in the Qur'ān when God addresses His most noble creatures to whom He grants respect and status. " Be patient with those who call on their God morning and evening, seeking His face, and let thy gaze on them not cease, nor be disturbed by the pomp of this world. Do not obey the calls of those who forget us, who follow their own desires, whose case is lost; but say, the Truth is from your Lord."[1] This is God's injunction to His Prophet Muḥammad the chosen.

My brother, it was not my desire to draw your attention to a privilege and a duty which you neglect, not to any suspected deficiency—surely God will guard you from any lapse or omission, from any deficiency or relaxation!—but God says: " Teach for instruction is of avail to those that believe."[2]

Now I began my letter to you with a view to establishing our closer contact, seeking your attention and your good graces and hoping that it would cause you to write back to me. So please do as I ask and grant me that further pleasure which would delight me. May God make you the instrument of aid to your brothers.

None the less, my brother—may you be guided on the right path!—there is just one minor point I should like to raise. It is one which I had first to learn myself and which I now venture to pass on to you in the hope that you too will add to it and in your turn teach it to me. And I should like to apologize in advance in the event of your not accepting it. Accept it only if it appeals to you as being true and accept it only as a piece of advice, since I present it to you as a suggestion for what it is worth: nor will I take exception to you if you reject it.

My brother, be cautious with your fellow men and be sure you understand your contemporaries. This is a primary consideration. Further, speak only after you are sure that you know your listeners.*

* Note: The manuscript ends here abruptly.

---

[1] Qur'ān 18, 28.

[2] Qur'ān 51, 55.

KITĀB AL-FANĀ'

A Discourse of the IMĀM ABU'L QĀSIM AL-JUNAYD IBN MUḤAMMAD—*may God sanctify his soul*[1]

"Praise be to God who severs the earthly bonds of those of His worshippers who seek Him and only Him and who grants the favour of His truths to those who reach Him, who find their support in Him, when He gives them (real) existence and grants them the favour of His love. Those that know Him does He list as His saints enjoying the various degrees of His benefactions. To them does He show the strength which emanates from Him and He endows them with something of His (divine nature) so that the passing thoughts which they encounter do not take possession of them. Nor do those qualities exist in them which might cause them ultimately to be lacking in the ability to achieve true unity with Him, *Tawḥīd*, to be completely divorced from this world. All this, then, is in accordance with God's call to them, their potentiality for intimacy with Him, the appearance of the Unseen and the proximity of the Beloved."

I heard Junayd continue as follows: "Allah granted me the favour of this intimacy and then veiled Himself from me with the veil of my corporal limitations. And I am myself the source of my tribulation. Woe is me! Allah first beguiled me[2] and then disappointed me (of His vision by my own physical weakness). It was my presence with Him which was the cause of my absence (from this world). My joy in my vision of God was the goal of my intense effort. But now my strength is gone and my spirit is departed. I have no taste for life nor can I savour the joy of His vision. I can no longer find true pleasure nor true pain. The world is become vapid. Yea, the very words I was wont to use have passed beyond my control. No phrases come to me, nor does any incentive invite me. That which was revealed to me has left me at the stage at which I was at the beginning."

---

[1] The title calls this work a *Kalām*, which may be translated "discourse." It seems to us that Junayd when writing this essay chose the literary form of the spoken word and of questions and answers.

[2] The Arabic word is اكادني which literally means "desired me."

Junayd was asked: " How is it possible for you to speak in this way since no phrase comes to you and no incentive invites you? " Junayd replied: " I spoke when I was absent from my normal state and then an overpowering vision and a refulgent brilliance took possession of me and induced in me a state of *Fanā'* creating me anew in the same way as He created me at first when I had no existence. Nor had I any sway over Him since no one can influence Him. Nor had I any knowledge of Him because He alone has this knowledge. Did He not obliterate my identity by His own nature and in this process my perception passed from me because I was close to Him. He is the Creator and the Re-Creator."

I asked Junayd: " What do you mean by the phrase ' He induced in me a state of *Fanā'* by creating me anew, in the same way as He created me at first when I had no existence '? " He replied: " Do you not know that God said ' When God took of the sons of Adam ' " and he quoted the verse as far as " We witness."[1] " In this verse God tells you that He spoke to them at a time when they did not exist, except in so far as they existed for Him. This existence is not the same type of existence as is usually attributed to God's creatures, it is a type of existence which only God knows and only He is aware of. God knows their existence, embracing them, sees them in the beginning when they are non-existent and oblivious of their future existence in this world. The existence of these is timeless. This, then, is a divine existence and a God-like conception[2] which becomes only Him.

" It is for this reason that we said, that when God granted existence to His worshipper, He caused, as it were, His desire to flow over him according to His will. This was possible because of God's divine and unique quality. This type of existence, then, is without doubt the most perfect and penetrating. It is the most significant, dominant and more fully described as conquering, victorious and genuinely overwhelming than the normal existence which appears in the worshipper, because in the divine existence his individuality is entirely obliterated and his worldly existence departs from him. This is

---

[1] Qur'ān 7, v. 171.
[2] *Idrāk Ilāhī.*

because no human quality survives nor does normal human existence continue, as we have made clear in describing the divine qualities of God's Truth and God's Victory.

" Now hand in hand with this spiritual metamorphosis goes a metamorphosis in values. Thus the pleasing is not of the accepted order of the pleasing, God's generosity is no longer of the usually accepted order of His generosity, because God neither feels nor is felt, He does not introduce variations into His nature. No one knows the nature of His kindness to His creatures, since it is a divine kindness which only God can know and do. In view of the foregoing we said that God has obliterated what appears to the worshipper and when He has overwhelmed him, God shows Himself as the most overpowering, the perfect conqueror, the completely victorious."

So I asked: " What can those, who have the quality described, find, in view of the fact that you postulate the removal of the essential nature of their existence and their knowledge? " He replied: " Their full spiritual existence is of God and from God and is revealed to them from God through His word and His complete sovereignty. This full spiritual existence is not achieved through their own unaided efforts, nor is it what they might imagine after complete subservience to God when their perception is removed and their soul annihilated, since God is separate from them and not bound to them. How can they find or describe what they have not experienced or lived through, or what they sought for and had no knowledge of? This is proved by the tradition which we have. It is related that the Prophet said: ' My servant draws nigh unto me by works of supererogation and I love him; and when I love him, I am his ear, so that he hears by me, and his eye, so that he sees by me.'[1]

" The Tradition continues in this wise but I have adduced an extract long enough to prove my point. That God is his ear so that he hears by Him and his eye by which he sees, is the formulation of a conception which is hard to comprehend. How can you bring it into the scope of your knowledge? If any one were to make such a claim it would be manifestly wrong, since

[1] This *Ḥadīth* is canonical, accepted by traditionalists. It goes back to Abū Hurayra.

this is knowledge of such a nature that cannot be perceived by means which are known to us and understood by us. The meaning of this tradition can only be that it is God who strengthens him, who enables him to achieve this, who guides him and who gives the vision of what He wishes in the manner He wishes so that he achieves rightness and is in accord with truth. This, then, is the act of God in him, the gift of God to him and only to him. It is not to be attributed positively to the worshipper, since it does not originate from him, nor out of him, nor through him. Nay: it comes over him from elsewhere and must therefore be attributed to another source. This, then, is a possible interpretation of this secret and independent state of the nature described above."

I asked: "How can this presence before God be the cause of his absence, and the enjoyment of the vision of God be the ultimate object of his efforts; seeing that it is well known that men do enjoy and find presence before God without strenuous effort, and are not absent?" He replied: "What you say is common knowledge and in the nature of human experience as it is usually described. But those endowed with special spiritual qualities, those who are the elect, those who have been singled out for their extraordinary spiritual capacity, they are those whose presence before God is absence, and whose enjoyment of the vision of God is the result of their strenuous spiritual efforts. This takes place because of the removal from them as they are, both of their physical and of their spiritual perceptions. This is since God has taken complete possession of them. He has obliterated their personality and annihilated their individual qualities. As a result it is God who functions in them in all their concerns, it is God who establishes the motives for their actions. This is but an aspect of his perfection and completeness.

"In this state they find God's grace though they are absent and enjoy an existence which differs from familiar existence when the ultimate truth of God is refulgent and His victory complete. When the spirit is without that indescribable bliss which is not felt by the soul, nor comparable with any other sensation, the spirit becomes used to this complete *Fanā'*, and finds that its *Fanā'* prevents it achieving *Baqā'*. But when God brings the spirit back to its normal state, he re-establishes it and gives it back to its own nature. Thus the experience with God and from God is hidden, the soul grieves, and becomes used to its normal state, because it has lost its first perfection and highest favour. It has been brought back to the shackles of reason and perception. Its regret is profound and its anguish for what it has lost continues in its conscious existence and present reality. This, then, is the reason for the soul's longing, its needs have returned to it: how can it not suffer by being banished from God? The soul was satisfied and now thirsts anew.

" Thus it is that the souls of those who have known God seek after the green pastures, the beautiful vistas, the fresh green gardens—but all other things which they long for echoing their experience before God are a source of pain for them because they serve only to remind them that they are unattainable and recall the lost Beloved. Sad indeed is their lot!

" The reference (in the Ḥadith) to God's gift of the faculties to His worshipper is explicit and not to be taken in a figurative sense. The exact nature of these faculties is known only to God. Those whom He endows with these faculties, those who are cognizant of them and have been chosen to enjoy them . . . for those so elect it is not seemly that human concepts should occur to them or human motives activate them. These faculties constitute a quality which persists after true *Fanā'*, when his human nature vanishes because he is the presence of God, overcome by God's victory, conquered by Him and completely possessed of Him, and that his individual characteristics are eliminated before the divine presence. Even so, in this divine state, he cannot find a way to reach the ultimate reality which now possesses him. It is only in this state that God can be seen in His exalted nature, His beatific names be appreciated. It is only after this stage has been achieved that it is possible for the worshipper to experience the " testing time "; he struggles and prevails and is faithful to God and then he is conquered by that which obliterates him, that same strength, that elevated spiritual stage, that noble relationship with God."

I said: " What you have told me is indeed remarkable. How is it then that those who enjoy this elevated relationship can also experience *Balā*? Please expound this for me." He said: " Know that at this stage when they seek God it is in accordance with

His will, and when they do not seek God, it is also in accordance with His will. At this stage, then, when God has complete possession of them, *Balā'* overtakes them because of their human qualities which still persist, because of their enjoyment of physical pleasures. This, then, is the veil between them and God which God has placed between them so that they can still retain a measure of their individuality and use both their physical and spiritual faculties in this environment of glory, in this consequence of praise (*dhikr*), in victory of God's conquest. How can this be known to you if none but the elect know it, and only they can discover it, and only they are capable of this knowledge? Can you understand how it is that they should seek God and yet not reach Him though they are helped by God's revelation to them, and are aided by the help of God's truths? It is because God has made them cognizant of an aspect of His existence and given them complete conviction of His hidden secrets which are the path to Him when the human qualities are obliterated and human needs are nullified. As a result, contact with God develops and the spiritual stages become elevated as the human perception is lost and the individuality passes away. He now presents them with effacement after they have lost their earthly individuality and reveals to them reality after they have found reality with God.

" This existence before God and vision of Him still emanates in some degree from themselves and is of the nature of a light veil or a thin curtain. When they come before it, they are overcome by grief for what they have lost and become aware of the intense effort they have made. This is because they have been overcome by that which is without cause and that which is not subject to external influence. Now at this stage the intimacy which they seek with God is in accordance with His will, and that from which they withhold themselves in their relationship with Him, is dictated by what He withholds. Their new knowledge of Him is that which God has inspired in them and not that which they know of Him as individuals. Then is their abode in strength and they attain true intimacy with God; they in themselves become fully preoccupied and there grow up in them, from God, the qualities of existence and non-existence. At this stage the anguish of the spiritual trial waxes."

I asked: " Then describe to me how *Balā'* envelopes them when they have fully achieved this wonderful state, when they are constantly near to God." He replied: " They have sufficient with what has already appeared to them and no longer have desires of the spirit. They have given over striving and donned the garb of God's victory which has come from His positive power and His awe-inspiring glory. At this stage they can view the world with their own perception and do not have recourse to the perception which comes from God since they are wholly separate and divided from Him, and use their own eyes—God being firmly established in His power and glory. When the manifestations of God appear to them, God drives them through their own qualities in His path of victory and glory. It is a stage which they leave without any claim to God, preferring their unique spiritual happiness, confident in their new-found intimacy, sure of access to God, they are free of formal obligations and will not be called to give account of their actions. It is at this stage of confident intimacy that God's test[1] is visited upon them suddenly and without warning."

I said: " You talk far above my head and have left me in a whirl. Please be simpler and speak so that I can understand." He said as follows: " When those who experience *Balā'* achieve that contact with God which He vouchsafes to them and when His behest comes to them, their inner spirit is metamorphosed and their spirit has lost its way, as it were, in eternity. The familiar places were not there for a refuge and the former homes of the body can no longer surround the new abode of the spirit. They are consumed with longing for Him who has brought them *Balā'*, and moan constantly in the *second* loss of their individuality. This loss has been a grievous wound to them, their new state has depressed them. They are very sorrowful, suffering deeply as they seek after God. They are overcome by a thirst which is all-consuming and constantly increasing. The pursuit of knowledge of God is now the constant preoccupation of the soul, it is entirely devoted to submerging its individuality in the attainment of intimacy with God. This thirst from God for God is an anguish even more

---

[1] The word *makara* means to scheme and sometimes to deceive. Thus we translate it. See Qur'ān 3, 54.

intense than the mourning for a near relative. God makes of every external form a sign. He gives to the soul the taste of poverty and renews for the soul knowledge of the experience of spiritual effort.

" The soul accepts the spiritual burden with its implication of suffering, seeks for its cure and is preoccupied with that divine revelation vouchsafed to it. As a result, it is able to view the remote with the eye of propinquity, to be closer to God because a veil has been removed and it is no longer completely concealed. Though the soul has *Balā'* it is not rejected. How can it be hidden from God by a veil when it is, as it were, a captive before Him, imprisoned in front of Him. God has allowed the suppression of the individuality when the man has *Balā'*. The soul no longer arrogates a degree of importance to its individuality but is amply satisfied with God's love and propinquity. Such, then, is the infinite duration of this newly found spiritual life and the intensity of the stage of *Balā* that the suppression of the individuality is completely swamped by the lightning flash of God's regard.

" As a result, the soul derives spiritual pleasure from *Balā* and is delighted with its *Balā'* with God, because it can enjoy propinquity with God and the sting of *Balā'* is assuaged. The soul is not bent down under the burden of *Balā'*, nor does it chafe at its spiritual load. Their experience makes heroes of them, because of the secrets revealed to them they stay conquered by God awaiting His commands ' That Allah designate what shall be done.'[1] Those who have experienced *Balā'* fall into two classes, on the one hand those who are at home with their *Balā'* and live constantly with God's desire . . . at the same time his interest in worldly affairs continues. None the less, he prefers to continue to have physical enjoyment as well as spiritual pleasure. God therefore makes a test for him in the continued choice between the two pleasures. It is a glorious trial. (As for the second class of those that experience *Balā'* and are not spiritually elevated, it is said that the reason for their departure from the state of grace is their lack of spiritual competence and the weakness of their spirit.)"[2]

---

[1] Qur'ān.

[2] This last passage has been added for the purpose of completing the course of thought.

KITĀB AL-MITHĀQ

IN THE NAME OF GOD THE COMPASSIONATE, THE MERCIFUL

What follows are Junayd's remarks on the Qur'ānic verse (Sura VII, verse 172): "When thy Lord took the descendants of Adam." In the opinion of the scribe, it is suitable to call these remarks Kitāb al-Mīthāq, i.e. The Book of Covenant. The reason for this choice of title is that Sahl also has a work on the same subject and that it carries the title proposed here, viz. al-Mīthāq.

Praise be to God who has made His graciousness to His worshippers, which is the revelation of His grace, a clear guide to knowledge of Him. This spiritual grace is in the measure of man's capacity to understand and to perceive. It is the capacity which enables him to communicate with God before his corporal existence. I praise Him throughout all eternity and I offer Him my gratitude everlastingly.

I testify that there is no God but God, the Unique, the One who is alone, the Eternal, the Holy. And I testify that Muhammad, may God's grace and peace be upon him, is the one who has been made perfect by prophethood, and the one who has completed (God's) mission. . . .

Now God has the elect among His worshippers and the chosen of those whom He has created. These are those whom He has chosen to be His saints and to be the recipients of His graciousness. He has thereby separated them from the mass of mankind unto Himself. But he has made their bodies to be of this world, their spirits of the nature of light, their apperception of the nature of spirit. He made their intellects bounded by the throne of God, but their understanding bounded by the veil. He has made the above of their spirits to be of the nature of the unseen in the very dwelling place of the unseen, and he has granted them freedom of access to the hidden corners of His Kingdom. He is their only refuge and with Him alone do they abide. In (their) timeless existence before Him and in (their) state of unity with Him, it is He who had granted them their being. When He called them and they answered quickly, their answer was a gracious and generous gift from Him, it was His answer on their behalf when he granted them their being, their function being that of interlocutors. He gave them knowledge of Him when they were only concepts which He had conceived. He then wished it, and made them like seeds which He transformed at His will into human seeds and put them in the reins of Adam. As we read: "And when He brought forth their descendants from the reins of the Sons of Adam and took them to witness against themselves, 'Am I not,' said He, 'your Lord?'" In this verse Allah has stated that He spoke to them when they had no formal existence. This is possible because Allah perceives them in their spiritual existence. This spiritual existence connotes their knowledge of God spiritually without in any way postulating their being aware of their own individuality. It follows, then, that at this stage God has existence of a sort which is known only to Him and recognized only by Him.

Now God, in recognizing their existence, comprehending them and seeing them, created them for the first time in a state of spiritual abstraction. Those who existed in the timeless existence are those who exist in the world which we know who are capable of abstraction from it and can abide with God. When they are completely imbued with the divine qualities, freed from the shackles of time, and have something of the nature of eternity, all these qualities dominate them when God desires their abstraction from this world so that they can abide with Him in the next, and He can instruct them to know His unseen, and so that he can show them the hidden corners of His knowledge and can grant them union with Him.

After their union with Him, He separates them from Himself (and grants them their individuality again), then He makes them absent (from this world when they are in union with Him), and makes them present (in this world) when He has separated them from Himself (and granted them their individuality again). Thus it is that their absence from this world is but a facet of their presence with God and their presence in this world is a necessary cause of their absence from God. (As sentient individuals) they are dazzled by the sight of the emanations from Him, but with the passing of the faculty of rational perception, their individuality passes too, and so He removes them from this world. He grants perfection to their *Fanā'* by granting them the state of *Baqā'* and perfects this *Baqā'* after *Fanā'* by *Fanā'*.

The circumstances of this world surround them in so far as God has willed it, since He wills it in His unique and elevated capacity. Whereas their first existence is completely real, is better, higher and more conducive to God's conquest and victory, and to their complete absorption in Him by means of that which He has granted them. In this state God wipes out all indications of their existence in this world and removes the signs of their corporal existence and their human existence vanishes. Moreover, they have no physical attributes, no perceptible existence, nor can the indications of their existence in this world be comprehended fully. All these indications conceal the timelessness of spiritual existence. The bliss of this spiritual existence is not comparable with human bliss. Though the same word is used, the meaning is different. In both cases the general nature of the bliss is the same, but the *signs and indications* are different. Whereas the external signs are pleasurable the taste is, in fact, marred by bitterness. Their thoughts are constantly directed towards their Beloved and their inward thoughts never cease from praising the Lord. At this moment the turbulent seas of the zealous God rage against them and severe indeed is their trial when they are on the verge of it, and their souls weaken while they wait patiently for it. Then that which was familiar to them becomes strange and that which they knew not becomes crystal clear. They are distinguished by their knowledge of truth before God when God creates in them the faculty of true knowledge of Himself. This faculty emanates from God and must be attributed to Him and *not* to the person in whom it is endowed. The possession of this faculty marks the fullness of endeavours before God.

At this stage God does not give precise definition to their trials, else they might rest back, nor does He indicate the exact nature of their endeavour lest they rest on their laurels. He makes His elect preoccupied independently of one another and separates them from one another. Thus, at the same time, they are both present and not in existence. The fullness of their endeavour is in their enjoyment of the vision of God, because, after He has obliterated in them every trace of corporal and spiritual existence, they can find Him themselves, and have vision of Him in their new state. In this state he has full possession of them and has destroyed their individuality (and has removed their characteristics) as we perceive it. In a word, perception of the truth comes from the Truth *par Excellence*, that is God, if and when God so wills it, and in the measure of His recognition of their worthiness and in His enabling them to achieve. God, as it were, replaces the faculty of perception which they had prior to His taking full possession of them.

He creates in them both the associated qualities and the faculty of perception which are in accord with His own type of perfection and completeness. As a result, the joy which they experience is not of the same order as normal human joy and has in it something of a trial. This is because Existence after complete personal suppression is not the same as normal human existence, the ultimate Truth of God is now refulgent and His victory is complete.

When the spirit is without that indescribable bliss which is not felt by the soul nor comparable with any other sensation, the spirit becomes used to this complete *Fanā'*, and the individuals are, as it were, cast into the desolation of destruction of the spirit's trials. Then they become familiar with this state after *Fanā'* and no longer are satisfied with their normal taste and cannot accept their previous type of existence. God absorbs them unto Himself without heeding their attributes or any characteristic whatsoever which may be attributed to them. He does not heed either those inclinations with which He has endowed them which create the describable qualities in them. Now these special qualities which enable man to come nigh unto God are lost in all his other qualities when man cannot find the path to achieve the approach to the highest existence in Truth (*Ḥaqq*) which God has enabled him to have. Thus, then, are His high attributes, the strength of His manifestation and the glory of His dominion.

Now it comes to pass that those who, having approached God and having stayed with God and having been certain of their contact with God, and not having deceived themselves about their own experience are put to God's test by the subsequent complete obliteration of their experience.

At this stage God endows them with strength, high degree, honoured intimacy and the glory of close relationship with Him. God's test is that He now presents them with effacement after they have already lost their earthly individuality, with reality after they have found Reality in God.

The severity of this test lies in the fact that, when brought face to face with ultimate effacement and true reality, then and only then, can they realize the degree of their inability to comprehend and the excessive brilliance of the vision which is beyond the confines of knowledge and which defies description.

Now at this stage the intimacy with they seek with God is in accordance with His will and that from which they withhold themselves in their relationship with Him is dictated by what He withholds.[1]

And their new knowledge of Him is that which God inspired in them and not that which they know of Him as individuals. Then is their abode in strength and they attain true intimacy with God; they are elected to the presence of God who had Himself witnessed their transmutation. What they have perceived is through God who unites each one's perception of Him and retains His separate entity. God is above human description and exalted far beyond a similarity with His creations.

ON DIVINITY

Said Abu'l Qāsim al Junayd—may God have mercy on him! God was in isolation with the elect and divinity was maintained in absoluteness for them alone. The first appearance of God's visitation was when He delivered to them the evidences of His causing them to appear and made them to dwell with divinity from its inception. God created timelessness, eternally continuous, lasting always, that which has neither end nor termination. Then God added to this the testimony of the power of His glory, the extent of His splendour, the display of His conquest, the height of His elevation, the dominion of His sovereignty, the intensity of His awe, the nobility of His majesty, the splendour of His rule. He is unique by these qualities and

---

[1] Literally: And they seek from Him concerning that which He sought from them and try to withhold from Him that which He formerly withheld from them.

thus allows himself to be distinguished. He is magnified and exalted by His greatness.

Thus, then, God in truth and by the measure of truth, is the ultimate truth, and God in truth and by the measure of all decisions, is the final arbiter. His unity in the uniqueness of His power is one, unique and eternal.

This, then, is the prime evidence that God has so inspired the elect that they can appreciate fully the significance of Uluhiya, that He has brought them near unto Him. In this state, God enables them further to know those of His fine attributes which He had withheld from them, which He had concealed within His protection. These attributes, some of which have been referred to and others of which have not been mentioned, describe union with God and separation from Him, according to God's will that they be revealed or withheld. Some of these true names of God are self explanatory, their meaning is implicit in their use, they are exalted in their ways, elevated in their dwelling places, and travel freely. These attributes are extinguished when God permits them to be absorbed into that which Truth had protected and concealed, had hidden and kept away, had covered up and screened from sight; Qualities which Truth has overcome and made its own, has conquered and made subject.

Then the manifestations of reality vanish in their division without being cut. When it is united (in God) it is extraordinarily elevated, magnified in its appearance and ennobled by the inviolability of its laws; awe inspiring with divine awe, glorious in God's glory, and victorious in God's victory. And if you ask how does the conception of "where?" apply to this, the answer is that, in so far as the word "where?" can apply to Him, the answer is not confined to the limits of our conception of space. This is because "where?" as applied to God is in proportion to His timeless continuance. Thus, then, the "where?" as applied to or for God is not the "where?" which we know, since it is only applicable to divinity. It is an aspect displayed by God when all the manifestations of reality are united.

God, then, it is that causes His elect to perceive the awaited evidence of His truth, these to whom this description applies. It is in His separate existence and peculiar knowledge.

The foregoing is but an indication of what cannot be further explained. Moreover, this of its very nature cannot be understood from indications, but only when you yourself are in the state which is described. I have wrapped up what is in it and have not elaborated it. Accept it, then, from the only source of it. If God wills He will guide you to its comprehension.

One of the features which God as creative Truth has implanted in the conception of the separate (human entity)[1] is that He causes to be intimately associated with the individual the manifestation of that wherewith He clothes His elect. He has clothed them with the manifestation of that wherewith He has them in His thrall. Thus the elect to whom God makes this revelation, are themselves the testimonies to the mysteries which He has concealed. Whenever He causes the elect to see something of the divine revelation He buries, as it were, the man who has achieved this spiritual state in the state of concealed mystery. The elect, when they see what God causes them to see, are in a state of continued exaltation inspired by God's revelation. At this stage, God's revelation is that of a secret cautiously and tremulously shown, in the unveiling of the hidden, before God enables the elect to see past the curtain which conceals this unusual divine aspect. Then God shows the evidence of His generosity, His predestined affection. He demonstrates this to them in the fact of His receiving them, in showing the glory of their dwelling place, in proclaiming the state of the achievement of fulfilment and the attainment of everything which was beloved, sought after and longed for. This, then, is the perfect gift of sincere companionship, the essence of the gift of God's proximity.

Then, when they are confirmed and confident in the stage where God has placed them, God grants them another grace in that He shows them how to lose the temporal shackles of their individuality, how to apprehend what He offers them, how to renounce the gifts generously given, and the affection

---

[1] Ismu'l Tafriqa literally " the name of separation " has been rendered as above, taking ISM as a technical term in logic when it is used to particularize a general ideas as in ISMU'L-JINSI, genus then generic.

bestowed on them as individuals. He grants to His elect the contrary of the former (Vision of God) since He desires to bring them to this new state of grace thereby and demands it of them.

If you were to see the elect at the instant of their vision of God and the state in which God has placed them, you would see nothing but the hostages of captive bodies, the physical relics of souls which are about in heaven. God has exhausted them by obliteration in the Kingdom of His glory and completely tired them out by His excessive trial in His absence from them . . . an absence which causes them to cry out in anguish, an overwhelming grief which makes them cry aloud. God stops their very breathing, imprisons their breath within them so that their life's breath circulates only in God, and they are, as it were, made one with Him. This is but part of the science of *Tawḥīd* which God indicates to His chosen.

KITĀB FI'L-FARQ BAIN AL-IKHLĀṢ WAṢ-ṢIDQ

In the Name of God, Most Gracious, Most Merciful, Praise be to God, and peace be on His servants whom He hath chosen.

Abu'l Qāsim al-Junayd—may God sanctify his soul and give light to his grave—says as follows:

May God grant thee the happiness of His nearness;

And may He at all times give thee new increase of His goodness;

And may He protect thee in the shade of His merciful wing;

And may He make your refuge near to Him, even where He has made to abide the souls of His privileged ones—those to whom He has given His protection, whom naught can overtake and naught can hinder and whose devotion to God naught can disturb;

The prayers and peace of God be upon His Apostle, his family and his companions.

You have asked me what is the difference between *Ikhlāṣ* (unquestioning submission to God, hence righteousness) and *Ṣidq* (a correct relationship with God, hence righteousness).

Ṣidq is to keep strict watch and ward on one's soul, after having performed one's religious duties and acted according to religious precepts. Further, it implies the public performance of all legal duties, and that this performance in the beginning be based in good will and devotion to God—may He be exalted and magnified.

Ṣidq is therefore an attribute of the Will and is present at the inception of the Will, at the performance of religious injunctions acting as the impulse to the Will inasmuch as God makes the way unto Himself. It is on this path that *Ṣidq* prevents you from acquiescing in the desire of your lower soul to relax in your religious duty. It impels you to accept religious precepts plainly without having recourse to complex interpretation.

Ṣidq therefore existed before the existence of *Ikhlāṣ*. In the Koran we have the phrase: " He will ask the Ṣādiqīn " (possessors of *Ṣidq*), that is once they have acquired *Ṣidq*, " what it meant to them." God has spoken of the Ṣādiqīn using the word in a different sense, when He says " This is the day on which *Ṣidq* will help the Ṣādiqīn."

Ṣidq, in the first passage, implies that God recognizes in the Ṣādiqīn a distinction between their *Ṣidq* and their *Ikhlāṣ*, because *Ikhlāṣ* exists as an attribute of man in two separate states—in the state of Conviction and Intention and, secondly, in the state of Action.

Ikhlāṣ, as an attribute of the Sadiq, is present in his Conviction; it has nothing to do with the nature of *Ṣidq*, since *Ikhlāṣ* is almost intuitive. A man who understands the meaning and purpose of all his actions and does not do those actions which do not conform with *Ikhlāṣ*—such a man is called *Mukhlis*.

Ikhlāṣ is primarily the recognition of the Unity of God with the Will, and, secondly, the recognition and avoidance of those actions which are evil.

(The term *Ṣidq* is used both of man and of God, but in different senses.) When it is used of man, the reference is to the order of his piety (*Ṣidq*) and not to his *Ikhlāṣ*. When it is used of God it connotes *Ikhlāṣ*. Thus one can say " so and so has *Ṣidq* " with reference to his knowledge of religious precepts and his assiduity to in their performance. But one cannot say " so and so has *Ikhlāṣ*." *Ikhlāṣ* is a purely personal and intimate quality which cannot be directly perceived by one's fellow men.

Ṣidq is, then, a patent attribute of its possessor, whereas *Ikhlāṣ* is not visible.

The Ṣādiq is so called because of the attributes he so patently possesses. We may call a man a Ṣādiq having observed his outward actions. He must also have some degree of *Ikhlas* inwardly. However, in order to show the qualities of Ṣādiq, the Ṣādiq has to understand the meaning of things, so that he can accept and do those actions which conform with his religious persuasions and reject those actions which do not conform.

Ikhlāṣ is superior to *Ṣidq*, in that implicit in *Ikhlāṣ* is the knowledge of the significance and ultimate purpose of all things, and, moreover, he who possesses *Ikhlāṣ* has the power to resist the evil suggestions of Satan because his heart is pure.

Nothing excels *Ikhlāṣ*, because for the worshipper there is no goal in devotion beyond *Ikhlāṣ*.

We do not say that there are degrees of *Ikhlāṣ*, because *Ikhlāṣ* is in itself an ultimate goal, whereas that there are degrees of *Ṣidq* is implicit in the verse in the Qur'ān when God is referred to as asking the Ṣādiqīn about their *Ṣidq*. He does not ask the Mūkhliṣīn about their *Ikhlāṣ*, since that is the essential quality which God demands of the true worshipper.

So *Ikhlāṣ* excels *Ṣidq*, and *Ṣidq* is inferior to *Ikhlāṣ*.

Now *Ṣidq* is used in three senses: the Ṣādiq in his words, the Ṣādiq in his action, the Ṣādiq in his intention. The Ṣādiq in words is one who tells the truth, whether it be in his favour or against him, who avoids specious interpretation and deceit. The Ṣādiq in action is one who never spares himself and does not consider his own personal comfort. The Ṣādiq in intention is one whose actions are dictated by the fact that his heart is turned towards God. A man, then, who possesses all these qualities is a true Ṣādiq.

However, it must be realized that *Ṣidq* is ever present with the Ṣādiq and never in any circumstances absent. (See my analysis on this point at the beginning of this book.) Thus, we have *Ṣidq* in pious action, in self-denial, in asceticism, in trust in God, in spiritual happiness, in love of God, in desire for God, in declaring the Unity of God in the Moslem sense, in the qualities of the (murīd) ṣūfī novice and the ṣūfī initiate both at the beginning of his meditations and after them. All theses stages of spiritual experience inevitably bear testimony to *Ṣidq*.

Now the meaning of *Ikhlāṣ* is complete and exclusive concentration on God. This focusing of intention towards God demands that the *Mukhliṣ* shall be aware of the implication of things and recognize that they change constantly. He will thus accept what conforms with the full focusing of his intention towards God and reject those indulgences prompted by either his worse self[1] or the Devil, which do not conform. In this state his personal vision departs and he realizes it is a gift of God which has replaced it. The *Mukhliṣ* will remain in a state of equanimity when his fellow men deride him because he recognizes God's gift of *Ikhlāṣ* to him, and he will be displeased when his fellow men praise him, since he fears that me may lose God's gift of *Ikhlāṣ*, and he no longer considers his fellow men when the spiritual state comes upon him. This is a sign which is visible to the vision of the *Mukhlis*, but does not exist in the vision of other beings.

Now the qualities of *Ṣidq* and *Ikhlāṣ* are both present in one who is a *Mukhliṣ*, whereas the man who is described as a *Ṣadiq* and therefore has the quality of *Ṣidq*, is only at the threshold of *Ikhlāṣ*. The ultimate quality to which we refer when we speak of 'Ubūdīya (true worship of God) in those seeking the path to God is *Ikhlāṣ*.

As for the genuine *Ṣādiq*, God may well grant him *Ikhlāṣ*, which is the next stage; in the same way the genuine *Mukhliṣ* may in his next stage be granted the ability (Kifāya)—which was lacking prior to this—to concentrate his spiritual perception on God (Baṣīra). The man who has attained this spiritual perception completely may well be granted in the next stage protection from his own evil instincts (Hiyata).

At this last stage God has full possession of His worshipper, He has overcome his faculty of reason and has annihilated his struggling individuality.

When God has full possession of the worshipper, He has endowed him with a new spiritual nature which replaces the

[1] In Qur'an.

individuality with which he formerly worshipped God. It is with this new and special faculty that it is now possible for him to worship God as One.

It is at this stage that the worshipper first realizes to the full the significance of the special *Tawḥīd* and that his acceptance of the reality of the physical world is replaced by his perception of reality itself. In the same way, the significance of the events in his life is that they are now in accordance with the will of his possessor, the external characteristics of these events being entirely without significance.

When the worshipper reaches this stage, he can no longer be described in rational terms; in fact, the promptings of reason to the worshipper who has realized to the full the special *Tawḥīd* are nothing but evil whispers which he must overcome.

It is Reason which formerly directed the worshipper in his worship when he worshipped God as an individual, but when he is completely possessed by God his individuality is suppressed. He is, at it were, transmuted. His external characteristics remain the same, but his individuality has vanished. Thus he is at once present and absent.

ANOTHER CHAPTER WHICH DEALS WITH *TAWḤĪD*

Know that the first condition of the worship of God—may He be exalted and magnified—is knowledge of God and that the basis of knowledge of God is the recognition of His being One (*Tawḥīd*), and that His unity demands the absolute negation of the possibility of describing God in answer to the questions "How?", "Where?" and "When?". It is through God that we can be guided aright to Him, and the means of this correct guidance is God's permission that we may succeed in finding Him (*Tawfīq*). When this permission is granted, the recognition of His unity follows. His *Tawḥīd* connotes belief in Him. From belief in Him follows confirmation which in turn leads to knowledge of Him. Knowledge of Him implies obedience to His commands, obedience carries with it the ascent towards Him which leads ultimately to reaching Him. When God is attained His manifestation can be expounded, from His manifestation there follows bewilderment which is so overwhelming that it removes the possibility of the exposition of God. As a result of losing this manifestation of God the elect worshipper is unable to describe God. And, when the worshipper is unable to describe God, he finds the true nature of his existing for God. From the true nature of such existence (for God's sake only) there comes the vision of God, together with the losing of his individual entity. Thus, with loss of his individual entity, his spiritual entity achieves absolute purity. In this state of absolute purity he has lost his personal attributes; by this loss he is wholly present (in God). By being wholly present in God, he is wholly lost to self. And thus he is present before God, absent in himself; absent and present at the same time. He is where he is not, and he is not where he is. Then, after he has not been, he is where he has been (before creation). He is himself, after he has not been truly himself. He is existent in himself and existent in God after having been existent in God and non-existent in himself. This is because he has left the drunkenness of God's overwhelming and come to the clarity of sobriety, and contemplation is once more restored to him, so that he can put everything in its right place and assess it correctly. Once more he assumes his individual attributes, after *Fanā'* his personal qualities persist in him and his actions in this world, when he has reached the zenith of spiritual achievement vouchsafed by God, he becomes a pattern for his fellow men.

ANOTHER QUESTION

If we consider a man whose knowledge is authoritative and genuine this religious knowledge demands punctilious performance and the man is completely devoted to it. He will find that the exigencies of that knowledge will not coincide with his instinctive spiritual desires. This gap, though he is aware, conscious and active, will lead him to have recourse to the science of the search after the return of God (Ḥaqq) while he is still aware, conscious and active. He then returns to God, humble, modest, poor and with little, and asks Him to carry his burden of genuine knowledge. At this stage he becomes able to carry out the exigencies of the second type of knowledge by the dominance of his instinctive spiritual desires over his actions and is no longer positively aware of his genuine knowledge of the first type, which bound him to the conditions laid down in its edicts. When the two types of knowledge (namely, the theoretical knowledge and the intuitive) are merged by the discovery of the reality of intuitive knowledge and the discarding of the reality of the first type, the elect has achieved true knowledge of the spiritual trial (*Balā'*). He tastes the bitter cup of God's censorship which makes it abundantly clear to him that he still has other characteristics and that, within himself, his nature still has hidden qualities; all this while he is going towards absolute and genuine *Tawḥīd*. *Balā'* diminishes in its rigour, in proportion as the intuition dominates and coincides with his natural desires (which are now elevated), as we have already described. At this stage, he comes to the obliteration of his individual instinctive desire for pleasure and also to the vanishing of his critical distinction with regard to the purification of his instincts through the disappearance of his desire for pleasure. Then he is able fully to comprehend the true indications towards God from the nature of events, the changes in things, without heed for mediums of understanding, since now his faculty of distinction coincides with a purified intuition.

ANOTHER QUESTION

Fear distresses me, Hope comforts me, Reality unites me with God, and Ritual[1] separates me from God.

When God distresses me with fear, he obliterates my existence and takes care of me.[2] When he comforts me with hope, he returns my existence to me after my absence and commands me to take care of myself. When He unites me with Him through the real (vision of God) He causes me to be present before Him and invites me. When God separates me from Him by ritual, He shows me that which is not my true self and covers me up (so that I cannot see Him). In all these states it is God who moves me without keeping me still, who makes me unfamiliar with my own spirit and ill at ease in these states.

When I am before God I taste the savour of my existence—

---

[1] The word *Ḥaqq*, according to Ibn Ajiba ( ) refers to those religious duties (*Ḥuqūq*) incumbent on the worshipper which can be performed only when the worshipper is in a state of tafriqa, separation from God, and not in a state of *jam'*, union with God. See *Tkaẓ-al-Himam*, v. 1, pp. 126 et seq.

[2] So that I need not take care of myself.

would that God would obliterate my existence and cause me to enjoy His vision, or that He would make me absent from myself and give me respite from that which is due to Him as formal ritual. Would that God would show me complete *Fanā'* in which is my eternal life.

My *Fanā'* is my *Baqā'*. In my genuine *Fanā'* God obliterates in me both my *Fanā'* and my *Baqā'*, so that when I am totally obliterated, I am without either *Baqā'* or *Fanā'* in my state of *Fanā'* and *Baqā'*. This is because the state of *Baqā'* and *Fanā'* apply to the existence of some being other than me, when I am obliterated.

ANOTHER QUESTION

Know that men are recognized by experience of their righteousness, their unsparing efforts to uphold the precepts laid down by God, persisting in their devotions from stage to stage until they reach the true and highest stage of worship of God. This is externally visible since they no longer have a choice in action, but are content to do God's will.

These, then, are the facts accepted by the community as indicating those combined characteristics which appear externally when the elect have reached that stage. This true and highest stage leads him to the vision of God, comprehension of God's guidance to Him, in modifying events for him to choose what God has chosen for him. These facts indicate that his fellow men have left him because his character has been modified for them and he is no longer aware of them. This is the stage of companionship. In the Qu'rān we have the verse in which God says to Moses: " I have taken you unto myself as a companion." In this stage of companionship, the range of his movements is limited, he can only go from God to God, for God and in God. He has *Fanā'* and this too is obliterated because he persists in *Baqā'* only through complete obliteration.

God desires to return his worshipper to the community and does so, making clear the evidence of His grace to him, so that the lights of His gifts in the return of his individual characteristics scintillate and attract the community to him who appreciate him.

ANOTHER QUESTION

Know that you are your own veil which conceals yourself from you. Know also that you cannot reach God through yourself, but that you reach Him through Him. The reason is that when God vouchsafes the vision of reaching Him, he calls upon you to seek after Him and you do so. When you have the vision of seeking after God, you will apprehend its nature and the effort required to achieve what you desire. At this stage you are veiled until your great need for God returns in the search for Him and He becomes your pillar and support in your intense search after Him and enables you to perform those duties which He has chosen for you in the knowledge of the search after God, to maintain those conditions which He has laid down, and to observe those things which you have been asked to observe.

Thus it is that for your sake God protects you from yourself and causes you to pass by obliteration to eternal life, so that you achieve your desire and live eternally with Him. This is because the unification of him who recognizes fully the unity of God lasts for ever, though the man himself is obliterated. At this stage you are your true self because you have lost the shackles of your human individuality and you achieve eternal life with God because you are obliterated.

There are three stages in *Fanā'* (obliteration).

First: The obliteration of attributes, characteristics and natural qualities in your motives, when you carry out your religious duties, making great efforts and doing the opposite of what you may desire and compelling yourself to do the things which you do not wish to do.

Second: The obliteration of your following after the enjoyment of the sensation of pleasure in obedience to God's behests so that you are exclusively His, without any intermediary means of contact.

Third: The obliteration of the consciousness of having achieved the vision of God at the final stage of ecstasy when God's victory over you is complete. At this stage you are obliterated and have eternal life with God and you exist only in the existence of God because you have been obliterated.

Your physical being continues but your individuality has departed.

ANOTHER QUESTION

Know that there are three types of people, the man who seeks and searches, the man who reaches the door and stays there, the man who enters and remains.

As for him who seeks God, he goes towards Him guided by knowledge of the religious precepts and duties, concentrating on the performance of all external observances towards God.

As for the man who reaches the door and stays there, he finds his way there by means of his internal purity from which he derives his strength. He acts towards God with internal concentration.

As for the man who enters before God with his whole heart and remains before Him, excluding the vision of anything other than God, noting every indication from God to him, ready for whatever his Lord may command. This readiness is characteristic of the man who recognizes the Unity (*Tawḥīd*) of God.

ANOTHER QUESTION

Know that *Tawḥīd* is found in four stages in people. The first is the *Tawḥīd* of the ordinary people, next is the *Tawḥīd* of those who are well versed in formal religious knowledge. The other two stages are experienced by the elect who have esoteric knowledge (*maʿrifa*).

As for the *Tawḥīd* of ordinary people, it consists in the assertion of the Unity of God, in the disappearance of any conception of gods, opposites, equals, likenesses to God, but with the retention of hopes and fears in forces other than God. This type of *Tawḥīd* has a measure of efficacy since the assertion persists.

As for the *Tawḥīd* of those who are well versed in formal religious knowledge, it consists in the assertion of the Unity of God, in the disappearance of any conception of gods, companions, opposites, equals, likenesses to God, combined with the performance of the positive commands and the avoidance of that which is forbidden so far as external action is concerned, all this being a result of their hopes, fears and desires; this type of *Tawḥīd* has a measure of efficacy since the assertion of the Unity of God is publicly proved.

As for the first type of esoteric *Tawḥīd*, it consists in the assertion of the Unity of God, the disappearance of the conception of the things referred to, combined with the performance of God's command externally and internally and the removal of hopes and fears in forces other than God, all resulting from the ideas which tally with awareness of God's presence with him, with God's call to him and his answer to God.

The second type of esoteric *Tawḥīd* consists in existence without individuality (*Shabaḥ*) before God with no third person as intermediary between them, a figure over which His decrees pass according as He in His omnipotence determines, and that one should be sunk in the flooding seas of His unity, completely obliterated both from himself and from God's call to him and his answer to God.[1] It is a stage where the devotee has achieved the true realization of the Oneness of God in true proximity to Him. He is lost to sense and action because God fulfils in Him what He hath willed of him. This implies that in his final state the worshipper returns to his first state, that he is as he was before he existed. The proof of this is the verse in the Qur'ān:

> " And when your Lord drew forth their descendants from the reins of the children of Adam and took them to witness concerning themselves, ' Am I not,' said He, ' your Lord? ' They answered ' but certainly you are.' "[2]

---

[1] This version follows the manuscript text of الحق which is in accordance with the preceding مع قيام مشاهد الدعوة والاستجابة and gives a significant distinction between the two esoteric stages. Sarrāj, Hujwīrī and Qushayri have the reading الخلق which puts an unnecessary strain on interpretation, noted by Anṣārī, the Merx and Hartmann al-Kuschajri, 1914, p. 50, note. In this same passage the reading commentator, شبح " a frame without a will " as found in our MS. is superior in the context to the reading in Nicholson's Hujwīrī since the شخص is the individual. Zhukovski (text p. 363) gives pride of place to شبح

[2] Qur'ān. *See* above, p. 76.

Who existed (at this time) and how could he have existed before he had existence? Did anyone answer other than the pure, fine and holy spirits in accordance with God's omnipotence and perfect will? His existence now is like it was before he had existence. This, then, is the highest stage of the true realization of the Unity of God in which the worshipper who maintains this unity loses his individuality (*dahab huwa*).

The Last Question on TAWḤĪD from the Discourse of JUNAYD—*may God be pleased with him!*

Junayd was asked what was the final goal of the worship of those who have knowledge of God. He replied: "The conquest of themselves." He expounded that God has set out the tasks for those who perform their religious duties, so that they achieve a stage which is from God and have not recourse to themselves. God makes the prophets look at their elevation with longing. He prefers them to the saints, and the angels praise them when they have left behind their own achievements and achieve the state with God through God alone. The station of the rest of mankind before God is through their own achievements without that grace which God grants them. Thus it is that God requites every man, according to his status.

RULES OF CONDUCT FOR ONE WHO IS DEPENDENT UPON GOD

Shaykh Abu'l Qāsim was asked concerning Rules of Conduct for one who is dependent upon God and he said: "Thou shouldst be satisfied with God under all circumstances, and thou shouldst not ask anyone except God." He was asked concerning the thought of Goodness (*Khāṭir*)[1] whether it is one thing or more and he said: "The thought which calls to obedience to God has three aspects—(a) the thought which comes from the devil, the cause of which is the suggestion of the devil (Satan), and (b) the thought which comes from the lower soul, the cause of which is desire and the longing for comfort, and thirdly (c) the thought which comes from the divine, the cause of which is the assistance given by God."

---

[1] By Khāṭir (passing thought) the ṣūfis signify the occurrence in the mind of something which is quickly removed by another thought and which its owner is able to repel from his mind. (Hujwīrī, p. 387.)

These thoughts may be confused one with another in the call to obedience to God, and one should clearly distinguish between them in order to perform right actions, because the prophet said: " For whom the gate of goodness is being opened, let him seize it," and one must reject the other two (i.e. thoughts). (a) As for the devilish thought, God said: " Verily those who fear God, when a thought of evil from Satan assaults them, they bring God to remembrance, when, lo! they see (aright) " (Qu. 7. 200); (b) the thought of desire is the thought of the lower soul and, as the prophet said: " Hell is surrounded by desires."

Each one of these thoughts has a sign, by which it can be distinguished from another; as for the thought from the lower soul, the cause of which is desire and longing for ease, desire can be divided into the mental, such as the desire for advancement and reputation, the assuaging of anger by revenge, the humiliation of opponents and things of this kind, and physical, such as the desire for food, drink, and lust for women, clothes, pleasures and things of that kind. For the human soul there is a need for these delights, in accordance with its distance from one or another of them and the strength of the attraction which each class (or category) exercises on it.

For the thought which comes from the lower soul, there are two signs which act as true signs for distinguishing the thought with which it is concerned. One of them is the presence of this thought together with the need for one of these things that are desired, such as the presence of marriage (in the mind) together with a strong desire for women, deluding him in this point that his intention was only to carry out the command of the prophet when he said: " Marry and be fruitful, I will multiply you on the day of resurrection " and in order not to transgress against the saying of the prophet " There are no monks in Islām "; and similarly in eating when there is a strong need for it, and sometimes it deludes you by calling upon you to abandon fasting or to acquire one of the desired things so that (the lower soul) says that, in keeping the fast, the mind is weakened from carrying out that which is obligatory for obedience to God; and that, if you invite a Muslim friend and you refrain from the desired good (in his presence), you make the heart of a Muslim sad, or sadden the heart of your family if you bring food for your family (and you do not share in it). And sometimes the thought deceives you in another form by saying to you: " Destroy this desire by obtaining this hateful thing in order that this thought may not persist in you and your worship of God become confused." And similarly in other desires, there is delusion and deception. And likewise when you are weary in worship and you keep on in obedience to God against your will, then the lower soul will point out to you that the prophet prohibited celibacy and wearying oneself as he said " You are only obliged to do what you are able " and as he said " He who rides ceaselessly does not finish his journey nor does he keep his camel." Nay, sometimes when you have exercised great restraint your soul is very weary and is withheld from its desires, it calls you to destroy it completely or restrain it from performing its functions so that the lower soul causes you to do that which leads to execution or prison and things of this kind, because it is thought that in these two circumstances (i.e. destruction or restraint) there is ease and an end to weariness. One of the two signs in this matter is that sometimes tiredness and weariness come together with the longing for ease and sometimes the need for something which is desired comes together with the motive or impulse of the desire. Then one should consider these two conditions and if one of these two conditions comes (to the mind) you know that the thought is from the lower soul and its need moved it (the lower soul) to call for it. The conclusion (of this indication) is that the thought comes from desire or the seeking of ease and it is therefore apparent that the thought is from the lower soul. And the second sign is the persistence of this thought and its unceasing nature so that it becomes continuous and, whenever you make an effort to thrust it from you, it persists in you and insists so that there is no use seeking refuge or taking precautions or being warned or turning away from it, nay it persists continually and this is one of the clearest signs that (the thought) comes from the lower soul. Just like the child, when he is kept back from something, the persistence of his longing for it is increased. These two conditions are true signs. When they are together, there is no doubt that the thought comes from the lower soul.

And the cure for (the lower soul) in this case is either complete opposition to and remorseless tiring out of it (the lower soul) and prohibiting it from ease when the motive of the thought is over-tiredness and weariness in worship or the imposition upon the lower soul of a task so heavy that it will repress it from moving in accordance with this thought. And if the thought comes from desire, the cure for it is deprivation of the thing which the soul desires or restraining oneself from something else which it desires in order to restrain oneself from the object of one's desire.

As for the thought which comes from the devil, it also has two signs. One of them is the awakening of some of the needs of the lower soul at the call of desire, or the call of ease at times when the soul is accustomed to get that for which it longs. And the difference between it (the thought which comes from the devil) and the thought coming from the lower soul is that the latter persists and does not go while the former goes and comes again, so that whenever a man is diverted from his desire because of inadvertence, it persists in him when the devil reminds him of the desire and the motion of the soul by this reminder (from the devil) is greater than that of the thought which is from the lower soul because the latter is only a passing one at the time when the need is strongly felt.

And the second sign is that this thought which comes from the devil originates in and comes suddenly to a man's mind, but the thought which comes from the lower soul moves continuously by nature towards desire or ease and this is because the suggestion of the devil only follows the course of speech between man and man so that the only difference between this and that is that man does not see him (i.e. the devil) and the soul can only move your heart through the sense of hearing at the time of speech or the utterance of sound, through the sense of sight at the time of making signs, through the sense of feeling at the time of touching. The devil (Satan) causes this through suggestion and touching the heart and passing through it. He (the devil) does not know that which is hidden, but he only comes to the lower soul through the characteristics which are normally virtue in the human being. And this is the difference between the thought which comes from the lower soul and that which comes from the devil.

As for the divine thought, it is indicated also by two signs, one of which, the most important, is the agreement of the Law with the thought and its (the Law's) testimony to the correctness of the thought. And the second sign is that at the beginning the soul is wearily reluctant to accept it until one finds a kind of alurement for it and this thought comes suddenly upon the lower soul without any preliminary steps like the thought which comes from the devil, but except for the fact that the lower soul is quicker in accepting the thought which comes from the devil (for the soul is readier to accept the devil's thought and lazier to accept the divine thought) because the devil comes to the lower soul only through its desires and relaxations, while the divine thought comes through the obligations, and the lower soul is in the habit of running away from obligations when they appear. This is the difference between this thought and the thought which comes from the devil and the thought which comes from the lower soul. And if a thought occurs to you, weigh it with these three weights and seek testimony as to every part of it according to the signs which we have indicated to you, so that the thoughts may be distinguished by you. Do with regard to the thoughts from the devil and the lower soul that which we have mentioned and repel them entirely and be ready to accept the divine thought, and lay aside preoccupation and waste of time, for time is short and conditions may change, and beware of the temptation of the lower soul and the suggestion of the devil, for as one of the gates of goodness has been opened to him (the devil) you must close it entirely in front of him from the beginning. As an example, if a thought occurs to you concerning fasting for part of a month, which is laid down by the law as a voluntary duty, or keeping vigil for part of a night, and you may say to yourself: " Let me leave this for the present until I can complete a whole night or a full month," then this is a deceitful temptation from the devil to shut the door of divine assistance which is wide open. In fact, the gate of divine assistance has been opened, and you should seize the opportunity from the beginning.

The divine thoughts do not linger but quickly change to

other thoughts and readiness to grasp the divine thought is a demand of the Law and in it (the readiness) there are two advantages. One of them is that one time is better than another time such as the times which we are told are favourable for God's forgiveness, and the times when God's mercy and pardon descend and the grace of God towards creatures is unlimited. And the second advantage is the training of the soul to be ready to carry out the commands of the Law and to obey God when blessing on work is to be hoped for. Moreover, there is the removal of the condition of slackness from the soul and this is readiness to put oneself in the condition to receive God's gifts of mercy and in this is an advantage also in the discipline of the soul to be ready to carry out the Law's commands. And God knows and decides.

This is the end of the rules of poverty from the sayings of Shaikh Abu'l Qāsim al-Junayd—may God sanctify his soul and illuminate his grave—and Praise be to the Lord of the Worlds and the prayer of God be upon Muhammad and his family and his companions, all of them, and an abundance of peace upon them.

EU Authorised Representative:
Easy Access System Europe Mustamäe tee 50, 10621 Tallinn, Estonia
gpsr.requests@easproject.com

Printed and bound by CPI Group (UK) Ltd, Croydon, CR0 4YY
03/06/2025
01891003-0001

رسائل الجنيد

حررها وصححها

علي حسن عبد القادر

فهـرسـت

صفحة

صفحة

١

[3a] رسالة لأبى القاسم الجنيد أيضا الى بعض إخوانه

صفا لك من الماجد الجواد جميل ما أولاك. وأخلصك بما خصّك به وحباك. وكشف لك عن حقيقة ما به بداك. وآثرك بما استأثر به عمن سواك. وقربك فى الزلفى لديه وأدناك. وبسطك بالتأنيس فى محل قربه وناجاك. وانتجبك بجميل أمره وصافاك. وأيّدك فى عظيم تلك المواطن وقريب تلك الأماكن بالقوة والتمكين والهدوء والدعة والتسكين؛ لئلا تقوى عليك البدائه الواردة والأنباء الغريبة القاصدة، فيلزمك لقوة ذلك عليك فى ابتداء خلوصه، إبهاتُ النهل لما لا يجد لما لا يقال منه محتمل، فكيف يحتمل ذلك أو تقف العقول بضبط ما هنالك، إن لم يمسكها بالكلاية ويكنف سرائرها بالرعاية؟ فأين أنت وقد أقبل بك كلك عليه، وأقبل بما يريده منك لديه؟ وقد بسط لك فى استماع الخطاب وبسطك الى رد الجواب؟ فأنت حينئذ يقال لك وأُنت قائل، وأنت مسؤول عن [4a] أنبائك وأنت مسائل، فى درر الفرائد[1] وترادف الشواهد بدوام الزوائد واتصال الفوائد، تهطل بغزر من المجيد عليك من كل جانب؛ فلولا إحلاله عليك النعمة وتمسيكه لقلبك بالسكينة؛ لذهلت عند كون ذلك القلوب، ولتمزقت عند حضوره العقول؛ لكنه جلّ ثناؤه وتقدست أسماؤه، جاد بالفضل على من أخلصه،

[1] MS. الفوائد

وعاد بالعطف على من اصطنعه ؛ فحمل عنهم ما تحمله إياه ، وحملوا ما أراده لهم وتفضل به من إدراكهم له ؛ جعلنا الله وإياك من أقرب أوليائه[1] لديه منزلا . إن ربي سميع قريب .

رسالة أبي القاسم الجنيد بن محمد الى يحيى بن معاذ الرازي رحمة الله عليهما

لا غبت بك عن شاهدك ، ولا غاب شاهدك بك عنك ، ولا حلت بتحويلك عن حالك ، ولا حال حالك بتحويله عنك ، ولا بنت عن حقيقة أنبائك ، ولا بانت أنباؤك بغيبة الأنباء منك . ولا زلت في الأزل شاهد الأزل في أزليتك ، ولا زال الأزل يكون لك مؤيدا لما زال منك ، فكنت بحيث كنت كما لم تكن ثم كنت ، بفردانيتك متوحدا ، وبوحدانيتك مؤيدا ، بلا شاهد من الشواهد يشهدك . ولا غبت لدى[2] الغيب من الغيب بغيبتك ، فأين ما لا أين لأينه ، إذ مؤين الأينات مبيد[3] لما أيّنه[4] وإذ الإبادة مبادة في تأبيد مبيد الإبادات ، وإذ[5] الاجتماع فيما تفرق ، والتفريق فيما جمع ، فرق في جمع جمعه ، وإذ الجمع بالجمع للجمع جمع فيما جمعه .

[1] MS. اولياه [2] MS. لدا [3] MS. مبيدا [4] MS. اينته

[5] MS. واذا

[رسالة لأبي القاسم الجنيد الى بعض إخوانه] [33 a]

لا زلت أيها الموجود بباب الله راتبا، وبه منه اليه لما يحبه منك طالبا، وله في آلائه وغريب أنبائه راغبا، فحبك به عليه فيما يحبه لك ويبلغك اليه، باصطفائه الى ما يريده منك، ليصطفيك فيما يوليك بما ينتخبه لك ويجتبيك، ثم يبديك فيما يوليك، ويخفيك في عزيز ما يبديك، إعلاء لك عن مصادفة النواظر لحقيقتك، وضَنٌّ بك عن معرفة القلوب لمكانتك، وضم لك بالاشتمال عليك الى مصون منزلتك، فكنت عند ذلك بحيث أرمس المكان مكونه، وطمس الدلائل عليه من وهم متوهمه، فكنت فيما هنالك بغيب لغيب، انتفت عن حقائقه الشكوك والريب، كما أن الحقائق بحق اليقين تعلم، وملاحظة[1] العيان لها محتجبة لا تتوهم، ومن وراء ذلك توحيد الموحد وربانية الألوهية المتفرد على أولية أزلية وبقاء سرمد الأبدية، وهنالك ضلت مقاليد الفهماء، ووقفت علوم العلماء، وانتهت إليه غايات حكمة الحكماء، وهذه غاية لما هذا نعته وسنا ذروه، وانتهت[2] الصفة الى صفته؛ ومن وراء ذلك برزخ الى يوم يبعثون. وإذا بعث الخلق بعد انقضاء مدة برزخهم وأحيوا[3] لحقيقة البعث بعد ميتتهم، عرفوا إحياء الحي لمن أحياه، وتركه في سرمد البقاء لمن أبقاه، وفيما أشرت به من ذلك شرح يطول وصفه، ولا يحتمل الكتاب نعته على كنهه.

[1] MS. وملاحظه [2] MS. انتهت [3] MS. واحيا

يا أخي رضي الله عنك، وصل كتابك السار ظاهره وباطنه وأوله وآخره، وسررت بما ضمنته من علم غريب وحكم عزيزة وإشارات واضحة منيرة، ولم يخف عليّ ما عرضت به مع ما صرحت به، وكل ذلك على علمي به وتسبقي الى فهم ما قصدت له بيّن عندي: [344] الى أين موئله والى أين نهايته ومصدره، ومن أين أوله وآخره، وكيف جرى على من جرى الحكم به؛ لا عدمت استعصامك به منه، وقيام عصمتك به له، غلبت غوالب قاهرة، وبدهت بواده باهرة، أودت بقوة سلطانها، تقاوم سلطانها بالتقاهر فيما قام منها، ثم حمل بعضها على بعض، فركدت متوارية، وهي في الحقيقة بالقوة متظاهرة، تحكمت بمنيع عز التصاول، بلا أين ولا الى أين متكون بكنه نهاية، ولاهوا[1] الى مواضع[2] محدودة، فتعرف لها غاية، إبادتها إبادة مستظلمة، وسطوتها للكل منتظمة. هيه ثم ماذا بعد ذلك، نصبهم غرضا للبلاء، وعرضهم للحَيْن والجلاء، وأنفذ عليهم المكاره بماضي القضاء، وجرعهم الموت صرفا، وأجرى عليهم بقدرته ما يشاء، فمن بين متمانع مستعصم مغلوب، ومن بين مستسلم مسلوب، فلا كان[3] المستسلم فيها باستسلامه ناجيا، ولا المتمانع بالاستعصام من طلبها خارجا، حبست أنفاسهم في أنفاسهم، فهم على فرط البلاء كاظمون،[4] وتخصصوا بتجرع المر المتلف، فهم على التلف مشرفون، فلو أطلقت الأرواح أن تفيض لكان في ذلك راحتها، لكنه في الموت ألم مذاق الموت حابسها، لا يأملون بعد الموت فرجا، ولا

[1] MS. ولاه [2] MS. مواضع [3] MS., omitted [4] MS. كاظمين

لهم قبل الموت من فرط البلاء مخرج[1]. يا أخى هؤلاء قوم هذه بعض صفاتهم، وكرهت الإطالة عليك فى نعت حالهم، وسمع سامعون ببعض نعت ما بلغ القوم إليه، وما القوم من حقائق ذلك كائنون[2] لديه، فسموا بالهموم انتهاء الى مطالبته، قبل النزول بالكون فى محض حقيقته. وشبه عليهم فيه كائنات المحظى[3]، وخفى عليهم المعزز[4] من كون التولّى، وجرت عليهم [348] أحكام أولئك فى أحكامهم، واستمر مترادف الزلل على مضى أيامهم، وكان عندهم أنهم أولئك وليسوا بأولئك، وقوي عليهم موهم حالهم أنهم فيما هنالك. هيهات هيهات ما أبعد من ذلك منالهم، وما أعظم ما يجرى عليهم من الخلل فى توهم حالهم، أعاذنا الله وإياك يا أخى من كل حال لا تكون لمحض الحقيقة متصادقة، ولا تكون لما أحكمه الحق مؤالفة.
ومع ما ذكرته من هذه الحال وما فيها، فهى واسطة بين حالين، والذى جرى منها فرق إذا انكشفت بين منزلتين، وليس مراد الحق بها ما هى بعينها، لكن ذلك على صحة كونه ليكشف بها ما وراءها. وعلم الأكابر ومنازل العظماء وأماكن الحكماء وصريح حقيقة فهم الفهماء بعد عبور ذلك وتجاوزه الى ما لو سنح سانح لتعبيره وجرى الحكم ببعض وصف تفسيره، «لخشعت الوجوه لِلْحي القيوم وقد خاب من حمل ظلما»[5].
يا أخى لا عدمت اشارتك بالحق على ما بسط الحق إليك[6]

[1] MS. مخرجا [2] MS. كائنين [3] MS. المحطى [4] MS. المعزر

[5] Qur. XX. 110 وعنت الوجوه; above not correct [6] MS. إليه

وقرت عيني فيك ببلوغ النهاية الى ما أطلعك[1] الحق عليه. أنت بعض أناسي، وشركاء رغبتي وكبير من كبراء إخوتي وخلّ من أخلاء قلبي بخالص محبتي. ألست أحد من بقي من كبراء إخواننا وأحد المشار اليهم من أبناء جنسنا، ومن عظمت نعمة الله علينا فيه فيما وهبه لنا منه. لا تدع يا أخي متفضلا متطولا محسنا مكاتبتنا ومواصلتنا نستريح عند ذلك الى طيب خبرك ونتفرج ببقاء أثرك ونبتهج بعظم ما وهبه الله لك، فإن كان ذلك عندك مما نستحقه فعلتهُ وإلا جعلت ذلك تطوعا منك علينا وامتنانا يصل منك الينا، وعليك سلام الله ورحمته وعلى جميع إخواننا.

[1] MS. اطلع

نسخة كتاب الجنيد الى عمرو بن عثمان المكى رحمهما الله تعالى

[35A]

أوتيت من العلم والحكمة أعلى منازله ؛ وتناهيت من الرسوخ فى المعرفة الى غاية أماكنها ؛ وأدنيت فى مجالس القرب الى أزلف مواطنها ؛ وتبوّئ بك من كمال جوامع الأنباء الى استيعاب معالمها، فجرى ذلك لك بالتمكين وأنت مستبصر؛ وعلوت فى سمو انتهائه مشرفا مستظهرا . قد تضمنته بقوة الاشتمال عليه فأفضى[1] اليك ؛ واستغنيت عن السعاية اليه بمنيع صولة التمكين، لأنك[2] لذلك كله بواضح الحق مستبين ؛ ولأنك فيما اختلف فيه من العلم على صحة اليقين ؛ وجعلك الله مع ذلك ممن سعد به إخوانه، ونالوا البغية من العلم بوصفه وبيانه، وانكشفت لهم الحقائق المشفية من تعبير لسانه، وأنس منهم من غاب أو حضر بشرف مكانه، بل جعلك الله نورا يملأ بسنا ضيائه الخافقين ويلوح مضيئًا طالعا على سائر الثقلين ؛ فينال عند ذلك كل فريق منهم حظه الكامل ويصل الى مراده الشامل الفاضل ، حتى تكون هذه الظواهر أموره التى ألبسها وبوادى أحواله التى أريد بها ، وقد نظر فيها فوقفت به الضنه عن ظهوره ، وتضمنه الصون والحجبة والكتم عن حضوره . وذلك سر تضل العقول عن الإشارة إليه؛

[1] MS. فأفضوا [2] MS. ولانك

وتنقطع الفهوم عن شئ من الورود عليه، هيهات هيهات طمست عن ذلك أطواق كوامل العلماء، وضلت عنه مقاليد أكابر الفهماء. فهو فى تفرد توحده عليّ، ويعزل قيومته تجرده. فكم من مومئ إليه بتوهمه، ومن مظهر التحقق[1] به بالطيب عنده أن يعرض لينطق به، تلجلج لسانه وتحير عند الإيماء به إلى بيانه. ويظن الجاهل إذا سمعه أنه قد أصاب وهو فى عمياء مظلمة عند الخطاب، يكون فى دعواه وحقيقة الحق تدفعه، ويوهم بوصفه السامع [35a] فى القصد إلى ما يقع الفهم به فى النفاذ فيما أمر به، والترك لما نهى عنه. وذلك بعض حق العلم على من حمله، فمتى اقتضيت لنفسك يقع العلم لها قبل إعطائك منها حق ما للعلم. واجب احتجب عنك نفعه ونوره وبقى عليك رسمه وظهوره، وذلك حجة للعلم عليك وإن كان رسمه ظاهرا[2] لديك، فاحذر أيها الرجل الذى قد لبس من العلم ظاهر حليته، وأومأ المشيرون إليه بجميل لبسته وقصر عن العلم بمحض حقيقته، ما وقعت به الإشارة إليك وانبسطت به الألسن من الثناء عليك فإن ذلك حتف لمن هذه الصفة صفته، وحجة من الله تعالى عليه فى عاقبته.

فلما سمع العالم من الحكيم ما نطق به، وقرع سمعه بيان ما شرحه له، أطرق مفكرا ثم انتحب بعد الفكرة باكيا، فطال بكاؤه وعلا نحيبه واشتد اضطرابه، فأقبل عليه عند ذلك الحكيم فقال له: الآن حين بدت شمس الحكمة تطلع عليك وواضح نورها يصل

[1] MS. ليحقق [2] MS. ظاهر

إليك، وعند ذلك تنجلى عنك ظلمات ما أعرضت عنه من علمك، واغفلته من موانع العلل لفهمك، وإنى أؤمل بذلك صلاح ما أفسدته والتلافى لحفظ ما ضيعته.

فلما سمع العالم إقبال الحكيم عليه بذلك، سكن من اضطرابه وهدأ من شدة بكائه، ثم أقبل على الحكيم فقال: زدنى من دوائك هذا فقد لاَوم جراحى، وقويت الأُطماع فى الوقوع لحجتى، فتخلصنى بلطيف حيلتك ورفق حكمتك من وبال ما أنت أعلم بماكُمن منه فى سرى، واستترعنى من خفيّ هوى الشر، فقد انطوى عنى فى سالف الأوقات الماضية خفيّ مستبطنات كانت فى السرائر كامنه وكشفْت لى عنها بجميل نعتك وأوقفتنى على ما بطن منها بلطيف رفقك.

قال له الحكيم: تحمد الله أبداً فيما أنعم به عليك من اطلاعه إياك [36a] على ذلك وإيقافه لك على مواضع خللك، فكن بالذل بين يديه خاضعا، وافتقر إليه بالاستكانة والخضوع ضارعا، فإنك لا تَخْفى مناجاتك له سامعا، وإنك إذا كنت كذلك كان لك إليه شافعا؛ واعلم مع ذلك أن ألْسنة الحكمة لا تنطق إلا من بعد أن يؤذن لها، وإذا نطقت وقع النفع لمن أُسمع بها، وإنما مثل ذلك من فضل الله على خلقه، مثل غيث سمائه الذى إذا أنزله وأحيا[1] به ميت أرضه، أما سمعت الله تعالى يقول «فانظر الى آثار رحمة الله كيف يحيى الأرض بعد موتها إن ذلك لمحيى الموتى وهو على كل شئ قدير»[2] وكذلك يحيى الله تعالى بألسنة الحكمة ما أمات الإعراض عنه من قلوب اهل الغفلة..

[1] MS. أحيا [2] *Qur'an, Sura XXX, 50*

قال العالم للحكيم : أجل إن الذى وصفته كما وصفته، وإنى أؤمل من الذى انتد بتنى بلسان حكمتك وجاد عليّ تعطف رحمتك، أن تستنقذنى من وبال التقصير بدلالتك، وتخرجنى من ذلة التخلف بمصادفة رؤيتك، وقد علمت الآن أن أربي الى التكشف لى عما لزمنى من وبال تركى للعمل بعلمى وتخلفى عما أوجبه حق العلم عليّ، وعما استتر فى نفسى وانطوى بالاستخفاء فى سرى ما لم أكن له مدركا ولا بما معى من العلم عليه واقفا، وقد أشرقت الآن بقدر ما أيّدنى الله تعالى به منك ومنّ بى عليّ، وكشفه لى بأسبابك على بعض ذلك، فبعلمى بالقليل من ذلك علمت أن عليّ منه كثيرا لم أدركه، وخفيّ مستبطنات لم أره ولم أعرفه، فاكشف لى أيها الحكيم من أمرى عما أنت أعلم به منى، فإن الطبيب أعلم بداء السقيم من نفسه، وأحق أن يصف له من الدواء ما يكون سببا لبرئه[1].

قال له الحكيم : قد بدت مطالعات الفهم تلحقك بمعرفة ما عليك من ذلك ولك، وبدت أوائل [368] معانى الصحو تلوح لعقلك، وبدت أوائل الإفاقة تسعى[2] بحركاتها لبعض ما فى سرك. واعلم أن ضرر الأديان أشر من ضرر الأبدان؛ وسقم الجوارح والأجسام أسهل من سقم القلوب والأفهام؛ لأن علل الدين والآفات المعترضة على اليقين سبب للبوار، ومورّدة لأهلها على النار، مؤدية الى سخط الجبار، وما عدا

[1] MS. لبروه   [2] MS. تسع

ذلك الى غيره وكان واقفا فيما سواه من الأمراض والأسقام الكائنة فى الجوارح والأجسام ، فذلك ضرر يؤمل برؤه ويزول مكروهه وشره ويرجى من الله تعالى ثوابه وأجره . وأعلم أن الطبيب العالم المجرب والحكيم الناصح المؤدب أعلم بدنف الأبدان والعلل المخامرة بآفاتها للأديان ، لأن المعبر عنهما يعبر عما يجد من ذاته ، والواصف لما حلّ به من بلائه ، مقصر عن بلوغ نعته لذلك ، مختلف عن الوصف لما هنالك ، ووصف المتطبّب الخبير المجرب البصير يكشف لأهل الأمراض عما وجدوه ، وينبئهم عن زوال ما فقدوه ، حتى كأن الموصوف بعبارة اللسان منظور إليه بحقيقة العيان .... وإنى أصف لك على أثر ذلك أمورًا تقوّى لك حالك وتبلغك غاية البغية من سؤالك والقوة بالله العظيم .

اعلم أيها المنسوب الى العلم بوقوع الصحو لك تتبين حيرة السكرة . وبكون الإفاقة تقف على وقت الغمرة ، وبصحة الذكر ينكشف لك وبال الغفلة ، وبالسلامة والعافية يتميز لك وقت العلة . فاعلم أن ذلك كله مشتغل فى حين كونه عن حقيقة معرفته ضار لأهله بما لبسهم منه عن وجود حيرته إلا بحمله ، عِلمٌ مزاجه اللبس والظلمة ليثبت الله تعالى بذلك عليهم الحجة ، فخلّ عن نفسك أيها المعنىّ بها والحريص على تعجيل [37A] استنقاذها وبال السكرة والغمرة والغفلة والحيرة باستعمال ما أصفه لك ، والاسراع الى ما أحثك عليه ، والمبادرة إلى ما أشير به إليك ، فإن صحة الصدق وجودة القصد يؤديانك الى المحل

الذى هو باب المدخل فيما تحبه والمخرج مما تكرهه، ولن يحجبك عن بلوغ ما تريد - والقوة بالله - إلا بتقصيرك عن المجاهدة فى واجب حق السعى عليك؟ فاحذر ثم احذر أن تكون على شيء من ذلك مقصراً، أو ألفاك وقتا وأنت عنه فاتر راجع، فإن مطيتك الموصلة لك الى بغيتك صدقك فى إقامة المناصحة فى محل مجاهدتك؛ فقد أوقفتك على وجه المنهج والمدرجة وقربتك من المسير على أوضح المحجة.

واعلم أيها الرجل الحاذر المحثوث المبادر أن الإقامة المانعة لك ولنظرائك بعد الحمل للعلم وطول السعاية فيه ودوام العناية بجمعه والاستكثار من الحمل له، الميل الى التأويل والدخول به فيما خفى من النفس من الميل الى الدنيا والركون إليها؛ وهم فى ذلك على معانى مختلفه: فمتأول متبين الأغماض والأعراض فيما استكن فى خفايا نفسه، فمضى فيه على ما عليه منه والعلم بنكته. ولا يتركه فى كثير من الأوقات ويستتر ذلك عليه فى بعض أوقاته. ومتأول قصد الصحة والتحقيق فيما تأوله، ولحقه فى ذلك الميل من حيث لم يستدركه، وانطوى عليه ما عليه فيما قصد له، وكان عنده الذى عمد له وتأوله أولى به من غيره فمضى على ذلك، وهذا نعت حاله، فكان مما قصد له فى التأويل على معنى الصفة الأولى[1] التى تبين لصاحبها خفي أغماضه وطوي ما فى نفسه إذ جعل العلم ذريعة وسببا الى ذلك، فلبس حليته وتجمل بلبوسه وأظهر بالتأويل أثر

[1] MS. الاوله

العلم [37B] ودعا إليه ونصب نفسه للشهرة به ليعلم الناس ما علم منه، فلما عُرف موضعه ومكانه وسُمع منه وأقبل الناس عليه نحوه، استحسن اجتماع العوام عليه وثناء الجاهلين بما ليس فيه، فقوي عليه بذلك سلطان التأويل وأوهم نفسه حظ اجتماعهم وانبساط ثنائهم وكثرة تعظيمهم وحسن قبولهم له، بما ظهر من نفسه وتحسّن به، مما يعلم الله تعالى منه خلاف ما أسرّه وأضمره، فلما استوى له ذلك عند العوام والجهلة، وكثرة حمد الحامدين بالغلط والغفلة، مال إلى ما فى نفسه من أخذ العوض على ما نشر من علمه، ورضى بما تعجله من ذلك ثوابًا لعلمه، وصار بائعا للعلم بالثمن اليسير والخطر القليل، ورضى بالدنيا عوضا من الآخرة ومن ثواب الله تعالى على الأعمال الصالحة، فى جملة من ذمّة الله تعالى فى كتابه وقصّ علينا من بيانه على لسان نبيه صلى الله عليه وسلم. قال الله عزّ وجلّ « وإذ أخذ الله ميثاق الذين أوتوا الكتاب لتبيننه للناس ولا تكتمونه فنبذوه وراء ظهورهم واشتروا به ثمنا قليلا فبئس ما يشترون »[1]. وقال تعالى « فخلف من بعدهم خلف ورثوا الكتاب يأخذون عرض هذا الأدنى ويقولون سيغفر لنا وإن يأتهم عرض مثله يأخذوه »[2]. فذمّهم الله تعالى وقصّ علينا فى كتابه وصرّح بذلك إلى العقلاء من عباده، وبيّنه بيانا محكما قويا لئلا يكون لمحتج فى ذلك حجة، ولا لقائل فيه مساغ ولا مدافعة. ثم إن الله تعالى قصّ علينا قصص

[1] Qur'an iii, 184 [2] Qur'an vii, 168

الأنبياء عليهم السلام وأخبرنا بما نعتهم به وبما أخذ عليهم من ترك الدنيا والتشمير الى الآخرة، وألا يأخذوا على شيء من ذلك ثمناً ولا يريدون عليه أجراً. ولأن حق العلم وحق تأديته إلى الخلق ألا يكون لشيء منه جزاء إلا ثواب الله عزّ وجلّ عليه [38a] والجنة التي جعلها دار من اتقاه وأطاعه قال الله تعالى لنبيه عليه السلام: «قل ما أسالكم عليه من أجر وما أنا من المتكلفين»[1]. وقال تعالى «قل لا أسالكم عليه أجرا إلا المودة فى القربى»[2]. وكذلك قصّ علينا فى قصص الأنبياء عليهم السلام، قال نوح «قل ما أسالكم عليه من أجر وما أريد أن أخالفكم إلى ما أنهاكم عنه»[3] وقال «إن أجرى إلا على الذى فطرنى»[4]. ومثل هذا كثير فى كتاب الله تعالى. وهذه سيرة الأنبياء عليهم السلام فى الأمم وسيرة العلماء فى الناس ألا يأخذون[5] على شيء من العلم ثمنا ولا يطلبون على شيء بما يعلمون أجراً وسيما [ما] أخذه العلماء على العلم سحتا وسيما ما أخذه الربانيون والأحبار مع نهيهم عن ذلك فقال تعالى «لولا ينهاهم الربانيون والأحبار عن قولهم الاثم وأكلهم السحت لبئس ما كانوا يصنعون»[6] والأخبار فى النهى عن ذلك كثيرة والاستقصا فى ذلك من الحجة يطول وصفه وقد تبين لك بعض ما فيه كفايه وبلاغ والله الموفق.

وأما الطوائف التى تأولت ورأت أن الذى تأولته هو الحق

[1] Qur'ān xxxviii, 86 [2] Qur. xlii, 23 [3] Qur. xi, 87 [4] ibid. 90

[5] MS. يأخذوا [6] Qur. iv, 63

فإنهم قوم لحقهم الزلل من حيث غاب[1] عنهم علم الحقيقة؛ ونالهم من المشتكلات التى لا تَبين لأهلها إلا بعد التورط فيها والانغماس فى مكروهها؛ جعل القوم أئمتهم فيما تأولوه رجالا[2] قلّت منا صحتهم لأنفسهم ولم يصادفوا صواب الحقيقة فيما عمدوه؛ قالوا: بالخلق إلينا فيما علِمناه أشد الحاجة؛ وعلمُنا إقامة الحق فى سائر الخلق؛ فمن ذلك تقديم الأئمة والمشورة عنهم والتقوّى بهم[3] وكذلك الأمراء والرؤساء وعظماء أبناء الدنيا؛ فجعلوا السعى الى الخلفاء والأمراء والحكماء وعظماء أبناء الدنيا عملا لهم يحتسبون به ويؤملون ثوابه وجعلوه من أجل الأعمال واعظمها قدرًا وأوفرها عندهم ثوابًا، فحملوا العلم إليهم وطرقوا به أبوابهم، وسعوا بما حملوه منه إلى من لم يطلبهم له ولم يدعهم اليه ولم يعرفهم به [38a] فلحقهم فى أول الأمر ذلّ السعاية والتوسل الى الحجّاب ومهانة الوقوف على ابوابهم، فمن بين مأذون له ومن بين مردود، قد لحقتهم المذلة، وعلتهم العقوبة، ولبستهم الذلة، ورجعوا بخضوع المذلة، فلم يزالوا كذلك فى نَصَبِ الغدو والرواح، وذلك سبب المهلكة والاجتياح، حتى وصلوا الى الذى قصدوا، ونسوا الأله الذى عبدوا، وأوردتهم الغفلة والنسيان موارد الأموات، وغمرتهم كثرة العلل والآفات واتصلت بأبصارهم وقلوبهم فتنة ما أعد أبناء الدنيا لأنفسهم وآثروه على أمور آخرتهم من بهجة رونقها ونضرة زينتها ولوعة زهرتها.

[1]MS. غابت [2]MS. رجال [3]MS. منهم

واعلم أيها الباحث عن واجب العلم وشرفه، والطالب للمصافاة بخالص الأعمال لسيده، أن أقدام القوم عن مناهج الحقيقة انحرفت، وأن قلوبهم على صحيح الإرادات ما استوت، وأنهم مالوا بخفي ما في النفوس على جميل ما أظهروه والى محبة علم الخلق به وتعظيمهم عليه وإجلالهم من أجله. وأحبوا اجتماع الخلق عليهم وإشارتهم إليهم[1]، حتى تصوّب آراؤهم وتصدق أقوالهم وتكبر غاياتهم ويتصل الثناء لهم؛ وإن قصر عن شيء من ذلك عنهم كرهوا وإن لم يقع لهم ما يحبون[2] غضبوا، ولا تسل عن فرط الغضب منهم والرضا والتعتب منهم على من خالف مواقع الهوى. وصفهم بكل ما هم فيه يطول به الشرح ويطول به الكلام، وقد شرحت لك من وصفهم ما انبسط به لساني. وأجرى لك من نعتي وبياني وفي ذلك كفاية.

فالبس الآن أنت جلابيب الحذر وتدرع بأدرع الخوف، وخذ على نفسك جنة التقوى، وقم لله تعالى على نفسك بدوام الرعاية، ودوام التفتيش وشدة المحاسبة وجودة التحصيل وصدق البحث، وصل سرا [39a] مع ذلك بدوام الذكر وقوي الفكر؛ فكن ممن جاهد في الله عزّ وجلّ حق جهاده، وممن أثنى الله تعالى عليه من صالحي عباده، مع ما يقع لك من الوعد الجميل والثواب الجزيل. قال الله عزّ وجل: «والذين جاهدوا فينا لنهدينهم سبلنا وإن الله لمع المحسنين»[3] وقال الله تعالى «ولو أنهم فعلوا ما يوعظون به لكان خيرا لهم وأشد تثبيتا»[4] فهاتان آيتان موجبتان لمنالات الخير ووقوع الهداية والرشد، فخذ بحظك الأوفر من العمل بهما واللزوم لما أمر الله

[1] MS. اليه [2] MS. يحبوا [3] Qur. xxix, 69 [4] Qur. iv, 69

تعالى فيهما . وكن على حذر من موافقة شئ مما تقدم به النعت من ذلك التأويل وخطأ الرأى، فإن ذلك مؤدى إلى إحباط العمل وشدة الندامة فى المنقلب .

قال له العالم : أيها الحكيم قد أتيت على الذى فى نفسى وبلغت مدى ما كان يجول فى صدرى وزدت على ذلك من الوصف أشياء عرفت فضلها، وانكشف لى صواب العلم بها وأرجو أن يكون ذلك من فضل الله تعالى ورحمته لى، وقد جعلك الله تعالى سببا لتنبيهى[1] على أمور لولا منة الله تعالى عليّ بك فيها لذهب بى التقصير عن العلم بها، حيث ذهب بمن تقدم وصفك له، فاوقفنى حقيقة علمك بها على ذلله وخطأ رأيه. وقد أنعم الله عليّ بما أيّدنى به منك، وعظّم عندى قدر ما جعلك الله له أهلا وموضعا من شرحك لما تقدم من نعته ووصفه، من أحوال الطبقات الثلاثة المتأولين، وما وقع لهم من الخطأ فى القصد والميل بالعمل الى غير منهجه، والى الانحراف فيه عن سواء السبيل وقد احتجت أن تصف لى العاملين لله تعالى بحقيقة العلم [39 B] القائمين بحقه، الصادقين فيما حملوا منه وفيما قلدوه من تأديته، الممدوحين بنشره وبما نقلوا الى من دونهم منه؛ والمحتسبين فى تعليمهم الناس على صحة الإرادة وصلاح[2] النية وجميل السيرة، الذين لم تمل بهم الأطماع ولم يفتنهم الاختداع، ولم تعرج بهم الأهواء، ولم تسترقهم إرادات النفوس؛ ولم تعطف بهم الدنيا؛ ولم يجر عليهم الزلل والخطأ، وكانوا فى ذلك كله على صحة المعنى . قال الحكيم: ابشر

[1] MS. اصلاح

بما فتح الله تعالى لك من باب السؤال، ويسرك له من صحة المقال، فإن ذلك إن شاء الله تعالى سبب لك إلى ركوب الأعمال ومباشرة جميل الأفعال، ومؤديا لما أؤمله لك الى تمهيد صدقك، فاخلص[1] الإرادة لله تعالى فى حقيقة قصدك، واجعل توسلك الى الحكمة واستدعائك لما تحب منها تحصين سرك من العلل المانعة عنها؛ واصلح الضمير بإجمامه لما يجب لها، فإن الحكمة لمن اشتملت عليه فيها الرغبة، واستولت على خالص سره المحبة، أشد عطفاً وحنيناً وميلاً من الأم الشفيقة[2] والأب الرفيق. وكأنى مع ذلك أرى سحابا من العلم غدقةً منبسطةً عليك، مونقةً قد أظلك غمامها، وقويت لك الآمال باستتمامها، فاستمطر[3] الغيث الكائن فيها بدوام الوقوف بحضرة فنائها، وأدم الاستغاثة بمنزِّل الغيث ومنشر السحاب وكاشف الضر ومعتق الرقاب؛ واعلم أنه جلّ ثناؤه يحيى بقطرة من غيث رحمته، موات ما أنزلها عليه من بريته؛ فتحرَّى[4] طلب الحياة تكون السقيا، فإن أوائل تلك الغمام توجدك الشفا، وإن غدق ما بها يغسل عن سرك الميل الى الدنيا، ومباشرته بجسمك [405a] يغسل عنك سائر الأدواء، وذوقك لسائغ طعمه يميت من نفسك الهوى. واعلم ان الله تعالى إذا أراد عبدا سهل له السبيل ووطّأ له التثقيل[5] وأسرع به فى الترحيل وبلّغه المنزل الفضيل ومنحه الحظ الجزيل. وإنى أؤملك من الذى عرضك لنجح السؤال وصحيح القصد فى المقال، أن يبلغك بفضله عليك ورحمته إياك، منازل المنتجبين من أوليائه، والأصفياء

[1] MS. واخلص [2] MS. الشفقه [3] MS. واستمطر [4] MS. فتحرا [5] MS. بالتثقيل

المستخلصين من عباده . وأنا واصف لك إن شاء اللّه تعالى ما سألت عنه ، من نعت أهل الحقائق من أهل العلم ، العاملين بـه ، الصادقين فى القصد اليه ، المجتهدين فى إقامة حقه ، المريدين للعلم لما وجب عليهم منه ، الذين لم تفتنهم فيما قصدوه أطماع الدنيا ، ولم تمل بهم عن الأخذ بحقيقته ، ولم يستفزهم الغواة من الأعداء ، « أولئك حزب اللّه الا ان حزب اللّه هم المفلحون »[1] اعلم أن أول ما أوتى[2] المحققين من أهل العلم من العمل فى أول الطلب اصلاحُ النية وصحة المراد والموافقة فيه للنفوس فيما بدا من إرادة الطلب ، فلم يبيحوا أقدامهم السعى ، ولم يتحركوا فى ذلك بالجوارح ، إلا من بعد ما أحكم جميل النظر لهم بالانبساط فيه ؛ فسعوا فيه على أصل ما أدبهم العلم به فى أول الأمر ، ومضوا على صحة الحال وشهادة العلم بذلك ؛ وألزم صحة ما يبدؤ[3] به الحق قلوبهم ، الإشفاق والحذر والتقية ، فضمّهم وجود ذلك ، وألزمهم حصر الجوارح وضبط السرائر ودوام الصمت ، وخافوا مع ذلك أن يكونوا قد قصروا عن واجب حق السعى فى طلب العلم ، واشتد تحصيلهم على النفوس ، وصحبهم جميل الذكر ودوام الفكر [40B] فى مواطن السعى فحماهم ذلك عن الانبساط عن معاشرة الطالبين له ، والساعين معهم فيه فكانوا بحال والحاضرين معهم بحال ، كلما بدا من غيرهم لغو أعرضوا ، وكلما بدا من سواهم غفلة أو لعب خافوا وحذروا ، وكلما ظهر لهم من غيرهم مزعج يجرى الى تأكيد حالهم وتشديد ضبطهم لما عليهم يدعون لمن حضرهم بالسلامة ، ويحبون لهم الصلاح والاستقامة ، لا يؤذون الناس ولا يحقرونهم ولا يغتابونهم

[1] Qur. LVIII, 22 [2] MS. اتوا [3] MS. يبدوا

ولا يذمونهم، بل يشفقون عليهم إذا رأوا منهم الزلل، ويدعون لهم إذا بدا منهم الخلل، يعرفون المنكر وينكرونه ويتجنبونه، ويعرفون المعروف ويحبونه ويستعملونه، لا يزدرون المقصّرين لكثرة وجوده، ولا يغمصون مَنْ دونهم لما به من حالهم حمدوه، بل يعرفون ذلك بدلالة العلم عليه، ولا يخفى عليهم من القوم ما نسبهم الحق اليه. فصواب ذلك وخطؤه لهم بالعلم مميز[1] والسلامة من رؤية مكروه ذلك لهم صاحب[2]، وفيما ألزمهم الاشفاق والتقوى شاغل[3] ولهم على طلب العلم مقبل[4]، ألسنتهم بحمد ربهم عند سماع العلم ناطقة، وقلوبهم الى اعتقاد العمل به مبادرة، وآذانهم بحسن الإصغاء اليه سامعة، وأبدانهم بالخدمة لله تعالى ساعية، أحسنوا على جميل السيرة جمعه، وبالوفاء بفضل الله تعالى عليهم فهمه، ولم يزالوا بدوام السعي اليه وشدة الإقبال عليه وبكثرة اللزوم لمن العلم حاضر لديه، حتى أخذوا منه بالحظ الأوفر والنصيب الأكبر، فلما بلغوا منه الى ما به يستعينون، وغاية ما اليه يحتاجون، وبحقائقه في سائر الأوقات يعملون، رجعوا الى تفتيش ما كتبوا والى البحث عما منه طلبوا، فكان ما نعاً لهم من السعاية[5] جامعا لهم الى الخلوة بالعبادة، ووقفت بالناس اليهم الحاجة، وعرف موضعهم بجميل الإرادة وعرف [41a] أماكنهم من العلم؛ وشرفت أحوالهم من الفضل، وانبسط ذلك ونشأ وظهر ذلك وبدا، فمن بين خال بعلمه متشاغل عن الخليقة بعبادته مؤثر[6] للعمل فيما فتح الله تعالى عليه منه، ولا يريد بإدامة الخدمة لله تعالى بدلا، ولا بالخلوة بما فتح الله تعالى له من ذلك حولا؛ ومن بين من حضرته في نَشْرِهِ العلم النية، وقويت له

[1] MS. مميزا [2] MS. صاحبا [3] MS. شاغلا [4] MS. مقبلا [5] MS. السقاية [6] MS. مؤثرا

على تعليمه العزيمة ، وسنحت له فى ذلك رؤية الفضيلة' فانبسط فى نشر العلم محتسبا ، وكان فى العمل لله تعالى بذلك مخلصا ، يرغب الى الله عزّوجلّ فى جميل الثواب ، ويؤمل من الله تعالى جميل العائدة فى المآب ' مصحوبا[1] فى ذلك بمصادفة الصواب ' إذا قال نطق بقوة العلم ' وإذا سكت سكت بوقار الحلم ' وإذا قصد الى البيان قرّب منال الفهم ، إذا كثروا عليه أحب نفعهم ، وإذا تفرقوا عنه نصحهم ، يؤدى اليهم ما حمل من العلم بلسان فصيح وبيان صحيح ، بقلب نصوح وقول صادق ، ولا يعجل على من جهل ، ولا يكافئ من زلّ وأخطأ ، ولا يواقف بالمراآة[2] أحدا ' يعفو عمن ظلمه ' ويعطي من حرمه ، ويحسن إلى من أساء اليه ، ويتجاوز عمن يتعدى عليه ' لا يريد على شئ من أعماله من الخلق أجرا ، ولا يميل الى مدحة ولا ثناء ، يجتهد لله تعالى فى إخلاص أعماله ويريد وجهه بجميل أفعاله ، لا يقبل الدنيا ممن يبذلها له ' ولا يعرج على من انبسط بها اليه ، يضع الدنيا حيث وضعها خالقها ، ويغنيه منها ما قسمه له رازقه ، لا يشتغل منها بما يزول ' ولا يعمل فيها بما لا يدوم ، منصرف بقلبه عن زينتها ، منحرف عن كل ما دعى اليها من بهجة رونقها ، يكفيه ما قلّ وصفا ، ويجزيه ما سلم واستوى ' يقف منها عند الشبهات ، وينصرف عن الأمور المشكلات ' بل هو للحلال البين تارك ' وفى الأخذ لما لا بد له منه [418] مقتصد ، قد آثر فيها وفى كل ما دعى إليها الزهادة ' ولزوم الكد والعبادة. يرحم من مال برغبته إليها ويرثى لمن أقبل بطلبه عليها ' لا يراها

[1] MS مصحوب [2] MS. مالمرآه

حظاً لمن طلبها، ولا ثمنا لسعي من اشتغل بها، ينظر إليها بعين زوالها، ويقرب انتقالها، فهذا محل الدنيا عنده، ومكانها فى العلم بها لديه؛ وهو مع ما وصفته لك دائم العزلة، كثير الخلوة، متصل الجد والخدمة، يجد راحة قلبه وقرة عينيه وسرور فؤاده، فيما خلص من صالح العمل إلى سيده، وأمل عائدة ثوابه فى معاده. فإذا ظهر للناس فى وقت اجتماعهم عليه، وطلبهم للعلم العتيد لديه، ظهر بجميل النية وصحيح الإرادة؛ فكان ذلك عنده بعض الأعمال المقربة الصالحة، فهو لا يخلو من حال هو بها فى الخلوة متعبدا، والى الله تعالى فيما يقرب اليه مجتهدا، ومن حاله أن تكون قد حضرته النية. ويبرز للخلق فيكون لعلمه ناشرا، ولهم مما علمه الله تعالى معلما. والوجل والخوف من الله عزّ وجلّ فى أحواله، والحذر والإشفاق دائما لا يفارقه، يقوم بشرائط علمه، ويعدل فى قوله وحكمه، هو من أقوم الناس بالأحكام وأعلمهم بالحلال والحرام، وأبصرهم بشرائع الإسلام، يقع على آثار المرسلين، ويتبع سنن الأولياء والصالحين، لا يميل إلى بدعة، ولا يقصر عن الأخذ بالسنة، بعلم بارع محكم قوي، وحال واضح بين مستو[1]، متوسط بجميع المذاهب، متحرى لأقوم الآراء، لا يميل إلى الكلام، ولا يخطر به منه اهتمام، لا يطعن على الأئمة ولا يذمها، ويحب لها من الصلاح ما يعمها، يرى السمع والطاعة ولا ينزع يدا من جماعة، يرى أن الخروج على الأئمة من فعل الجهلة الفاسقين، والغواة المارقين، الذين يريدون الفتن، ويبتغون الفساد فى

[1] MS. مستوى

الأرض، أولئك العداة والفساق والظلمة المراق، الذين سلكوا غير سبيل الهدى، واستصحبوا الغواية والردى،[428] ومالوا بالفتنة إلى الدنيا. وقد رفع الله عزّ وجلّ عن ذلك أقدار العلماء، وجعلهم أئمة هداة نصحاء، أخيارا أبرارا أتقياء خلصاء سعداء نجباء سادة أجلة عظماء حلماء كرماء أولياء، جعلهم الله أعلاما من الحق منشورة ومنارًا للهدى منصوبة، ومناهج للبرية مضروبة، أولئك علماء المسلمين وأمناء المؤمنين وأجلة المتقين، فبهم فى نوائب الدين يقتدى، وبنورهم فى ظلمات الجهل يهتدى، وبضياء علمهم فى الظلماء يستضئ، جعلهم الله عزّ وجلّ رحمة لعباده، وبركة على من نشاء من بريته، يعلم بهم الجاهل ويذكر بهم الغافل، ويرشد بهم السائل، ويعطى بهم النائل، ويزيد بهم العامل، ويبلغ بهم الى المحل الفاضل، ويحث بهم الراحل، ويمكن بهم القوى الكامل؛ أولئك الذين عمروا بالذكر لله تعالى أعمارهم. وقطعوا بالعمل الفاضل الزكيّ آجالهم، وبقوا بذلك للخليقة محمود آثارهم، ووضحت للبرية ضياء أنوارهم، فمن اقتبس من سنا نورهم استضاء، ومن قفا على آثارهم اهتدى، ومن أتبع سير ما هم عليه سعد، ولم يشق، أحياهم الله تعالى حياة دائمة، ويتوفاهم وفاة سالمة، وأنسوا بما قدموا به إلى الآخرة؛ جعل الله خواتم أمورهم أفضلها، وأحوالهم التى قُبضوا عليها أجملها.

وبعد أيها السائل عن نعت المحققين من العلماء العاملين بالعلم فى مدة البقاء، فقد وصفت لك بعض أحوالهم ونَعَتّ لك كثيرا من جميل أفعالهم، ولو أردت بلوغ الاستقصاء لوصفهم،

وذكر ما يستحقونه من نعتهم، لطال بذلك كتابى، واتسع به جوابى، وفيما أجرى الله تعالى ذكره من ذلك كفاية لمن اهتدى، وبلاغ لمن عمل بما هو أولى.

قال العالم للحكيم: أيها الأستاذ العطوف[1] الرحيم والمعلم الناصح الحكيم، لقد أزعجت بوصفك [42 B] للقوم قلبى، وملأت بالخيفة صدرى، وعرفنى بذلك موضعى وقدرى، وخفت أن يعجز عن حمل ما عرفته صبرى، لما بينته من شدة تقصيرى، ودوام تخلفى، فاحتقرت عند المعرفة نفسى، وأيقنت بليتى ونقصى، فكيف لى بما أكون به من ذل التخلف خارجا، وعن مذموم أخلاق نفسى راحلا، وفى أوائل طريق القوم داخلا، فإنى أرى الوقوف عن ذلك مأثما، والبقاء مع الحال التى أنا عليها مغرما.

قال له الحكيم: لقد سألت عن شأن عظيم وأمر عال جسيم، يسهل على العاملين بفضله ركوب الأهوال فى طلبه، وحمل الأثقال والتغرب من الأوطان، والخروج عن الأموال، وقلّ من قويت فيما عند الله تعالى رغبته، إلا سهل عليه بذل بدنه ومهجته، ولم يعظم عليه شئ فى بلوغ بغيته، فكن أيها السائل عن منازل النجباء ودرجات العلماء وأحوال الأئمة العظماء المقفين على آثار الأنبياء، على ترك لكل سبب عن منهاج القوم يعطفك عن سبيل الهداية والرشد ويمنعك، فكن إلى الله تعالى راغبا فيما إليه يرفعك، واعلم أن ملاحظتك بالرغبة إلى ما قلّ من الدنيا أو كثر، حجاب لك عن الآخرة، وعلة على ملاحظتك فى حين نفاذ البصيرة؟ فنحّ عن ملاحظة الضمير ما يورثك رؤيته النقص والتقصير، وصفّ الضمائر

[1] MS. العطيف

وطهر السرائر بتجريد الاعتزام وإجمام الاهتمام، تفردا منك بما له قصدت، وفي إدراكه رغبت، فإن في إصلاحك لما بطن من سرك إحكام لما أعلن وظهر من جهرك. فإياك أن تميل إلى شئ وإن قل خطره، فيميل بك عن محمودٍ وضح لك أمره، فإن أغبن الغبناء من باع كثير ما يبقى، بقليل ما يفنى، ومن شغل نفسه عن أمور الآخرة بأمور الدنيا. واجعل أيها الرجل الطالب لفضل الأحوال والمذاهب أول ما تبدأ من عملك، وتقرب بفعله إلى ربك، الزهد في الدنيا والإعراض عن كل ما مالت اليه النفس من قليل أو كثير، فإن قليل ما ملت به إليها، يأخذ من سرك [43A] ويشغل من قلبك ويعترض على ذكرك، وعلى قدر قوة ما معك من مواد القليل منها وضعفه، كذلك تكون قوة المعترض منه وضعفه، وعلى حسب الواقع من ذلك، يحتجب عنك فهم ما قصدت الهمة، وإنما تؤثر الأعمال وتحصن القلوب، إذا انقطعت عوارض الدنيا عنها، فإذا اعترض منها شئ وإن قل، فهو المراد والعمل معا، وكان ذلك يبعد المحاضر والأفهام، ويوقف الحال عن لحوق الاستتمام، فاحذر ما عاطفك منها، ومال بك وان قل قدره إليها، تخلص[1] بتخلصك من ذلك الى سوىّ الحال وصحة الفعل والمقال، فقال له العالم: وضعت لنصحك خدى، وجمعت له همى وفرغت له قلبي وتبينت فيه رشدى، وقد أملت برشد هدايتك وحقيقة دعايتك وصدق مناصحتك، أن يبلغني الله تعالى الى كل ما أؤمله وغاية ما أطلبه، وقد رأيت ينابيع الحكمة الجارية من مكنون سرك على لسانك، واصلة إليّ ببعض ما

[1] MS. يخلص.

تقصدنى به ، وقد ذقت سائغا من مائه ، فأوجدنى انتعاشُ تبينه محبةَ نفعك لى به ، فزدنى منه ما تقوى به الحياة الباعثة لى ، من موت ما مضى من الحال، إلى مستقبل ما وقع من الانتقال، فإنى لم أجد شيئا أرجع به فيك الى الله تعالى، إلا مناجاتى له بجميل مجازاتك عنى ومكافأته لك بما هو له أهل وولي، وبعد إيقاظك لى أيها الحكيم من رقدة الغفلة، وإنباهك لى من وسن السهـو والسِّنة ، فقد وجدت[1] استقلالا إلى استدراك الفهم عنـك ، يحملنى ما وجدت منه إلى العمل ببعضه، ووجدت مطالعات ما بقى عليّ من التقصير، يزجرنى عن الوقوف عنها لمحكم بيان وعلم إيقان، فأما ما بين ما سنح من تيسير الله تعالى للعلم، وبين ما نبه العلم عليه من النهوض الى ما بقي . . . . .

[1] MS. وجب

نسخة كتاب الجنيد إلى أبي يعقوب يوسف بن الحسين الرازي رحمهما الله تعالى

كشف الحق لك عن حقيقة أنبائه، وتولاك بعظيم منته وآلائه، وتضمنك في ضمه إياك إلى سوابغ نعمائه، وجرت عليك برفعه لك إليه وإعلائه، فكنت بحيث لا تكون الأغيار لك إليه سببا، بل تكون بما يوجد به منك منتسبا، قد أخلصك بما اصطفاك به من خلصاء صفوته، وأوحدك بالانتحال[1] ممن خصه بولايته، وتخيرك بالاجتباء من كبراء أهل مودته، الذين آثرهم بالاصطفاء لعظيم خلته، فكانت أوائل أقدامهم المجردة لديه، الموضوعة على مناهج الورود عليه، النزوع عما دونه إليه، فسبقت إليه به كل سابق، وسمت إليه وحده عن سنيات المطالب، على أنوار فواتح البذل، تخر عليهم خريرا، وتدر بمنائح الأفضال عليهم درورا، بسكب غيث هاطل منهمل، ومدرار غلف بغرائب البر متصل، [43a] يذهل ببوادي وروده عقول من لاحظه به، ويبهر بأوائل شهوده من أراده له، فإلى أين وبماذا يتخطى[2] ذلك قلوب المكرمين به، وكيف وأنى تتحاماه عقول المصادفين له، وذلك لا يكون بفعل مكون، وإن كان مكرما، ولا ينفذ عنه بتخطيه سر ولي وإن كان ممكنا، ولن يحمل ذلك عن أهل مجالسه وأنسه إلا الحامل بقوته وقدرته حملة عرشه، فهو ولي المحاماة عمن اصطنعه لنفسه، فعند ذلك إذا أراد ذلك دعا إلى

[1] MS. واوجدك كما بالانتحال

[2] MS. يتخطا

إخلاص ذكره، وأقبل بمن تفرد به عليه، وأوى[1] بمن استأثر بمكنون سره إليه، فكان ما جمعه لأهل الزلفى لديه والمقربين عنده لهم تبعا، وسائر أوليا ه فيما عاطفوا من ذلك شيعا. لهم منه ما بذله من عظيم عطائه، وجاد به من جليل مننه وآلائه، فذلك حظهم المبذول، وعطاؤهم الدائم الموصول، وذلك كله على عظيم قدره، وجليل ما خصهم الله تعالى به من نفيس بره، حجاب عما أخلص به المنفردين بخالص ذكره، مع حقيقة وجود ذلك، والكون بالنزول فيما هنالك يبدو[2] أوائل علم من تفرد به وأراده بالاختصاص لما يوجد له، ولن يصلح لمعاينة ذلك عين بقيت عليها منها بقية، ولن يلامح طرف مواقع لرزية، جعلنا الله واياك يا أخي ممن اصطنعه لنفسه، واستأثر به عمن دونه.

كتابي إليك يا أخي وسبل الحق مسهلة المناهج، وطرق الرشد زاهرة قد وطئت بالتمهيد لأقدام السالكين، وفسحت بالتوسعة لسير الطالبين، وزينت ببهجات الأنوار لقلوب الراغبين، وهي مع ذلك لقلة القاصدين إليها ولقلة السائرين بالصدق عليها، كالعشار المتعطلة، والمواطن القفار الخربة، ليس لها على ما عظّم الله من قدرها، ووعد من جزيل الثواب على سلوكها، من أكثر الناس عامر، ولا في عظيم خطرها من الخلق راغب، واني أرى العلم مع كثرة منتحليه وانتشار طالبيه [44 ٨] بقلة صدقهم في قصده، وتركهم العمل بواجب حقه، كالعازب المتغرب البعيد المنفرد، وأرى الجهل والدعاوى على كثير من الناس غالبا، وقلة العلم للمنتحلين للعمل بيّنة،[3] وأرى هموم أكثر الخليقة على الدنيا عاكفة، ولما تعجل من حطامها

[1] MS. واوا [2] MS. يبدوا [3] MS. بين

طالبة ، ولقليل ما تعجل منها مؤثرة ، وقد انكفت العقول والقلوب بالانكباب على طلبها ، وانصرفت إلى الرغبة فى القليل منها ، وأراهم بشر المراد وكثرة الفساد وقلة العمل للمعاد ، فى غمرة سكرتها ، وحيرة هوالك ما استولى عليهم منها ، ليس فيهم لغلبة ذلك عليهم مفيق ، ولا راجع إليك أن وعظته بتحقيق ، قد اشتملت عليهم الفتنة بالعاجلة فتحيرت عقولهم عن أمور الآجلة . وبالخلق يا أخى إذا كانوا كذلك أشد الحاجة الى عالم رفيق ، ومؤدب مناصح شفيق ، وواعظ يدلهم على الطريق ، وأنت يا أخى رضى الله عنك بقية ممن مضى ، وأحد من يشار إليه من العلماء ، وجليل من أكابر الحكماء ، وقد علمت رضى الله عنك أن الله عزّ وجلّ قد أخذ الميثاق على أهل معرفته وأولى العلم به الذين آثرهم بكتابه ، وفتح لهم فى الفهم عنه ، وخصهم بما استخلصهم به من تبيان ، وقلدهم من عظيم آماناته أن يبيّنونه للناس ولا يكتمونه ، وقال جلّ ثناؤه « والربانيون والأحبار بما استحفظوا من كتاب اللّه[1] » ، وقال تعالى « لولا ينهاهم الربانيون والأحبار عن قولهم الاثم وأكلهم السحت لبئس ما كانوا يصنعون »[2] وأنت يا أخى أحد من بقى ممن قلد من ذلك ما قلدوه ، وعرف من أنباء الحكم بعض ما عرفوه ، وعليك عندى تبيان ما وهبه اللّه جلّ ثناؤه لك ، والقول بعظيم ما أنعم به عليك ، فاعدل رضى اللّه عنك الى المريدين بهمك ، واقبل عليهم بوجهك ، وانصرف [44B] إليهم بحجتك واعطف عليهم بفضلك وأثر على غيرهم بدلالتك ، وجميل دعايتك ، وابذل لهم منافعهم من علمك ومكين معرفتك ، وكن معهم فى ليلك ونهارك ، وخصهم

[1] Qur. v, 47 [2] Ibid. 66

بما عاد به عليك ولك، فذلك حق القوم منك، وحظهم مما وجب لهم عليك؛ أما سمعت الله جل ثناؤه وذكره وهو يقول لأعظم خلقه عنده قدرا، وأعلاهم لديه منزلا « واصبر نفسك مع الذين يدعون ربهم بالغداة والعشي يريدون وجهه ولا تعد عيناك عنهم تريد زينة الحياة الدنيا ولا تطع من أغفلنا قلبه عن ذكرنا واتبع هواه وكان أمره فرطا وقل الحق من ربكم »[1] فهذه وصية الله جلّ ثناؤه لنبيه المجتبى محمد صلى الله عليه وسلم المصطفى.
يا أخي رضي الله عنك لم أنبهك على حظ كنت عنه غافلا، ولا على أمر رأيتك عنه مقصرا، وأعيذك بالله من كل هفوة وتقصير، وعن كل نقص وفتور، لكن الله عزّ وجلّ يقول « وذكّر فإن الذكرى تنفع المؤمنين »[1]. وقد بدأتك بكتابي هذا متوسلا به إلى مواصلتك، ومستزيدا به من إقبالك عليّ ومؤانستك، ومتسببا به إلى مكاتبتك، فكن حيث أحببته منك، وزدني فيما رغبت فيه إليك، جعلك الله سببا لنفع إخوانك، ومع ذلك يا أخي هديت لرشدك، فقد سنح لي شيء أريد أن أقوله، بدأت بنفسي فيه قبلك، وأحب أن أكون فيه تبعا لك بعدك، وأقدم مع ذلك الاعتذار إليك، إن لم يقع مقبولا لديك، فخذه إن كان له في الحق موضعا، وكن له على المناصحة مستمعا، فهو لك مني على المناصحة مبذول، وإن رددته علي فهو لدي مقبول، يا أخي رضي الله عنك كن على علم بأهل دهرك، ومعرفة بأهل وقتك وعصرك، وابدأ في ذلك أولا بنفسك، وكن عاطفا بعد احكامك فيه بحالك....

[1] Qur. li, 55

[54b] بسم الله الرحمن الرحيم

الحمد لله وصلواته على محمد وآله وسلم تسليما

كتاب الفناء

كلام الإمام أبى القاسم الجنيد بن محمد قدس الله روحه: الحمد لله الذى قطع العلائق عن المنقطعين اليه، ووهب الحقائق للمتصلين به المعتمدين عليه، حين أوجدهم ووهب لهم حبه، فأثبت العارفين فى حزبه، وجعلهم درجات فى مواهبه، وأراهم قوة أبداها عنه، ووهبهم[1] منه من فضله، فلم تعترض عليهم الخطرات بملكها، ولم تلتق بهم الصفات المسببة للنقائص فى نسبتها، لانتسابهم الى حقائق التوحيد، بنفاذ التجريد، فيما كانت به الدعوة، ووجدت به أسباب الحظوة[2] من بوادى الغيوب وقرب المحبوب؛ ثم سمعته يقول: وهبنيه ثم استتر بى عنى فأنا أضرّ الأشياء عليّ، الويل لى منى، أكادنى وعنه بى خدعنى، كان حضورى سبب فقدى، وكانت متعتى بمشاهدتى كمال جهدى. فالآن عدمت[3] قواى لعناء[4] سرى. لا أجد[5] ذوق الوجود ولا أحلو[6] من تمكين الشهود، ولا أجد نعيما من جنس النعيم، ولا [أجد] التعذيب من جنس التعذيب، فطارت

1 MS. ووهبه 2 Margin. Text has الحظره 3 Margin. Text has عزمت 4 Thus the text. Margin amend to لفناء 5 Margin. Text has لاجد 6 MS. أخلوا

المذاقات عنى ، وتفانت اللغات من وصفى،[1] فلا صفة تُبدى ولا داعية تُحدى . كان الأمر فى إبدائه كما لم يزل فى ابتدائه. قلت : فما أبان منك هذا النطق ولا صفة تبدو[2] ولا داعية تحدو؟[3] قال : نطقت بغيبتى عن حالى،[4] ثم أبدى[5] علىّ من شاهد قاهر وظاهر شاهر [55a] . أفنانى بإنشائى كما انشانى بديًا فى حال فنائى ، فلم أوثر[6] عليه لبراءته من الآثار ، ولم ولم اخبر عنه إذ كان متوليا للإخبار . أليس[7] قد محى رسمى بصفته ، وبامتحائى فات علمى فى قربه ، فهو المبدئ كما هو المعيد . قلت : فما قولك افنانى بإنشائى كما أنشانى بديا فى حال فنائى ؟ قال : أليس تعلم أنه عز وجل قال " وإذ أخذ ربك من بنى آدم " الى قوله " نشهدنا " [8] فقد أخبرك عز وجل أنه خاطبهم وهم غير مرجودين إلا بوجوده لهم ، إذ كان واجدا للخليقة بغير معنى وجوده لأنفسها ، بالمعنى الذى لا يعلمه غيره ، ولا يجده سواه ، فقد كان واجدا محيطا شاهدا عليهم بديا فى حال فنائهم عن بقائهم ، الذين كانوا [فى الأزل] [9] للأزل ، فذلك هو الوجود[10] الربانى والإدراك الإلهى الذى لا ينبغى إلا له جل وعز ؛ ولذلك قلنا إنه إذا كان واجدا للعبد يجرى عليه مراده من حيث يشاء بصفته المتعالية التى لا يشارك فيها ، كان ذلك الوجود أتم الوجود وأمضاه لا محالة ، وهو أولى وأغلب وأحق بالغلبة والقهر وصحة الاستيلاء على

[1] MS. وضعى [2] MS. تبدوا [3] MS. تحدوا [4] MS. مالى [5] MS. أبدا
[6] MS. اوشر [7] MS. ليس [8] Qur'an vii. 171. [9] Added in Kitab Al Mithaq, 58 b. [10] MS. الموجود

ما يبدو[1] عليه، حتى يمحي[2] رسمه عامة ويذهب وجوده، إذ لا صفة بشرية ووجود ليس يقوم به لما ذكرنا، تعاليا من الحق وقهره، [3]إنما هذا تلبس[3] على الأرواح [ما لها من الأزلية][4] نعيم ليس [من] جنس النعيم المعقول، وسخاء بالحق لا من جنس السخاء المعلوم، إذ كان عزّ وجلّ لا يحس ولا يُحس ولا يبدل ذاتيته، ولا يعلم أحد كيفية لطائفه فى خلقه، وإنما معنى ذلك ربانى لا يعلمه[5] غيره ولا يقدر [55b] عليه إلا هو، ولهذا قلنا إن الحق أفنى[6] ما بدا عليه، وإذا استولى كان أولى[7] بالاستيلاء وأحق بالغلبة والقهر. قلت: فما يجد أهل هذه الصفة، وقد محوت اسم وجودهم وعلومهم؟ قال وجودهم بالحق بهم وما بدا عليهم بقول وسلطان غالب، لا ما طالبوه فأذكروه وتوهموه بعد الغلبة، فيمحقها ويفنيها، فإنه غير متشبث بهم ولا منسوب اليهم، وكيف يصفون أو يجدون مالم يقوموا فيحملوه، أو يقاربوه فيعلموه، وإن الدليل على ذلك من الخبر الموجود، أليس قد روي عن النبى صلى الله عليه وسلم أنه قال: قال الله عزّ وجلّ "لا يزال عبدى يتقرب إليّ بالنوافل حتى أحبه فاذا أحببته كنت سمعه الذى يسمع به وبصره الذى يبصر به". وفى الحديث زيادة فى الكلام غير أنى قصدت الحجة منه فى هذا الموضع؛ فإذا كان سمعه الذى يسمع به وبصره الذى يبصر به

1 يبدوا 2 MS. تمحا 3-3 MS. فاذا كان هذا تلبسا 4 Added in Kitab Al Mithaq, 58b 5 MS. يعلم 6 MS. أفنا 7 MS. أولا

فكيف تكيّف ذلك بكيفيته أو تحده بحد تعلمه؟ ولو ادعى ذلك مدع[1] لأبطل فى دعواه ، لأنا لا نعلم ذلك كائنا بجهة من الجهات تعلم أو تعرف ، وإنما معنى ذلك أنه يؤيده ويوفقه ويهديه ويشهده ما شاء كيف شاء بإصابة الصواب وموافقة الحق، وذلك فعل الله عزّ وجلّ فيه ومواهبه له،[2] منسوبة اليه لا الى الواجد لها ، لأنها لم تكن عنه ولا منه ولا به ، وإنما كانت [3]واقعة عليه[3] من غيره ، وهى لغيرها أولى وبه أحرى، وكذلك[4] جاز أن تكون بهذه الصفة الخفية، وهى غير منتسبة به على النحو الذى ذكرناه . [56a] قلت: كيف يكون الحضور سبب الفقد والمتعة بالمشاهدة كمال الجهد، وإنما علم الناس ها هنا أنهم يتمتعون ويجدون بالحضور، لا يجهدون فى ذلك ولا يفقدون؟ قال: ذلك علم العامة المعروف، وسبيل وجودهم الموصوف، فأما أهل الخاصة والخاصة المختصة، الذين غُربوا لغربة أحوالهم ، فإن حضورهم فقد، ومتعتهم بالمشاهدة جهد لأنهم قد محوا عن كل رسم ومعنى يجدونه[5] بهم أو يتشهدونه[6] من حيث هم، بما استولى عليهم فمحاهم، وعن صفاتهم[7] أفناهم، حتى قام بهم وقام عنهم بما لهم ، وثبت دواعى[8] ذلك عليهم وفيهم من جنس كماله وتمامه، فوجدوا النعيم به غيبا بأمتع الوجود على غير سبيل الوجود، لاستئثار[9] الحق واستيلاء القهر، فلما

[1] MS. مدعى [2] MS. وما وهبه [3-3] MS. واقفة به [4] MS. وكما
[5] MS. يجدوه [6] MS. يشهدوه [7] MS. صفاته [8] MS. رواع [9] MS. لاستينار

فقدت الأرواح النعيم الغيبي الذى لا تحاسه النفوس ولا تقاربه[1] المحسوس ، ألفت فناها عنها ووجدت بقاها يمنعه فناها. فإذا أحضرها أنيتها[2] وأوجدها جنسها،[3] استترت بذلك عما كانت به وكان بها ، فغصت[4] بنفسها وألفت بجنسها ، إذ أفقدها التمام الأول والاكرام الأكمل ، وردت الى تعلم وتعقل ، فالحسرة فيها مستكنة وغصة الفقد بها متصلة فى حال حضورها وكائن وجودها ، ولذلك تاقت الى الشهوة ورجعت الى الحاجة . وكيف لا يكلمها اخراجها[5] بعد غيابها وتوقانها بعد امتلائها . فمن ههنا عرجت نفوس العارفين الى الأماكن النضرة والمناظر الأنيقة[6] والرياض الخضرة ، وكان ما سوى ذلك عذابا عليها[7] مما تحن اليه من أمرها الأول الذى تشمله الغيوب ويستأثر به المحبوب. ويحك إن اشارته [566] الى الصفة إشارة لا يشارك فيها ، ومراده فيها ومنها هوما استأثر به عليها . فمن كان مستترا أو ذاكرا لها أو مختصا بها ، كان لا ينبغى للمراد بذلك حضور البوادى عليه ولا البواعث منه اليه ، فتأمن[8] صفته عن الفناء بحقيقته،[9] ذاهبا[10] عن الحضور ما هو به ، اقتدارا من الغالب له القائم به المستولى عليه . حتى إذا أحضر وأشهد ضمن حضوره الاستتار[11] وامحت فى شهوده الآثار،[12] حتى لا يجد السبيل الى درك الشفاء على خالص الوجود المستولى عليه [13]من الحق تعالى[13] كذلك يرى[14] فى صفته

[1] MS. تقاومه [2] MS. البتها [3] MS. جبسها [4] MS. فعصت
[5] MS. ما اخرجها [6] Margin Text has الأنقة [7] MS. عليهم
[8] MS. فيا من [9] MS. بحققته [10] MS. وذاهبا [11] MS. الاستار [12] MS. فى الاثار
[13-13] MS. تعالى من الحق [14] MS. ير

العليا وأسمائه الحسنى![1] وإنما جرت سنة[2] البلاء على أهل البلاء من ههنا، حتى جاذبوا وأقاموا ولم يتخدعوا، أقيم عليهم ما محقهم فى نفس القوة وعلو المرتبة وشرف النسبة.

قلت: فما أعجب ما أخبرتنى به وإن أهل هذه النسبة العالية ليجرى عليهم البلاء؟ فكيف ذلك حتى أعلمه؟ قال: افهم: لما طلبوه فى مراده ومانعوه عن أنفسهم، فطلبوا له فى استيلائه[3] عليهم ببساط البلاء على صفاتهم، لأن لذة الأشياء فيهم سترهم به ليقضوا[4] بأنيتهم ويحترفوا[5] بحسوسهم ويلذوا[6] برؤية[7] أنفسهم فى مواطن الفخر ونتائج الذكر وغلبات القهر. وأنّى لك بعلم ذلك، وليس يعلمه إلا أهله ولا يجده سواهم ولا يطيقه غيرهم. أو تدرى لما[8] طالبوه ومانعوه فتوسلوا بما منه بدا اليه واستعانوا فى التوسل بالحقائق عليه؟ لأنه أوجدهم وجوده لهم وثبت فيهم وعليهم غيب سرائره الواصلة اليه، فامتحت[9] الآثار، وانقطعت[10] الأوطار، حتى [57a] توالت النسب، وتعالت الرتب، بفقدان الحس وفناء النفس.

ثم أحضرهم[11] الفناء فى فنائهم، وأشهدهم الوجود فى وجودهم؛ فكان ما أحضرهم منهم وأشهدهم[12] من أنفسهم سترًا خفيًا وحجابًا لطيفًا، أدركوا به غصة الفقد وشدة الجهد، لاستتار ما لا تلحق به العلل، إحضار ما يلحق العلل به وتليق الآثار بصفته. فطالبوه

[1] MS. الحسنا [2] MS. سنت [3] MS. اسنيلاه [4] MS. اليقضون [5] MS. ويحترفون [6] MS. ويلذون [7] MS. برية [8] MS. لمن [9] MS. فامتحا [10] MS. وانقطع [11] MS. أحضرها [12] MS. واشهد

فيما كان مطالبهم ، وما يعرفه[1] من نفوسهم ، لأنهم حلوا بمحل القوة ، ونالوا حقائق الحظوة ، فأقيم عليهم مشتغلا لهم ، فنشأ منه فيهم تمام كان ولا كان على الصفة ، وإن كانت غصة[2] البلاء تزيد. قلت : فصف لى تلوين البلاء عليهم فى موطنهم العجيب ومنزلهم القريب. قال: إنهم استغنوا بما كان بدا ، فخرجوا عن الفاقة ، وتاركوا المطالعة ، وألبسوا الظفر بجهد الاقتدار وصولة الافتخار ، وكانوا بذلك ناظرين الى الأشياء بما لهم ، دون التعريج على ما له ، بإقامة الفرق والفصل ، لما رأوا ووجدوا[3] بالعينين ، فاستولى بالأمرين[4] ، فإذا بدت عليهم بوادى الحق ، ألجأ منه لهم ما لهم ، على التجريد اقتدارا وافتخارا . خرجوا عن ذلك غير مشاكيين له ، مؤثرين لما انفردت به متعتهم ، دالة عليه ويقينا بالسماحة ، لا يرون رجوعا عليهم ولا مطالبة تجرى عليهم . فإذا كان ذلك أحاط بهم المكر من حيث لا يعلمون .

قلت : قد أغربت على عقلى ، وزدت فى خبالى[5] فادن من فهمى. قال : إن أهل البلاء[6] لما اتصلوا بحادث الحق فيهم ،[7] وجارى حكمه عليهم ، تغربت أسرارهم ، وتاهت أرواحهم عمر الأبد ، لا تأويها المواطن ولا تجنّها الأماكن ، تحنّ الى مبتليها حنينا ، وتئن[8] [57b] بفناء النائى عنها أنينا ، قد شجاها فقدانها وذلها[9] وجدانها ، أسوفة عليه ، موجعة لديه ، متشوقة فى الوجد اليه ، أعقبها بها

[1]MS. يعرفها [2]MS. عنده [3]MS. يوجد [4]MS. الامرين [5]MS. حبابى [6]MS. البلى [7]MS. فيها [8]MS. تان [9]MS. وذللها

ظمأ، ويزيد الظمأ فى أحشائها نماء، فهى الكلفة بمعرفتها، السخينة بفقدها. أقام لها عطشها اليه مع كل مأتم مأتما، ورفع لها فى كل كسوة علما، يذيقها طعم الفقر، ويجدد عليها رؤية احتمال الجهد، مالة مع آثار المؤن، تواقة الى [1] مثلات الشجى [1] طلابة لشفائها، متعلقة بآثار المحبوب فيما يبدو، [2] وكل إبعاد تراه بعين الدنو. خفيت [3] خفاء لفقد سترها فما استترت، وابتلاها فما نكلت. وكيف تستتر، وهى مأسورة لديه، محتسبة له بين يديه. سمحت له بهلاكها فيما أبدى عليها من ابتلائها، ولم تعزم على الاهتمام بأنفسها استغناء بحبه وتعلقا به فى محل قربه. ترى مقادير الألحاظ منه فى سرعة يقظتها، يستغرق هلاكها بالجارى عليها فى دوام البقاء وتشديد البلاء، [4] حتى امتنعها بلاؤها، وآنسها به بقاؤها، لما رأته قريبا لمنعها واتيا بلسعتها. فلم تلو عن حمله كلا لا ولا برمت به ملالا. هم الأبطال فيما جرى عليهم لما أسر اليهم. أقاموا فى قهره، انتظار أمره، ليقضى الله أمرا كان مفعولا.

وأهل البلاء [5] يقسمون [6] على قسمين: فمنهم من أوى [7] الى بلائه، فساكن مراده، وما بلى هواه فى الأشياء إيثارا لمتعة نفسه وتمتعه بوجود حسه حتى انكى [8] به ومكر به وأزال بالمكر عنه مزايلة حالة، واعتد ببلائه شرفا، ورأى [9] أن سبب الخروج عنه سبب النقصان والضعف...

[1-1] MS. ممثلات الشجا [2] MS. يبدوا [3] MS. حلف [4] MS. البلى
[5] MS. البلى [6] MS. يقسموا [7] MS. أوا [8] MS. الجا [9] MS. وروى

تم كتاب الفناء وكانت النسخة المنقول منها نسخة أعجمية كثيرة السقم جدا فلتتوقع نسخة مرضية للتصحيح بها إن شاء الله . والحمد لله وصلواته على سيدنا محمد وآله وصحبه وسلم

[58A] بسم الله الرحمن الرحيم

ومن كلام الجنيد رحمه الله فى قوله تعالى « وإذ أخذ ربك »[1]
قال كاتبه : يليق بهذا الكتاب أن يسمى « كتاب الميثاق »
ولسهل رحمه الله كلام فى ذلك سمي بكتاب الميثاق

الحمد لله الذى جعل ما أنعم على عباده من إبزاغ نعمته دليلا هاديا لهم إلى معرفته ، بما أفادهم به من الأفهام والأوهام التى يفهمون بها رجع الخطاب ؛ أحمده دائما ديموميا ، وأشكره شكرا قائما قيوميا[2] ؛ وأشهد أن لا إله إلا الله الفرد الفريد الأحد الوحيد الصمد القدوس ، وأشهد أن محمدا صلى الله عليه وسلم الكامل بالنبوة والتام للرسالة صلى الله عليه وعلى آله أجمعين .

ثم إن لله عز وجل صفوة من عباده وخلصاء من خلقه ، انتخبهم للولاية واستخلصهم للكرامة وأفردهم به له ، جعل أجسامهم دنيوية[3] وأرواحهم نورانية وأوهامهم روحانية وأفهامهم عرشية وعقولهم حجبية ؛ جعل أوطان أرواحهم غيبية فى مغيب الغيب . جعل لهم تسرحا فى غوامض غيوب الملكوت ؛ ليس لهم مأوى[4] إلا إليه ، ولا مستقر إلا عنده ؛ أولئك الذين أوجدهم لديه فى كون الأزل عنده ومراكب الأحدية لديه ؛ حين دعاهم فأجابوا سراعا ، كرما منه عليهم وتفضلا ؛ أجاب به عنهم حين أوجدهم ؛ فهم الدعوة منه ؛ وعرفهم نفسه حين

[1] Qur. vii, 171 [2] MS. قيوميا . Corrected in margin [3] MS. دنيابيه
[4] MS. مأوا

لم يكونوا إلا مشيئة أقامها بين يديه ؛ نقلهم بإرادته ثم جعلهم كذر أخرجهم بمشيئته خلقا فأودعهم صلب آدم عليه السلام فقال جلّ وعزّ « وإذ اخذ ربك من بنى آدم من ظهورهم ذريتهم وأشهدهم على أنفسهم ألست بربكم »[1] فقد أخبر جلّ ذكره أنه خاطبهم وهم غير موجودين إلا بوجوده لهم، إذ كانوا واجدين للحق من غير وجودهم لأنفسهم، فكان[2] الحق بالحق فى ذلك [58a] موجودا بالمعنى الذى لا يعلمه غيره ولا يجده سواه ؛ فقد كان واجدا[3] محيطا شاهدا عليهم برأهم فى حال فنائهم، الذين كانوا فى الأزل للأزل أولئك هم الموجودون الفانون فى حال فنائهم الباقون فى بقائهم ؛ أحاطت بهم صفات الربانية وآثار الأزلية وأعلام الديمومية ؛ أظهر[4] هذه عليهم لما أراد فناءهم[5] ليديم بقاءهم[6] هناك، وليفسحهم فى علم الغيب غيبه ؛ وليريهم غوامض مكنونات علمه ويجمعهم به. ثم فرقهم ثم غيبهم فى جمعهم وأحضرهم فى تفريقهم، فكان غيبهم سبب حضورهم وحضورهم سبب غيبهم. اختطفهم بالشواهد البادية[7] منه عليهم حين أحضرهم، واستلبهم عنها حين غيبهم ؛ أكمل فناءهم[8] فى حال بقائهم وبقاءهم[9] فى حال فنائهم. أحاطت الأمور بهم حين أجرى عليهم مراده من حيث يشاء بصفته المتعالية التى لا يشارك فيها. فكان[10] ذلك الوجود أتم الوجود، وهو أولى وأعلى وأحق بالقهر والغلبة وصحة الاستيلاء على ما بدا منه عليهم حتى يمحى أثرهم ويمتحى رسومهم ويذهب وجودهم ؛ إذ لا صفة بشرية ولا وجود معلومية

[1] Qur. vii, 171 [2] MS. كان [3] MS. وافرا, see Kitāb al-Fanā' [4] MS. ظهر [5] MS. فناهم [6] MS. بقاهم [7] MS. البادى [8] MS. فناهم [9] MS. بقاؤهم [10] MS. كان

ولا أثر مفهومية ؛ إنما هي تلبيسات[1] على الأرواح ما لها من الأزلية ؛ ذوق وجود نعيم لا كالنعيم ؛ مستحيلة في المعاني متفقة الأسامي متصادقة في ذوق نعيمها متلونة في رسوم شواهدها ، تبدو[2] بنعيمها في طوالع شواهدها وتتلون في ذوق مرارات طعمها ؛ لَهَجُ أفكارهم في محبوبهم وتدمّت أذكارهم في أسرارهم ؛ هاجت عليهم عند ذلك بحار الغيرة تتلاطم أمواجها ، عَظُم البلاء عند تصفحهم لواردها ، واضمحلت نفوسهم عند توقعهم إياها ، وقام عليهم كل معلوم نكرا وثبت كل نكر[59A] معلوما ؛ برزوا بعلم الحقيقة لدى[3] الحق ؛ حين أوجدهم حقيقة الحق نسبة منه لا الى الواحد لها ؛[4] كان ذلك كمال الجهد لديه ، ثم لم يجعل لبلائهم أسامي ليستريحون ؛ ولا لجهدهم معلوما فيتنعمون ؛ شغل بعضهم عن بعض ؛ وأفرد بعضهم عن بعض ؛ فهم في حضورهم فقدٌ ؛ وفي متعتهم بالمشاهدة كمال الجهد ، لأنه قد محى عنهم كل رسم ومعنى يجدونه[5] بهم ؛ ويشهدونه[6] من حيث هم لما استولى عليهم فمحاهم وعن صفاتهم أفناهم ، وإنما معنى ذلك أن تؤدي الحقيقة من الحق ما يشاء ، كيف أثبت بهم وعليهم وقام عنهم بما لهم وثبت دواعي[7] ذلك عليهم وفيهم من جنس كماله وتمامه ، فوجد النعيم من غير جنس النعيم ووجد البلاء في معلوم النعيم ووجد الوجود في غير سبيل الوجود ، باستتار الحق واستيلاء القهر ، فلما فقدت الأرواح النعيم الغيبي الذي لا تحاسه النفوس ولا تقارنه المحسوس ، ألقت فناها عنها وطرحتهم في مفاوز مهلكات بلواها ، ثم ألفت بعد إلفهم

[1] MS. ملبوسات [2] MS. تبدوا [3] MS. لدا [4] MS. واجده إليه [5] MS. يجدوه [6] MS. يشهدوه [7] MS. رواع

للفناء فناء، لأن لا يجدوا طعم معلوم ولا يستريحوا الى موجود، امتلأ بهم بلا إشارة إلى صفاتهم، ولا رسوم من رسوم الموصوفات ولا البواعث منه إليها، وامتحت شواهده في الآثار حين لا يوجد السبيل إلى درك الشفاء على خالص الوجود المستولى عليه من الحق تعالى[1]، كذلك مَن في صفته العليا وقوة شاهده بوارد سلطانه؛ وإنما جرت سنة البلاء على أهل البلاء، حين جاذبوا وأقاموا[2] وثبتوا ولم يتخدعوا، أُقيم عليهم ما محقهم في نفس القوة وعلو المرتبة وشرف المنزلة وسناء النسبة، ثم أحضرهم الفناء في فنائهم وأشهدهم الوجود في وجودهم، فكان ما أحضرهم منهم وأشهدهم الوجود في وجودهم [سترا خفيا وحجابا لطيفا][3] أدركوا به عظيم الفقد [59a] وشدة الاستينار ما لا يليق به العلم ولا [تليق][4] الآثار بصفته، فطالبوه فيما كان مطالبهم، ومانحوه ما كان مانحهم، وتعرفوا منه ما عرفوه إليهم لا بهم، حلوا بمحل القوة، ونالوا حقائق الحظوة، وتعالوا إلى حقيقة الحضرة، فأقام عليهم شاهدا منه فيهم، وأدركوا منه به ما أدركوا، وأوقف كل واحد منهم عند إدراكه، وأفرد كل ما انفرد منه تعالى الله عن صفة الخلائق، وعز أن تشتبه به الخلائق علوا كبيرا.

تم بحمد الله ومنّه

[1] MS. تعالى من الحق [2] MS. وقالوا [3] Added from Kitāb al-Fanā' [4] Added from Kitāb al-Fanā'

[59B] بسم الله الرحمن الرحيم

ومن كلام الجنيد قدس الله روحه
فى الألوهية

قال أبو القاسم الجنيد رحمه الله تعالى: اعتزل الحق بهم، وجرّد الألوهية لهم، فكان أول وارد الحق بتأدية شواهد إبرازه لهم وإنزاله إياهم فى أول الألوهية، أنزل الأزلية على سرمد الأبد، فى ديمومية البقاء إلى ما ليس له غاية ولا منتهى، ثم أتبع مع ذلك بشاهد منيع العز وطول الفخر وظهور القهر وشامخ العلو وقاهر السطوة وشدة الصولة وعظيم الكبرياء وجليل الجبرياء، فاعتزل منفردا بذلك وتكبر وتعالى بالعظمة، فكان الحق بالحق للحق قائما، وكان الحق بالحق للحكم حاكما، وتوحد فى تفرد جبروته أحداً فردا صمدا، وهذا أول شاهد إنزاله من أنزل فى غلبة هذا الاسم عليه وأحلّه به لديه، وتابع مع ذلك ما أمكن فى إجنان صونه به له من أسمائه الحسنى ما وقعت إليه الاشارة [60A] وما لم يقع من أسماء الجمع والتفرقة على ما شاء من الإبداء والإخفاء، فمنها ما بدت فى شواهدها، وظهرت فى مطالبها، وعلت فى مذاهبها، وسرحت فى مساكنها، وترددت فى مراكبها، ثم تفانت[1] النعوت بجواز الاحتواء على ما تكيفته الحقيقه فسترته، وكمنت فيه فغيبته، وطوت عليه فكتمته،

[1] MS. تفاقت

وتمكنت منه فأتلفته، وغلبت عليه فقهرته، ثم تذهب بواديها[1] على الانفصال من غير انفصام، وعلا بالإلف من غير جنس النظام، فعالى بظاهره وبظافر أبداه بتمكين أحكامه، فتصاول عند ذلك الصول، وتفاخر الفخر، وتقاهر القهر، فأين الأين عند ذلك وليس يحين أينه، وأين ذهاب الأين على دوام أزليته، وأين ما لا أين له ولا أين فيه على تفرد الألوهية، وهو بعض ما لوح الحق به فى اسم الجمع، ثم يجرى فيهم ما توقع منهم به النظر، فى شواهد ما لاقى[2] الحق به مَن هذا نعته على اسمه المنفرد وعلمه المجرد، فهذه إشارة ما لا يقع به الشرح أكثر، ثم لا ينال فهم ذلك من جنس الإشارة إلا بتقدم الكون فيما تقدم به النعت، وقد طويت[3] ما فيها ولم أفصح به فخذها من حيث لا تنال به إلا به إن أدرك الحق بإدراكك فى إدراكك، ومن بعض ما أوجد الحق فى اسم التفرقة أن حبس به إظهار ما ألبسهم وألبسهم إظهار ما به حبسهم، فكانوا فى إبدائه[4] شواهد مكنون إخفائه، فكلما طالعهم بما لاحظهم أرمس مستدرك المكان بكون خفي الكتمان، وهم فى شواهد ما يطالعهم به على ترادف ما أطلعهم به عليه، ثم يطالعهم فيما به يطالعهم، مطالعات سر المحتز المرتجف عليهم به فى إظهار ما كمنه، وذلك قبل أن يشرف [60 a] بهم[5] على حجاب غريب هذه الصفة، ثم يبدى[6] لهم شواهد البذل ومستعطفات سوابق الأمر، ويظهر لهم به عند إقباله به عليهم وإجلاله[7] منزلة لديهم بأنباء كون دوارك الوفاء، والاحتواء على كل محبوب ومطلوب ومرغوب، باستتمام كمال المصافاة واتحاد

[1] MS. بوادها [2] MS. لا قا [3] MS. طوى [4] MS. ابتدائه [5] MS. به [6] MS. يبدا
[7] MS. اجلاله

منح الموالاة ، ثم يعطف عليهم فى قرار أمن ما أحلهم فيه بإشهاده إياهم الغيبية عنهم ، والأخذ بما أقبل به عليهم ، وانتزاع لكل ما آنسهم من منحه وعطف عليهم به من بذله ، وأوقف عليهم لما يريد أن يبلغهم إليه ، ويطلبهم به ، أضداد الشواهد المتقدمة ، فلو رأيتهم بعين إشهاده إياهم وكون فيما فيه أحلهم ، لرأيت رهائن أشباح أسرى واجتناح جوائب[1] أرواح سرى ، قد رهقوا بالمحو[2] فى ملكوت عزه ، وأرهقوا بفرط ابتلاء الحق لهم بفقده ، مما هم به منه يصرخون ، وبه إليه فى غمرات الكرب يضجون ، قد جمع أنفاسهم فى أنفاسهم ، وحبس أرواحهم فى أرواحهم ، فهم به عليه يترددون ، ومنه به إليه يتوحدون ، وهذا بعض علم التوحيد مما لوح[3] إليه به صفوته . تم بحمد الله ومنه وصلى الله على محمد وآله وسلم تسليما .

وكانت نسخة الأصل أعجمية سقيمة
جدا فلتتوقع نسخة صحيحة للمقابلة
إن شاء الله تعالى

[1] MS. واجتياح جراقب [2] MS. بالحو [3] MS. لوج

من كلام الإمام أبى القاسم الجنيد بن محمد قدس الله روحه ونور ضريحه

فى الفرق بين الإخلاص والصدق

[61b]

بسم الله الرحمن الرحيم، الحمد لله وسلام على عباده الذين اصطفى.
قال الشيخ الإمام ابو القاسم الجنيد قدس الله روحه ونور ضريحه:- آنسك الله بقربه، وجدّد لك فى كل وقت من الزيادة فى برّه، وسترك فى ظلال جناح رحمته، وجعل مأواك فى جواره[1] الذى أسكن فيه[2] أرواح[3] أهل خاصّته، الذين تولاهم بحياطته، فلم يلحقهم لاحق، ولم يقطعهم قاطع، ولم يشغلهم شاغل؛ وصلى الله على نبيه وعلى أهل بيته وأصحابه وسلم. أمّا بعد فإنك سألت عن الفرق بين الإخلاص والصدق، فمعنى الصدق القيام على النفس بالحراسة والرعاية لها، بعد الوفاء منك بما عليك ممّا دلّك العلم عليه، فى إقامة حدود الأحوال فى الظاهر، مع حسن القصد إلى الله عزّ وجلّ فى أوّل الفعل؛ فالصدق موجود فى حقيقة صفات الإرادة، عند بداية الإرادة، بالقيام بما دُعيت إليه فى حقيقة إرادتك، ممّا طرق الحق لك اليه، والمبادرة فيه بالخروج عن موافقة النفس لطلب الراحة، مع انتصاب العلم

[1] MS. جوازه   [2] MS. فيها   [3] MS. ازواج

لك وموافقتك له، بخروجك من التأويل . فالصدق موجود قبل وجود حقيقة الإخلاص، وقد قال الله عزّ وجلّ « ليسأل الصادقين[1] » ثم سألهم بعد ما أوتوا بالصدق : ما أرادوا بصدقهم، وقد سمى الله الصادقين فى موضع آخر على غير هذا المعنى فقال عزّ وجلّ : « هذا يوم ينفع الصادقين صدقهم »[2] فكان الصدق فى الأوّل علما للخلق وفصلا بينهم وبين الإخلاص، لأن الإخلاص موجود فى صفة الخلق عند حالَيْن : حال الاعتقاد والنية، وحال الفعل والعمل [به 62] فالإخلاص فى صفة الصادق موجود فى العقد غير منسوب الى الصدق الّا بوجود[3] [أوائل الإخلاص فى باطنه][3]، وباق عليه علم موارد الأشياء عند ممارسة الفعل بالجوارح والتخلص لفعله عن عوارض اضداد الإخلاص حتى سمّى مخلصا . فأوّل الإخلاص أن يفرد الله تعالى بالإرادة، والثانى أن يخلص الفعل من الآفة، فالصدق الذى هو عند الخلق صدق، فرق بينه وبين الإخلاص، والصدق الذى عند الله تعالى هو الصدق مع الإخلاص، وقد يقال فلان صادق لما يرى عليه من صفات العلم وبذل المجهود منه، ولا يقال فلان مخلص لغيبة الخلق عن علم إخلاصه، فالصدق مشهود فى صفة الصادق، والإخلاص معدوم من مشهده، فالصادق موصوف بحسن صفات شاهده، منسوب الى الصدق بدلائل ظاهره، مع وجود أوائل الإخلاص فى باطنه، باق عليه علم

[1] Qur'ān xxxiii. 8 [2] Qur'ān v. 122 [3]–[3] Added as it is in the text after.

موارد الأشياء عند وروده ، يقبل[1] ما وافق الأول من معنى قصده ، ويردّ ما خالف علم ظاهره ، فالإخلاص يعلو[2] الصدق لوجود زيادة العلم ، مع وجود قوة الردّ لما عارض من وسواس العدو ، لوجود صفاء القلب ، ولا يعلو الإخلاص شئ ، لأنه لا غاية في العبودية من حيث العبد فوق الإخلاص ، ولا يقال إخلاص المخلص ، لأنه لا غاية بعد الإخلاص ، وقد قال الله تعالى « ليسأل الصادقين عن صدقهم » ولم يقل ليسأل المخلصين عن إخلاصهم ، لأن غايته من الخلق فيما استعبدهم به ، فالإخلاص[3] يعلو الصدق والصدق دونه .

والصدق على ثلاثة أشياء : صادق بلسانه ، وهو القائل بالحق له كان أم عليه بخروجه عن [62b] التأويل والتدليس ، وصادق في فعله ، وهو الباذل للمجهود من نفسه بإخراج وجود راحته ، وصادق بقلبه وهو القصد اليه في فعله ، فعند وجود هذه الخصال يكون صادقا ، مع أن الصدق موجود من الصادق في كلّ حال لا يستغنى عنه في حال من الأحوال . وقد فسرت جملة في أوّل الكتاب ، فالصدق في التورع والتزهد والزهد والتوكل والرضا والمحبّة والشوق والتوحيد لأهل الصلاة ، في صفات المريد والمراد ، والذاكر والمذكور ، وكلّ ذلك لا بد من أن يتولد له شاهد ظاهر يشهد له بالصدق . ومعنى الإخلاص إفراد النية لله عزّ وجلّ وحسن القصد اليه ،

[1] Margin text has يقول [2] MS. يعلم [3] MS. الاخلاص

بحضور العقل عند موارد الأشياء، وبيان تلوين الأمور عليه، بما وافق الأوّل فى معنى صحّة قصده، وردّ ما خالف ذلك من موارد النفس والعدو، مع ذهاب رؤية النفس بوجود رؤية المنّة، مع وجود حسن العزاء عند المذمّة من الخلق، لوجود حسن المعرفة بالفضل، ووجود الكراهة عند المحمدة، لخوف فساد المعرفة بذهاب رؤية الخلق عند مصادفة الأحوال، فهذا علم مشهود عند شاهد المخلص معدوم عند شاهد الخلق. فالصدق والإخلاص يتفقان فى حال المخلص، وينفرد الصدق بالصادق، مع أوّل وجود الإخلاص، فغاية وصف الموصوفين بالعبودية فى الاستعباد هو الإخلاص، والصادق فى حقيقة صدقه يتولى بالإخلاص، والمخلص فى حقيقة إخلاصه يُتَولّى بالكفاية، لوجود نفاذ البصيرة، وذو البصيرة فى حقيقة نفاذ بصيرته يُتَولّى [63a] بالحياطة من جميع ما يخشى فساده، ثم وقع الاستيلاء بالتولّى بعد ذلك، فقهر العقل فأفناه عن مقاومة الواجد. فعند وجود حقيقة التولّى بالخصوصية، خرج عن عبادته للّه بالنموسية، ودخل فى عبادته عزّ وجلّ بالوحدانية، فكان ذلك أوّل وجوده حقيقة توحيد الخصوص، بذهاب رؤية الأشياء لقيام رؤية الحق. فجرت الأحوال عليه فى مجارى صفاتها، (لمراد مليكه فيها، بسقوط صفاتها)[1] منها، فعند وصول العبد الى هذا، خرج عن صفة وجود ما يوصف بالعقل، فصارت عوارض العقل عند وجود حقيقة التوحيد، وساوس تحتاج الى أن يردّها، لأن العقل

[1] Added from the margin.

كان قيّم العبد عند قيام العبد بالمعبودية، من حيث العبد، فعند وقوع حقائق الملكة من الله عزّ وجلّ له، ذهب العبد فى العبودية من غير المعدن[1] الأوّل، فكان موجودا فى الصفة معدوما من المشرب، فصار عند ذلك موجودا مفقودا.

باب اخر فى التوحيد

اعلم أن أوّل عبادة الله عزّ وجلّ معرفته، وأصل معرفة الله توحيده، ونظام توحيده نفى الصفات عنه بالكيف والحيث والأين، فبه استدلّ عليه، وكان سبب استدلاله به عليه توفيقه، فبتوفيقه وقع التوحيد له، ومن توحيده وقع التصديق به، ومن التصديق به وقع التحقيق عليه، ومن التحقيق جرت المعرفة به، ومن المعرفة به وقعت الاستجابة له فيما دعا اليه، ومن الاستجابة له وقع الترقّى اليه، ومن الترقى اليه وقع الاتّصال به، ومن الاتصال به [63b] وقع البيان له، ومن البيان له وقع عليه الحيرة، ومن الحيرة ذهب عن البيان، ومن ذهابه عن البيان له انقطع عن الوصف له، وبذهابه عن الوصف وقع فى حقيقة الوجود له، ومن حقيقة الوجود وقع فى حقيقة الشهود بذهابه عن وجوده، ويتفقّد وجوده صفا وجوده، وبصفائه غيّب عن صفاته، ومن غيبته حضر بكليته، فكان موجودا مفقودا ومفقودا موجودا. فكان حيث لم يكن، ولم يكن حيث كان. ثم كان بعد ما لم يكن حيث كان كان، فهو

[1] Margin. Text has معدن

هو بعد ما لم يكن هو، فهو موجود موجود بعد ما كان موجودا مفقودا، لأنه خرج من سكرة الغلبة الى بيان الصحو، وتردّ عليه المشاهدة لإنزال الأُشياء منازلها ووضعها مواضعها لاستدراك صفاته، ببقاء آثاره والاقتداء بفعله، بعد بلوغه غاية ما له منه.

مسألة أُخرى

رجل انتصب له العلم بحقيقته، وانتصبت المطالبة عليه بحدّتها، وانتصب للعمل بكليته، فلم يقع الائتلاف بين الصفة والعلم فى المطالبة، فاستدرك عند الاختلاف بينهما مع حضوره وجمعه وانتصابه، علم مراد الرجوع الى الحق مع الانتصاب والحضور والجمع، فرجع اليه الصغار والذلّة والافتقار والقلّة بالسؤال، بحملان أثقال ما انتصب عليه من علم الحقيقة، فكان موجودا عندما انتصب له من العلم الثانى، بخروج صفته للعمل فيه، وغير واجدلما انتصب عليه من حقيقة علم الأوّل، لأُثقال ما انتصب عليه من شروط أحكامه، فاستدرك عند اجتماع العلمَيْن بوجود حقيقة الثانى وفقد حقيقة الأُوّل - عَلِمَ وقوع [ه64] البلاء بحقيقته؛ بتجرع كأس المراقبة لإيضاح بقايا صفاته وإيضاح خفايا طبعه، بالخروج الى صفاء حقيقة التوحيد، بانحطاط وقوع البلاء، على حسب ما تقدّم من الموافقة للصفة، بوجود لذّة الطبع، فخرج عند ذلك بفناء الصفة من الهوى، الى وقوع تجريد

الحكم على صفاء الصفة ، بذهاب الهوى ، فانبسط بالإشارة بالحقيقة الى الحق عند حوادث الأمور وتلوين الأشياء ، بذهاب الوسائط ، بوقوع صفاء الحكم على صفاء الصفة .

مسألة أُخرى

الخوف يقبضنى . والرجاء يبسطنى . والحقيقة تجمعنى . والحق يفرقنى . فإذا قبضنى بالخوف أفنانى عنى بوجودى ، فصاننى عنى . وإذا بسطنى بالرجاء ردّنى علىّ بفقدى ، فأمرنى بحفظى . وإذا جمعنى بالحقيقة أحضرنى فدعانى . وإذا فرقنى بالحق أشهدنى غيرى فغطانى عنه . فهو فى ذلك كلّه محركى غير ممسكى ، وموحشى غير مؤنسى ، بحضورى أذوق[1] طعم وجودى ، فليته أفنانى عنى فمتعنى . أو غيبنى عنى فروّحنى وللفناء أشهدنى . فنائى بقائى . ومن حقيقة فنائى أفنانى عن بقائى وفنائى فكنت عند حقيقة الفناء بغير بقاء ولا فناء ، بفنائى وبقائى لوجود الفناء والبقاء ، لوجود غيرى بفنائى .

مسألة أُخرى

اعلم أن دليل الخلق برؤية الصدق وبذل المجهود ، لإقامة حدود الأحوال بالتنقّل فيها ، لتؤديه حال الى حال ، حتى يؤديه الى حقيقة العبودة فى الظاهر ، بترك الاختيار والرضا بفعله ؛ وهذه مواضع [64b] قبول الخلق لدلائل صفات علم الظاهر[2]

[1] MS. لذوق [2] MS. الظاهره

عليه، واجتماع صفته، ثم تؤديه حقيقته الى مشاهدة الحق وإدراك إشارته إليه، بتلوين الأمور لاختيار اختياره لـه؛ وهذه مواضع ذهاب الخلق عنه، لتلوين صفاتـه فيهم، ومواضع تغييبه عنهم، وهذا مقام الاصطناع، قال الله عزّ وجلّ لموسى عليه السلام « واصطنعتك لنفسي »[1] فمن أين الى أين، فمنه واليه وله وبه فنى، وفى فناؤه، لبقـاء بقائه بحقيقة فنائه، فإن للحق فيه مرادًا، برده عليهم، أخرجه اليهم بتظاهر نعمائه عليه، فتلألأ سناء عطائه برد صفاته عليه لاستجلاب الخلق اليه وإحسانهم عليه.

مسألة أخرى

اعلم أنك محجوب عنك بك، وأنك لا تصل اليـه بك، ولكنك تصل إليه به، لأنه لمّا ابدى اليك رؤية الاتّصال به، دعاك الى طلب له فطلبته، فكنت فى رؤية الطلب برؤية الطلب والاجتهاد لاستدراك ما تريده بطلبك، كنت محجوبا، حتى يرجع الافتقار اليه فى الطلب، فيكون ركنك وعمادك فى الطلب بشدّة الطلب، وأداء حقوق ما انتخب[2] لك من علم الطلب، والقيام بشروط ما اشترط عليك فيه، ورعاية ما استرعاك فيه لنفسك، حماك عنك، فيوصلك بفنائك الى بقائك لوصولك الى بغيتك، فيبقى ببقائه، وذلك أن توحيد الموحِد باقٍ ببقاء الواحد، وإن فنى الموحِّد، فحينئذٍ أنت أنت، إذ كنت بلا أنت، فبقيت من حيث فنيت والفناء ثلاثة:

[1] Qur'ān XX 41 [2] MS. انتخت

فناء عن الصفات والأخلاق والطباع، بقيامك بدلائل [٥٤a] عملك، ببذل المجهود ومخالفة النفس، وحبسها بالمكروه عن مرادها. والفناء الثانى فناؤك عن مطالعة حظوظ، من ذوق الحلاوات واللذّات فى الطاعات، لموافقة مطالبة الحق لك، لانقطاعك اليه، لتكون بلا واسطة بينك وبينه. والفناء الثالث فناؤك عن رؤية الحقيقة من مواجيدك بغلبات شاهد الحق عليك، فأنت حينئذٍ فانٍ باقٍ، وموجود محقق لفنائك، بوجود غيرك عند بقاء رسمك بذهاب اسمك.

مسألة أُخرى

اعلم أن الناس ثلاثة: طالب قاصد، ووارد واقف، أو داخل قائم، أمّا الطالب لله عزّ وجلّ فإنّه قاصد نحوه، باسترشاد دلائل علم الظاهر، معامل الله عزّ وجلّ بجد ظاهره؛ أو وارد للباب واقف عليه، متبيّن لمواضع تقريبه إياه، بدلائل تصفية باطنه، وإدرار الفوائد عليه، معامل لله عزّ وجلّ فى باطنه، أو داخل بهمّه، قائم بين يديه، منتف عن رؤية ما سواه؛ ملاحظا لإشارته اليه، مبادرا فيما يأمره مولاه، فهذه صفة الموحِّد لله عزّ وجلّ.

مسألة أُخرى

اعلم أن التوحيد فى الخلق على أربعة أوجه: فوجه منها توحيد العوامّ، ووجه منها توحيد أهل الحقائق بعلم الظاهر،

ووجهان منها توحيد الخواصّ من أهل المعرفة؛ فأمّا توحيد العوامّ فالإقرار بالوحدانية بذهاب رؤية الأرباب والأنداد والأضداد[1] والأشكال والأشباه، والسكون الى معارضات الرغبة والرهبة ممن[2] سواه. فإن له حقيقة التحقيق فى الأفعال[3] ببقاء الإقرار. وأمّا توحيد حقائق علم الظاهر فالإقرار بالوحدانية بذهاب رؤية الأرباب والأنداد والأشكال والأشباه، مع إقامة الأمر والانتهاء عن النهى [65b] فى الظاهر، مستخرجة ذلك منهم من عيون الرغبة والرهبة والأمل والطمع، فإقامة حقيقة التحقيق فى الأفعال لقيام حقيقة التصديق بالإقرار. وأمّا الوجه الأوّل من توحيد الخاص فالإقرار بالوحدانية بذهاب رؤية هذه الأشياء مع إقامة الأمر فى الظاهر والباطن بإزالة[4] معارضات الرغبة والرهبة ممن سواه، مستخرجة ذلك من عيون الموافقة[5] بقيام شاهد الحق معه[5] مع قيام شاهد الدعوة والاستجابة. والوجه الثانى من توحيد الخاص، فشبح قائم بين يديه ليس بينهما ثالث، تجرى عليه تصاريف تدبيره، فى مجارى أحكام قدرته، فى لُجَج بحار توحيده، بالفناء عن نفسه وعن دعوة الحق له، وعن استجابته له، بحقائق وجود وحدانيته فى حقيقة قربه، بذهاب حسّه وحركاته، لقيام الحق له فيما أراده منه، والعلم فى ذلك أنّه رجع آخر العبد الى

[1] MS. واضداد [2] MS. مم [3] MS. والافعال [4] MS. بانزاله [5] MS. القيام شاهد الحق معه مع قيام شاهد الحق معه

أوّله ، أن يكون كما كان إذ كان قبل أن يكون ، والدليل فى ذلك قول الله عزّ وجلّ « وإذ أخذ ربّك من بنى آدم من ظهورهم ذرّياتهم وأشهدهم على أنفسهم ألست بربّكم قالوا بلى »[1] فمن كان وكيف كان قبل أن يكون ، وهل أجابت الّا الأرواح الطاهرة العذبة المقدسة ، بإقامة القدرة النافذة والمشيئة التامّة ، الآن كان إذ كان قبل أن يكون ؛ وهذا غاية حقيقة توحيد الموحِّد للواحد بذهب هو .

آخر مسألة التوحيد من كلامه رضى الله عنه

سئل الجنيد رحمه الله الى أين تنتهى عبادة أهل المعرفة بالله عزّ وجلّ ، فقال: الى الظفر بنفوسهم ، نصب الحق لهم أعمال أدلّة العمّال ، فوقفوا مع ماله دون التعريج على مالهم ، فتشوّق اليهم الأنبياء ، [66a] وانتسب[2] بهم للأولياء ، وسبحت لهم الملائكة ، فتركوا مالهم ووقفوا مع ما لله عزّوجلّ عليهم ،[3] وسائر الناس وقفوا مع مالهم وتركوا ما لله عزّوجلّ عليهم[3] فرد الله عزّوجلّ كلّا الى قيمته .

[1] Qur'ān vii. 171. [2] MS. والنسب [3] From the margin

أدب المفتقر إلى اللّـه

بسم الله الرحمٰن الرحيم

وسئل الشيخ أبو القاسم رحمه الله عن أدب المفتقر إلى اللّه عزّ وجلّ فقال: أن ترضى عن الله عزّ وجلّ في جميع الحالات، ولا تسأل أحدا سوى اللّه تعالى. وسئل عن خاطر الخير هل هو شيء واحد أو أكثر، فقال: قد يقع الخاطر الداعي للطاعة على ثلاثة أوجه: خاطر شيطاني باعثه وسوسة الشيطان[1]، وخاطر نفساني باعثه الشهوة وطلب الراحة، وخاطر رباني وباعثه التوفيق. وتشتبه هذه الخواطر في الدعاء إلى الطاعة، ولا بد من تمييزها لأعمال الصواب منها، لقوله عليه السلام (من فتح له باب من الخير فلينتهزه) ولا بد من رد الآخرين. أما الشيطاني فبقوله تعالى (إن الذين اتقوا إذا مسهم طائف من الشيطان تذكروا فإذا هم مبصرون)[2] والشهواني الذي هو خاطر النفس بقوله صلى الله عليه وسلم "حفّت النار بالشهوات"، ولكل واحد من هذه الخواطر علامة يتميز بها عن صاحبه. اما الخاطر النفساني فباعثه الشهوة وطلب الراحة، والشهوة تنقسم الى نفسانية كمحبة العلو والجاه والتشفي عند الغيظ وإصغار المعاند وأمثال ذلك، والى جسمانية كالطعام والشراب والنكاح واللباس والمنزه وأمثال ذلك وللنفس

[1] MS. للشيطان [2] Qur. vii, 200

احتياج إلى هذه الملاذ بحسب بعدها عن كل واحد منها وشدة توقانها إلى كل جنس جنس منها ، فلخاطر النفس منها علامتان قائمتان مقام شاهد عدل على تمييز الخاطر المختص بها: أحدهما حضور هذا الخاطر عند احتياجها إلى بعض هذه الأشياء المشتبهات مثل حضور التزويج عند شدة حاجتها إلى النكاح وتلبيسها ذلك عليه بأن تقصدها إعمال قوله صلى الله عليه وسلم [٦٦أ] تناكحوا تناسلوا فإنى مكاثر بكم الأمم يوم القيامة، وتجنب قوله صلى الله عليه وسلم « لا رهبانية فى الإسلام » ، ومثله فى الطعام عند شدة حاجتها إليه ، فربما لبّست عليك هذا مدعائك إلى ترك الصيام أو تناول بعض المشتهيات ، بأن تقول إن فى سرد الصيام إضعاف النفس عن الأمر المحتاج إليه فى الطاعات، [وأن] فى ترك تناول هذا الطعام المشتهى ما كسر قلب المسلم إذا دعى إليه الصديق [أو] قلب العيال إذا كان مما جلبته أنت لعيالك . وربما خدعتك بلون آخر بأن تقول لك اكسر هذه الشهوة بتناولها هذه الكره لئلا يلج عليك هذا الخاطر فيشوش عليك عبادتك وأمثال ذلك فى سائر الشبهات[1] ، كل هذا من تلبيسها وتدليسها . ومثله عندما تكدها بالعبادة وتلزمها على الكراهية الطاعة، فتختار لك نهى النبى صلى الله عليه وسلم عن التبتل وعن اتعاب النفس مثل قوله عليه السلام (اكلفوا من العمل ما تطيقون) ومثل قوله عليه السلام (إن المنبت لا أرضا قطع ولا ظهرا أبقى) ، بل ربما دعتك عند إكثارك إتعابها ومنعها شهواتها إلى ما فيه إهلاكها رأسا أو منعها من تصرفاتها،

[1] MS. المشهيات Corrected in margin.

فتحملك إلى ما يؤدى إلى القتل أو السجن وأمثال ذلك ، لما يتخيل فى هاتين الحالتين من الراحة وزوال التعب عنها . فأحد الشاهدين فى هذا الباب أن يكون قد تقدم لها الكد والإتعاب عند طلبها الراحة وتقدّم لها الحاجة إلى الشئ المشتهى عند باعث الشهوة ، فيعتبرها بهذين الحالين ، فإن كان قد تقدم أحد هاتين الحالتين ، علمت أن الخاطر من النفس ، وحاجتها إلى ذلك هو الذى حركها الى الدعاء اليه ، ومجموع ذلك أن يكون الخاطر شهوانيا ، أو لطلب الراحة ، فالغالب على هذا الخاطر أنه من النفس . والشاهد الثانى إلحاح بهذا الخاطر [678] وعدم انقطاعه ، حتى يأتى مواليا كلما جاهدت فى دفعه عن نفسك ألحّ عليك ولج ، ولا ينفع فيه الاستعاذة ولا التخويف ولا التحذير ولا الترغيب ، بل هو ملح دائم الإلحاح ، فهذا من أكبر الدلائل على أنه من النفس ، إذ هى كالصبى متى منع من الشئ ازداد لحاجا فى طلبه ، فهاتان الحالتان شاهدا عدل متى اجتمعا لا تشك فى أن الخاطر من النفس . ومداواتها عند هذه القضية بالمخالفة المحضة والاتعاب الشديد ، فتمنعها الراحة عند ما يكون الباعث للخاطر كثرة الكد والإتعاب بالعبادة ، أو بوصف وضعه أثقل ، ليكون ذلك أقمع لها من التحريك لمثل هذا الخاطر ، وإن كان شهوانيا جعل دواؤه الحرمان للشئ الذى طلبته ، أو تمنع من مشتهى آخر لها ، ليكون ذلك أمنع لها . وأما الخاطر الشيطانى فله أيضا علامتان : أحدهما تنبيهه ببعض ما تحتاج النفس إليه بداعى الشهوة أو داعى الراحة فى الأوقات المألوف[1] تحصيل

[1] المؤلوفات .MS

النفس مطلوباتها فيها[1] ، والفرق بينه وبين النفسانى فى هذا الباب أن النفسانى يلح ولا يذهب، وهذا يذهب تارة ويكر، فكلما لهى الإنسان عنه بسبب فتور النفس ألح عليها بالتذكير للشهوة، وتكون حركة النفس عند هذا التذكير أكثر من الخاطر النفسانى إذ الخاطر النفسانى إنما خطر لشدة الحاجة، والثانى أن هذا الخاطر الشيطانى يبتدئ ويطرأ على عقله، والخاطر النفسانى متصل متحرك للطبع نحو الشهوة أو الراحة، وذلك أن وسوسة الشيطان إنما هى تجرى مجرى مخاطبة الإنسان للإنسان، غير أن الفرق بين هذا وذاك ألا يراه، والإنسان يحرك قلبك من جهة حاسة [68a] الأذن عند الخطاب، أو التصويت والبصر عند الإشارة، والحس عند الغمز، والشيطان يحرك ذلك من الوسوسة وغمز القلب والخطور فيه، وهو لا يعلم المغيب، وإنما يأتى إلى النفس من جهة الأخلاق التى ألف انفعالها له؟ فهذا الفرق بين النفسانى والشيطانى. أما الخاطر الربانى فإنه يستدل عليه بشاهدين أيضا: أحدهما وهو المقدم موافقة الشرع للخاطر وشهادته بصحته، والثانى فتور النفس عن قبوله ابتداء، حتى يحصل لها نوع الترغيب، وهو الهجوم على النفس من غير مقدمات له كالشيطانى، إلا أن سرعة النفس لموافقة الخاطر الشيطانى أكثر، وهى له أبدر، وهى عن هذا أكسل، إذ الشيطان انما يجيؤها[2] من شهواتها وراحاتها، وهذا يأتى من جهة التكليف وتنفر نفرة من التكليف عند وروده عليها، فهذا الفرق بين هذا

[1] MS. فيه [2] MS. يجيها.

[وبين][1] الخاطر الشيطاني والخاطر النفساني، فإذا خطرلك فزنه بهذه الموازين الثلاث، واستشهد في كل فصل منه بالشواهد التي أشرنا لك فتميز لك الخواطر فاصنع في الشيطاني والنفساني ماكنا ذكرناه لك في المدافعة[2] الحاسمة لهما وبادر لهذا الخاطر الرباني ودع التشاغل والتضييع فإن الوقت ضيق والحال يتحول[3]، وإياك وتسويل النفس ووسواس الشيطان، فإن هذا الباب من أبواب الخير قد انفتح [4]لك فارحبه حتى تستأنفه[4] من أوله، ومثاله أن يكون قد خطر الخاطر في صيام بعض شهر قد حث الشرع على صيامه، أو قيام بعض ليلة، فتقول دع هذا حتى استكمل الليل بأوله أو الشهر بتمامه، وإنما ذلك مخادعة ليسد باب التوفيق المجزى[5]، فإن هذه الخواطر لا تدوم، وإنما هي سريعة الاستحالة، والمبادرة لإمساك الخاطر الرباني [68a] مأمور الشرع، وفيه فائدتان: أحدهما أن يكون وقت أكمل من وقت، كنحو الأوقات التي ورد الخبر عن مسامحة الله عز وجل وتنزل الرحمة والغفران، ونظرات الحق سبحانه وتعالى إلى الخلق لا تحصى. والأخرى ايلاف النفس للمبادرة لامتثال الأوامر والطاعات عندما ترجى بركة العمل، وفيه إزالة حال التكاسل بها، وذلك للتعرض لنفحات رحمة الله تعالى، وهذا في رياضة النفس على المبادرة الى امتثال الأوامر مفيد أيضا، والله أعلم وأحكم.

آخر أدب الفقر من كلام الشيخ أبي القاسم الجنيد قدس الله روحه ونور ضريحه والحمد لله رب العالمين وصلى الله على محمد وآله وصحبه أجمعين وسلم تسليما كثيرا.

[1] Omitted. [2] MS. المداومة [3] MS. تحول [4-4] MS. له فا رتجه حتى اسابقه
[5] MS. المجرى